ordin-ary saints

ordin-ary saints

Living Everyday Life to the Glory of God

SQUARE HALO BOOKS

P.O. Box 18954
Baltimore, MD 21206
www.SquareHaloBooks.com

ISBN 978-1-941106-29-7
Library of Congress Control Number: 2022949388

Printed in the United States of America

This book is a celebration of twenty-five years of
publishing "extraordinary books for ordinary saints."
It is both a gift to our friends and readers who have
supported us over the years, and an offering of thanks
and praise for these good works which God prepared
beforehand that we should walk in them.

. . .

Let the favor of the Lord our God be upon us,
and establish the work of our hands upon us;
yes, establish the work of our hands! (Ps. 90:17)

Contents

ORDINARY SAINTS

The ordinary saints, the ones we know,

Our too-familiar family and friends,

When shall we see them? Who can truly show

Whilst still rough-hewn, the God who shapes our ends?

Who will unveil the presence, glimpse the gold

That is and always was our common ground,

Stretch out a finger, feel, along the fold

To find the flaw, to touch and search that wound

From which the light we never noticed fell

Into our lives? Remember how we turned

To look at them, and they looked back? That full-

-eyed love unselved us, and we turned around,

Unready for the wrench and reach of grace.

But one day we will see them face to face.

FOREWORD

A Brief History of Square Halo Books: An Unlikely Convergence of Random Events

Square Halo Books finds its roots in a collection of small, seemingly disconnected events that started long before our incorporation on September 24, 1997. The first random event took place in the summer of 1981 when Alan and I married and moved from Baltimore, Maryland to Media, Pennsylvania where Alan accepted a call to pastor a church plant. Here began the convergence of the Bauer/Bustard relationship with thirteen-year-old Ned Bustard.

Ned's love for art, comic books, and storytelling was evident even at his young age. I spent wonderful afternoons listening to Ned develop intricate story lines about the children in our congregation. He created and drew each character based on their real-life characteristics, then wove them into a C.S. Lewis-like story. Ned's stories and drawings were delightful. Eventually, Alan and I left Church of the Covenant and returned to Baltimore, where Alan began his career as a seminary professor.

In the fall semester of 1995 Alan was asked by the seminary to teach Revelation. This began an unsettling time as our family discussions focused on the end of human history. We talked about the coming of intense lawlessness, the love of most believers growing cold, and the death of the church. Focusing on end times burdened my soul.

However, God had much goodness waiting for us in this random act. Because of this class, Alan was able to systematize his carefully researched lectures and write a book called *The End: A Reader's Guide to Revelation.* We tried shopping the book around to publishing houses; but, they would only consider Alan's manuscript if he agreed to make major changes. They wanted Alan to write a comparison of the various views of eschatology that also included Alan's innovated ideas. I believed changing Alan's manuscript was a ridiculous idea. Why should Alan change his carefully exegetical work to fit someone else's point of view in order to sell books? Alan's students loved his principles of interpretation, glossary of terms, and compelling view of the end of human history. I told Alan it was time for us to start our own publishing company! Here began one of our most passionate marital fights . . . to start or not to start!

Eventually, Alan agreed and we put in motion the legal structure needed to launch it. Neither of us had a whit of experience in publishing, nor did we ever imagine God was building something grander than just a start up publishing company to publish one book. As Alan has said, "In the beginning, God decided He wanted a new publishing company, but it was a complete secret to those of us who would build it." Our beginnings were random and very unlikely.

As Square Halo grew, Alan took on the role of CFO. Under his watchful eye, Alan kept us solvent while he continued to teach and work. During those years he also wrote *The Beginning: A Second Look at the First Sin,* as well as an essay for *The City for God: Essays Honoring the Work of Timothy Keller.* His latest book is titled, *How to See: Reading God's Word With New Eyes.*

The mosaic depicting Pope John VII, from the collection of the Vatican Museum, which inspired the Square Halo logo.

But back to our history. The Bauers and the Bustards stayed connected throughout the years. By the time we agreed to start a publishing company in order to print Alan's book, Ned had grown up, married the lovely Leslie Anne Symons, and begun raising his darling Bustard chicks. As we put the legalities in place for our new company, I recalled my experience with Ned's artistic creativity when we lived in Media, Pennsylvania. Who else would we turn to but Ned Bustard to help birth our company? Alan's book was essential for the church at large, and we needed Ned's artistic creativity to help develop our fledgling company. Who would ever guess that a brief encounter with a thirteen-year-old would ever turn into Square Halo Books?

We remember the crazy phone call where Alan offered Ned a third ownership in our company in exchange for his expertise in book layout and cover art which would allow us to move forward with Alan's book. Ned was reluctant at first, but eventually came around to our vision (he jokingly made his one stipulation for surrendering to my grand vision—he would be given the title of "creative director."). Several weeks later, we sat on the Bustards' plaid couch in their living room, choosing our logo and composing our mission statement. Looking over Ned's several sketches for possible names and logos took me back to those lovely afternoons in Media. God collected what appeared to be random acts and merged them together for His glory. However, one cannot justify a newly formed publishing house with just one title.

Then came our third random act in 2000. Since college, Ned voraciously read all that he could on Art and Faith. When he finished the last book (or so he thought) on the topic, he wanted to go deeper. So he pitched the idea for our second book, *It Was Good: Making Art to the Glory of God.* This book established Square Halo Books as a boutique publishing company dedicated to explore the intersection between Art and Faith. Ned also edited other books for us, including *It Was Good: Making Music to the Glory of God, It Was Good: Performing Arts to the Glory of God,* and *Revealed: A Storybook Bible for Grown-Ups.*

While Ned, Alan, and I were figuring out the ins and outs of our new business, Leslie was raising their daughters, teaching, working, and homeschooling. Initially, Leslie served Square Halo as a "tie breaker" when the three of us disagreed. However, as her role in her family changed, Leslie became more active in the company.

Today, Vice President Leslie is the face and voice of Square Halo Books. She has planned enormously successful conferences. She hosts an informative and delightful podcast that features our contributors. Additionally, she co-wrote and edited *Wild Things and Castles in the Sky: A Guide to Choosing the Best Books for Children* and penned a golden collection of poetry, *The Goodness of the Lord in the Land of the Living.* Leslie brings a sense of beauty, warmth, and inclusion to Square Halo that is unmatchable. Her involvement with various literary organizations and conferences enhances her ability to thoughtfully contribute to and guide Square Halo Books.

Even I, the self-appointed and very pushy president of our company, was challenged by this unlikely convergence of random events orchestrated by God. Not only did I write an essay on music and suffering for *It Was Good: Making Music to the Glory of God,* I also wrote, *Speaking CODE: Unraveling Past Bonds to Redeem Broken Conversations,* based on what I do as a CCEF-trained biblical counselor.

As of this printing, Square Halo Books has published forty titles and already have several titles prepared for release next year. But when we look farther ahead, what do we imagine the future holding for Square Halo Books? We have no idea . . . but at least we know God will converge unlikely events for His glory. Will we still be as surprised by these unlike events as we have in the past? Oh yes, and may it always be so for Square Halo. And we will continue publishing relatively unknown authors who never get an opportunity to see their work in print. What we do know is Square Halo will stay committed to our mission statement written twenty-five years ago:

> In Christian art, the square halo identified a living person presumed to be a saint. Square Halo Books is devoted to publishing works that present contextually sensitive biblical studies, and practical instruction consistent with the Doctrines of the Reformation. The goal of Square Halo Books is to provide materials useful for encouraging and equipping the saints.

Indeed, Square Halo Books remains an unlikely convergence of random events. It is God's work, for His glory and our good.

GLORY

What's This Book All About?

Johan Sebastian Bach, the great Lutheran church musician, is universally recognized as the greatest contrapuntalist (and by some as simply the greatest composer) who ever lived. He wrote endless anthems and cantatas for church worship ("Jesu, Joy of Man's Desiring"), a number of "secular" concert pieces (*The Brandenburg Concertos*), and a popular keyboard primer (*Notebook for Anna Magdalena Bach*). Yet he treated all of them the same. At the top of the first page of the manuscript he started with the Latin initials for *Jesu juva*, "Jesus, help me." And at the bottom of the last page he finished with *Soli Deo Gloria*, "Glory to God alone." What did Bach understand that we need to recapture if we want to celebrate God's glory today? I summarize it in what may seem a radical claim:

God's purpose in the salvation of sinners is His own glory.

That is not the first answer most of us would give if we were asked why God saves sinners. We would probably respond that it is out of love, and we would not be wrong. "For God so loved the world that he gave his only Son, that whoever believes in him should not perish, but have eternal life" (John 3:16). But there is something else going on too: God works in everything, and especially in salvation, supremely for His own glory—or the Father does it with the glory of the Son, and the Son with the glory of the Father, in mind: "Father, the hour has come; glorify your Son, that the Son may glorify you" (John 17:1).

This perspective is conspicuously absent from much contemporary preaching, but it is essential to an accurate understanding of the gospel and of why the gospel is good news. It is emphasized three times in the first chapter of Paul's epistle to the Ephesians as a kind of refrain. Paul is giving a summary of the plan of salvation, of all that the whole Trinity has done to save us. Why did God the Father conceive the plan of salvation and elect us to sonship? To the praise of His glorious grace (v. 6). Why did God the Son redeem us through His blood? That we should be to the praise of His glory (v. 12). And why did God the Holy Spirit seal us for redemption as a pledge of our inheritance? To the praise of His glory (v. 14).

But this doctrine is not just here: it is a major theme of the whole Bible. It is implied or stated in passages such as Exodus 3:12, 7:3–5, 9:16, 40:34; Psalm 19:1, 79:9; and Isaiah 48:9–11. Israel was brought out of Egypt that she might *worship* in the wilderness. The purpose of the plagues was that Pharaoh would know that Yahweh is God, and Yahweh alone. By allowing Pharaoh to live, God demonstrated His power and proclaimed His name through all the earth. The glory of the Lord filled the tabernacle, and then the temple, at their dedications. The very heavens broadcast His glory, as the firmament proclaims His handiwork. Why does God delay His wrath? For the sake of His own name! "For my own sake, for my own sake I do it, for how should my name be profaned? My glory I will not give to another" (Isa. 48:9–11). But the climax of the theme appears in the Lord's great high priestly prayer, in John 17:1. What was foremost in the mind of Christ as He faced the great crisis of His life, at the fulfillment of His purpose for coming into the world? What was foremost on His mind as he faced the cross and spiritually prepared Himself for it? "Father the hour has come; glorify your Son that the Son may glorify you."

Yes, God loves us, and yes, salvation has our good in mind. But the emphasis is inescapable: God's *ultimate* purpose is His own glory. We see it first in the creation of the universe: what God ultimately achieves in creation is His own glory. The universe accomplishes this purpose simply by existing in all its intricate design and glorious splendor, but it accomplishes it even more profoundly as the setting for a narrative through which God's glory achieves even more piercing clarity: the creation, fall, redemption, adoption, and glorification by grace alone of God's ultimate creation, made in His very image. God's greatest glory comes from His greatest work, and His greatest work is the salvation of sinners. And so God's *ultimate* purpose in our salvation, what He ultimately achieves in our salvation, is His own glory—not incidentally but by design. God's glory is the ultimate purpose of every atomic particle, every creature, every event that has providentially been allowed to happen.

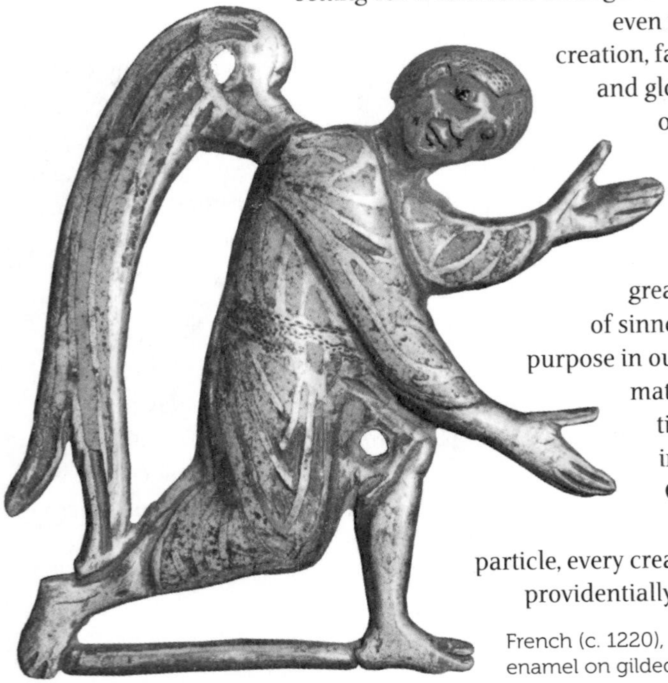

French (c. 1220), *Kneeling Angel*, enamel on gilded copper

It all works together for His glory as much as for the good of those who love Him.

This makes the glory of God an awfully important concept. We had better get it right. What then do we mean when we talk about God's glory? What does it mean to say that it is the ultimate purpose of creation, culminating as the ultimate purpose of salvation? If we were to trace the word "glory" through the Bible, we would find it associated with the presence of God and the nature of God. It burns from the top of Sinai so that people have to be warned not to touch the mountain (Ex. 19:16–25, 24:9–18). Moses has to be protected even from the trailing edge of it by the cleft of a rock as God passes by and proclaims His name—that is, the essence of His nature, of who He is (Ex. 33:18–23). His glory fills the tabernacle and then the temple so that the priests cannot stand to minister within them (Ex. 40:3–38, 1 Kings 8:10–13). It shakes even the heavenly Temple in Isaiah's vision as he hears the seraphim crying out, "Holy, holy, holy is the LORD of hosts! The whole earth is full of his glory!" (Isa. 6:1–3) It shines from the face of the ultimate revelation of God, Jesus Christ (2 Cor. 4:3–6) because it was the fruit of the climax of His saving work at the cross (John 17:1).

How do we put all of this together? *God's glory is the manifestation of His perfect and holy character in all its awesome and majestic splendor throughout the whole of creation. Manifestation*: Angels and men were created so that God's glory could be seen, understood, marveled at, and worshipped. *His perfect and holy character*: It is His very nature and essence, His personality and His heart, in so far as they are sharable at all with finite beings, which are to be revealed. *Awesome and majestic splendor*: Words fail to capture how great, how weighty, how shatteringly good this revelation is. *Throughout the whole of creation*: No canvas could be sufficient for this painting, no screen for this film, but all the vast reaches of space and time are there to impress us small ones with as much of it as we can grasp. From the mightiest super-galaxy cluster to the smallest quark, it all has the same message: behold the glory of the Lord!

What then does it mean to say that God's glory is the purpose of salvation? It means that for God's character to be revealed to men and angels is the greatest good conceivable, the highest value imaginable, the ultimate reason for which the world was made. That is why creation glorifies God: the heavens declare His glory and the firmament proclaims His handiwork (Ps. 19:1). "For his invisible attributes, namely, his eternal power and divine nature, have been clearly perceived, ever since the creation of the world, in the things that have been made" (Rom. 1:20). The world's stubborn persistence in existence despite its utter contingency; its elegant design; its fine tuning for life: all speak eloquently not just of its Maker's existence but of his dynamic creative energy and incomprehensibly brilliant intelligence.

As impressive as the voice of the universe is, the most profound way God is glorified in the history of this creation is through the salvation of sinners—those persons created in the image of that inscrutably glorious Maker, capable of their own derivative creativity, which made possible art and culture and even gave them the capacity to depart from His commandment and fall. Then comes the utterly unpredictable response to that fall: the history of Abraham and the people of faith who followed him, who were redeemed from slavery, received the law, and gave the world a Hope that could overcome even the depths of its fall.

And then we have the fruition of that Hope: the virgin birth, sinless life, atoning death, and triumphant resurrection of Christ, and the work of the Holy Spirit in calling out of the Gentiles a people for His name—regenerating them, sanctifying them, uniting them in one body, the Church, and keeping them for final union with Christ. All this reveals the nature and character of God and writes it indelibly on the pages of space, time, and history in the fullest and deepest manner conceivable. At the cross we see the justice of God demanding the death penalty for sin, the love of God taking that penalty on Himself, the wisdom of God reconciling the apparently contradictory claims of love and justice, and the power of God in the resurrection of the crucified Savior. What could manifest the depths of God's character, the heart of who He is, more profoundly? Nothing. But it does not end there.

The fullness of the provision for His own, the work of the Spirit on behalf of the Son to convict them of sin, call them to faith, regenerate them, sanctify them, keep them, and finally unite them to the Son in such a way that they share his glory forever: "Please, Aslan," said Lucy, "can anything be done to save Edmund?" "All shall be done," said Aslan.[1] In all of this, then, God is glorified. For God's ultimate purpose in the salvation of sinners is His own glory.

There is no contradiction with God's love here. Pursuing His own glory does not make God selfish. We tend to think it would, because we know that pursuing our own glory is wrong, and we naturally transfer that wrongness to Him. But the analogy does not hold. He is the Creator, and we are the creatures. He deserves all worship, adoration, and praise, and we do not. He belongs in the center, and we do not. Because of who we are, it would be wrong for us to seek our own glory. Because of who He is, it would be (if we can say it this way) wrong for Him not to. In the final analysis, the glory of God is not just His greatest good; it is the greatest good. That God should be glorified is the greatest good conceivable. And therefore it is our greatest good. To pursue His own glory is the most loving thing God can do for His creatures. To realize that truth is to find the fulfillment of our creation.

Soli Deo gloria! Amen.

1 C.S. Lewis, *The Lion, the Witch, and the Wardrobe* (1950; New York: Harper Collins, 1978 , orig. publ. 1950), p. 141.

This essay first appeared in Touchstone: A Journal of Mere Christianity 35:5 *(Sept./Oct., 2022): 19–21, and is used here by permission.*

HOME REPAIRS

Better and More Beautiful

One of my earliest memories involves wallpaper: not the pattern but the process. When I was four, I moved with my parents and two younger sisters to a small brick house on Jersey Street. In my mind, it seems we had hardly unpacked our boxes before my parents were wallpapering the dining nook (it hardly qualified as a room). The care they lavished on this corner spot where two walls hugged our heavy, dark dining suite had a quality of reverence. Of course, I would not then have used that word. I only knew that in a period of immense transition (*which* box held my enormous mustard-yellow teddy bear?), this papering of the dining nook, this careful measuring of mitered corners for a wooden chair rail that would frame the new paper like art, mattered in ways I accepted but could not yet understand.

My father was a university campus minister. When I think of him then, he holds a soft, leather Bible and he is leading a small group discussion, or he is gardening, or he is repairing or redecorating our house. I cannot say these things held equal value to him, but as his firstborn observer, they seemed to me to lie on a single plane of importance. We loved Jesus, which meant we invited people into our home, which meant we took care with our home, which meant wallpaper was sacred, though sacred was not a word we used in our family.

My own first foray into home repairs came around the age of ten when, after much begging from his three daughters, my father built for us a plywood dollhouse. My sisters and I had begun collecting miniatures after discovering a dollhouse shop while away from our Texas home on a Colorado vacation. My first miniature was a tiny bakery cake, dolloped with tiny plaster frosting, that looked real enough to eat, though one swallow would have taken care of it. The tiny cake was followed by a tiny ice-cream parlor seating set. The two chairs had swirly wire backs and the table legs were swirls of golden wire. These were soon followed by a ceramic kitten lapping up a ceramic puddle of milk, a set of three old-fashioned flour bags, and half a dozen paper books about the size of my father's thumbnail. Obviously, these precious possessions required a home of their own.

That Christmas I was entrusted with my mother's glue gun, which allowed me to attach rows of tiny wooden shingles to the plywood roof of the gift I now shared with my sisters. I can remember standing on a chair in my blue denim jumper and daubing each shingle with glue before adding it to an overlapping row. My best friend at the time shared my love for tiny replicas. Her parents were not "in ministry" so her exquisite dollhouse came ready-made from the fanciest dollhouse shop in the greater Houston metro area. Every item was perfectly to scale, which meant that when I peered into the rooms, I felt suddenly aware of myself as a giant before slipping seamlessly into the doll family's point of view. I especially envied my friend the soft felt fuzz of her wall-to-wall carpeting. My own dollhouse was carpeted with remnants from my father's redecorating, which meant that the pile was so deep my doll family's feet would entirely disappear into it.

My best friend and I grew apart in middle school. We briefly reconnected after high school graduation, but our reunion was short-lived. While we were both still teenagers, my friend was killed in an accident involving cars and alcohol and a courtroom trial of which the only thing I can recall is sitting between my mother and her mother and noticing our fifth grade teacher sitting with the jury. *Was this allowed? Our former teacher on the jury, the one who had read* Where the Red Fern Grows *to both of us?* Who knew what was right in this strange, new world. Immediately after my friend had died and long before the trial, my mother and I went to her home to *pay our respects,* and I sat with a group of old school friends and our mothers in the dining room where the only sign of my friend's life was her dollhouse sitting on the floor in a corner of the room. I did not ask to see it, but everything in me wanted to move to the floor, open the swinging front panel of the house I knew so well, and grow small again.

Not long after, I married my high school sweetheart, graduated from college, and moved away from Texas, but I would return every year or so to see family. Sometimes I would run into my friend's mother at the shopping mall in my small hometown, and I felt guilty with each new update I gave, acutely aware that my friend had not lived long enough to marry or move away or become a mother. On one of those visits home, I despaired at the sight of my old dollhouse sitting, dilapidated, in my parent's garage. After I grew up, it had been played with by so many visiting children—my parents' ministry hospitality was legendary—that it hurt to look too closely at the rundown house. I collected a few of the best bits and pieces and brought them home to my own firstborn daughter.

Eventually my little girl added the bakery cake and the kitten lapping milk to a dollhouse her grandfather, my husband's father, built for her from a dollhouse kit. Her house was a clapboard Queen Anne with wooden shutters painted red. I don't think my own child lay in bed at night mentally rearranging dollhouse furniture as I had once done, but she played with that house and she played hard. Strange new dolls and out-of-scale items were always being added. I sometimes joined her and tried to contribute my own aesthetic finesse. *Shall we pick tiny flowering weeds and arrange dollhouse bouquets in upside down china thimbles? Shall I glue strips of lace to the window tops for curtains?* When we moved from Florida to Pennsylvania, the dollhouse was given its own special moving crate, constructed around it in our seashell-stuccoed home and carefully removed once we arrived at our red brick farmhouse. But daughters grow quickly, and the dollhouse was carried down to the basement not long after. I imagined we might carry it up again when my youngest child and second daughter was old enough, but she never showed any affinity for miniature worlds, preferring her own magic world where she, with a unicorn horn glued to her headband, waved rainbow streamers and galloped with flying ponies.

I sometimes remembered my child's dollhouse while I lay in bed trying to fall asleep. I would picture the sheet-draped lump in the corner of our dirt-floor basement and imagine uncovering it, repairing it, maybe repainting those red shutters green. Only now my own house is an 1880 farmhouse where the plaster keeps failing in new places and the wood floors give us frequent splinters. Glue guns are no use against this perpetual decay. Of course this real, right-sized house must take precedence over a toy. What kind of fool paints tiny doll shutters when her own shutters need a good scrub and a new paint job? When the planks of her own front porch are once again rotting through? And so, I paint, my husband wallpapers, we bring in helpers for the really big jobs. Whereas my daughter's house had only two tiny terra cotta pots filled with felt roses on the front porch, I keep adding new garden areas and then feeling overwhelmed by the upkeep. The work of making this Pennsylvania home has always felt beyond us, but it has also buoyed us. It is right and good to make a place better and more beautiful.

Breezy Brookshire, *Dollhouse*, dip pen and ink wash

Home repairs in an old house can feel unending. Scratch one to-do from your list, and three more appear. And yet, somehow over this past decade we made enough progress to invite my husband's parents to live with us. In June, they put their own Texas home on the market. In July, they sold it. In September, they moved into the guest barn that sits just beyond our kitchen door. In October, my father-in-law's health declined. In November, he died at home, and we realized that he would not use the woodworking tools we had arranged in a shed for him. He would not attend his grandson's Eagle Scout ceremony or his granddaughter's high school graduation. And he would never know that I had uncovered the dollhouse and moved it to a folding table. He would never know that I had plugged in a task lamp in that corner of the basement. He would never see the dollhouse repair supplies I had already gathered, things like new wallpaper with miniature patterns and a dollhouse electrical kit with light bulbs right-sized for mice.

Home repair is my family legacy. Building and beautifying are sacred work. As a child I sensed this. My parents may not have spoken of it, but they demonstrated how much it mattered. It wasn't enough to open our Bibles and invite people into our homes. We must also vacuum the floors. Wallpaper our walls. Build decks and grow flowers. It is easy to tell myself that my love for miniatures was simply the child-sized version of the work I watched my parents do, as if I were "playing house" and in some way practicing for adult life. But if dollhouses are childish things, they are childish things I feel compelled to take up again.

This year when the garden goes back to sleep and the evenings draw in, I intend to take myself to the basement. I will finally remove the sheet, turn on the task lamp, and plug in my glue gun. I will tell myself that a grandchild might play with this house one day, and while true, this is not truly the reason for the work. The reason is that miniature worlds are marvels that help us marvel at the right-sized world again. Loving and losing over a lifetime can take the shine off ordinary life. We grow weary. We lose touch with wonder. But I once learned to care for houses and gardens and cakes and kittens by holding them in my hands. I need to hold these things in my hands again, cup them entirely in my palm, like God holding me, like God holding the whole world in His hands. The work of dollhouse repair doesn't matter in any conventional sense. There is no real need for it. I am not doing great things for God if I repaint these shutters green. But when I work on this house, I will be a maker as God is a maker and in this miniature way, I will reflect God's image and God's glory until the day when I lay down my tiny paintbrush and call this house, made by many hands, good.

KARAOKE

The Song We're Headed Toward

For Norbert Weiner,
a signal was something
that ought to be filtered
from noise, but for God,
at least in this life,
the signals merge with
the noise, and although
maybe that's just God's
way, it's possible God
is more like Gwen Stefani
in that he expects us
to hear, over the din
of the hip hop club
of this world, him shouting
"Holla back, girl!"
and wants us to holla
back somehow, through
prayer, or maybe just
lives of self-sacrifice.

—Aaron Belz,
"Signal Versus Noise"
from *Lovely, Raspberry*

There are places in my life I thought I'd never leave. Places I've experienced a slice of eternity—either in the never-ending time-ticking way, or the pure goodness of the experience. Like the science classroom, under florescent high school lights—fifty minutes that felt just long enough to stretch on forever. Flights from east to west coasts that make you wonder if you should pitch a tent and hang some art because this is your home now. And singing karaoke.

When I was ten, my sisters and I received a karaoke machine for Christmas from our favorite aunt and uncle. The summer before, we sang karaoke songs and stayed up late in their living room, drinking soda and eating pizza (probably after a trip to the Disney store).

This story doesn't start there, it starts fifteen years later on the corner of NW Hoyt and NW Twenty-First Street, at Voicebox Theater, in Portland, Oregon. When I moved to Portland to teach elementary school, I found a wonderful Anglican church. And, as an embarrassment of riches, there were six young, single, post-college adults, reading from the lectionary, serving with the children's ministry, setting up chairs, and filling in for one another when the greeter or the offering-counter didn't show. There were Old Fashioneds at our fellowship meals, and TV show illustrations in our sermons. It was a young congregation. Our pastor and his wife, the music director, invited everyone out to Voicebox one evening after church.

It would be the first of many nights that included cleaning up from our four o'clock service, getting dinner together, and eating quickly so we could speed across town to make our eight p.m. slot.

Perhaps to some, the idea of karaoke means tossing back tequila shots in a sad dive bar, howling into a questionable microphone, venting your deepest sadness over a four-bar musical intro.

But plastered-sad-old-man doing an off-key "Margaritaville," this was not.

Voicebox is a venue with five or six separate rooms, with restaurant service and karaoke set-ups in each room. Participants add songs to the queue using a link on their phones. The seven or eight of us sang nineties country ballads, classic rock hits, and songs from *Prince of Egypt.* We danced to pop songs we queued for each other. That first night I attempted a Lauryn Hill track, and as I struggled my way through the spoken verses (it turned out I did need to follow her voice), everyone shouted a word or two from the screen to help me or remained graciously engaged in conversation. At last we faded the song out, amid hoots and applause, and picked a different one.

The best moment wasn't when I was singing a favorite song (or one I didn't totally choke on) but the moment when the music started—a song everyone knew—and we would all sing. We sang in other capacities: some in choir at church, harmony parts on hymns, and some of us were former worship leaders at other churches. Karaoke was an extension of sacred singing together.

I had never shown much interest in typical group activities in Portland, which included rock climbing, frisbee in the park, or hiking. But if you're looking for someone to sing the second part on "Islands in the Stream"? Sign me up.

I love each stage of karaoke, starting with choosing a good song. I began to keep a list of them on my phone. The best songs are the ones that bring people together. Not too slow, not a super-sad ballad, not a song that subjects the audience to your glory-grab number that we can tell makes you relive that one solo, that sounds like a single spotlight in an empty theater. A good karaoke song makes you a community DJ. It's singable, danceable—a song other people are excited to hear when you're up. It's not too long. (Unless it's Queen, which the group will carry.) Next favorite part: cheering people on.

For birthday parties, or when friends came to visit, I ventured out to other karaoke venues in the city. With stages where other people sang, too. This did up our likelihood of encountering tequila-soaked strangers processing past lovers through an Adele song onstage. A slurry Sinatra. Or singers of the tuneless variety, picking a song by their favorite artist to sing with their bachelorette party. No matter who was at the mic, the audience cheered, sang along, and rooted for them.

Back home, my friends and I are loud singers. We grew singing up together in each other's living rooms, at school, and at church hymn-sings.

In the liturgy of our time together, we have Cher impressions, and top-of-your-lungs Whitney choruses danced at wedding receptions. We have shared playlists, albums always played on long drives, even favorite tunes from childhood choir concerts in our repertoire. In our annual holiday visits together, if one of us starts singing (while driving or brushing our teeth) the rest chime in, finishing together in frothed, minty harmony. Music is one of the ways we spend time together, a part of our spiritual countenance—including an exuberant love of life, a strong likelihood of breaking into song, the joyful unselfconsciousness of finishing the verse someone started from across the house. Karaoke, then, was not an out-of-the-ordinary activity when I began to request it every birthday party and cross-country reunion. I probably wouldn't have been able to articulate why I loved it so much, at first. Something about the songs people picked and getting to sing them together. Something about singing together being a level up from even the best conversations: we were working together in the same tune.

What if there are no unsacred spaces in making a joyful noise?

What if we held to Kuyperian karaoke theology: "There's not a square inch in the whole domain of human existence over which Christ, who is Lord over all, does not exclaim, 'Mine'!"[1]

Growing up, my relationship to music was weekly cello lessons and orchestra practice, harmonizing with my sisters at local coffee shop gigs, and singing soprano on the top of the risers at the school Christmas concert. When my sisters and I fought on our summer road trips, the consequence was singing something in three-part harmony.

These days, my relationship to music and making music has changed. I am a musical consumer and a car-singer, for the most part. I pay for a monthly subscription to find the songs I want to listen to, at any given moment, and curate them into playlists with clever names, sonic laundry baskets of emotion and arrangement, so I never have to not hear the thing I want to hear right then. I rent a corner of the music complex.

But as a writer, I am moved by songwriting (first, the beauty of the word) and the unnecessary-essential beauty of writing a song. Who needs it? How could we live without it?

If, indeed, we are currently being sung over by the Creator of the cosmos (Zeph. 3:17), what could that mean for ordinary playlist listeners like us?

If we lived into our beloved reality how would we get to live?

Perhaps singing back: belting verses with the people you love at weddings or on long drives or over toothpaste or walking up on that stage, shaky, fearless, and ready to kill it.

What if karaoke is one of the last recreational community experiences we can have with music? Concerts, churches with a robust singing culture, sitting around with other people and instruments, and singing in a windows-down car with your friends, all a close second.[2]

My parents grew up into music when records made music accessible, and later, radio. A solo experience with music meant closing the door to your room with a 45 spinning. Being able to hear the song you wanted to listen to meant waiting by the radio with a cassette player to push the red record key when it played, or listening to the Top 40 at the roller rink.

I developed my love of songs and the people who made them when a young artist could get a record deal through their YouTube fame. When the ubiquity of personal music technology meant that the majority of the hours you spent listening to music were hours spent alone with music (sans the loading and reloading of CDs). There have only been a few years of my life when I wanted to hear a song and wasn't able to access it immediately.

In an everyday sense, most of our experiences with music are solitary ones. Unless you spring for concert tickets or play with a group or belong to a church. Or get a group together for karaoke on Sunday nights. In only a few of these scenarios are you more than a consumer. Karaoke combines our two strongest glimpses of God's goodness: music and community.

Music is the way I connect with God. I grew up singing the psalms in church and playing folk songs on ukulele and mandolin with friends after school. Three voices in harmony, I think, when someone talks about holiness.

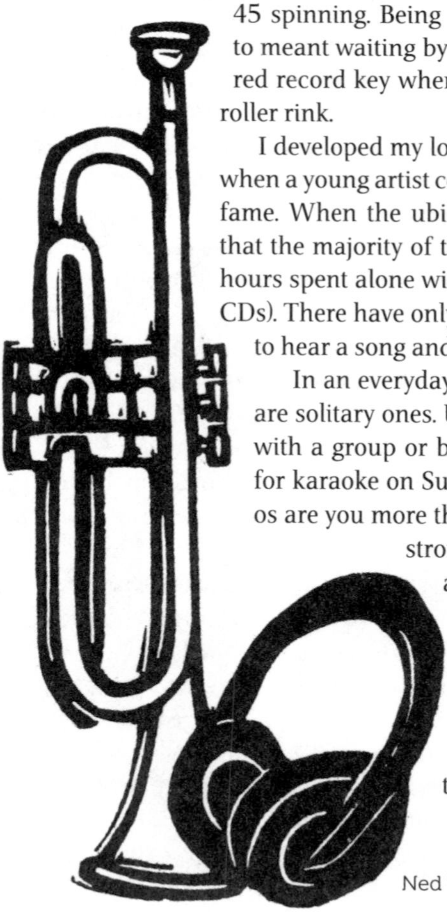

Ned Bustard, *Brother Gregg* (detail), linocut

There's something about singing the same song. Readers of the tuneless-singer variety may disagree but, regardless of ability, who among us hasn't felt like she might levitate at the finale of a musical number, or felt a thrum of hope upon hearing an intro to a song beloved for decades while walking through the grocery store?

It's the closest I get to understanding the writer of Ecclesiastes, when he said that God,"put eternity into our hearts" (Eccl. 3:11).

On Earth, an echo of this could be the multi-part voices singing the Doxology, as church is dismissed, but anything else on the sacred periphery counts.

. . .

"Good times never seemed so good . . ." The bar shook with the song from the stage. The infamous Nashville haunt, alive with sound, held shiny businessmen and groups of tourists in bright boots who threw back their heads and sang along with the chorus, belting as they made their way to the bar to order, as another crowd walked through the door, and as they left to find another spot down the street. "Everyone is singing the same song? This is what heaven will be like," I thought, wondering if anyone else was thinking about heaven in this honky tonk.

I know it's a feeling I'll get to feel again, without end. An experience that won't just be piped through earbuds while I finish my homework, or through an out of the ordinary night on the town. I won't have to worry when I should be getting back, and "Sweet Caroline" won't be the one we'll all be singing to.

In living memory of my dad
pastor, writer, and leader of the band
Gregg Strawbridge (1964–2022)
who read this essay
about heaven and karaoke
on a Monday night in January,
and got to hear the song
we're all headed toward,
only two days later.

See you at the table.

1 Abraham Kuyper (1837–1920, in his inaugural address at the founding of the Free University of Amsterdam.)

2 In addition to building community, songs are the closest thing we have to time travel. More than a photo or the smell of an old sweatshirt, when I hear that one Maggie Rogers song, it suddenly feels like June 2019.

PIPES

Smoking My Pipe

I am an inveterate pipe smoker. No, *inveterate* is not the right word; it sounds pejorative, a concession to a weakness or a vice. On the contrary, the long, settled, rich pleasure of pipe-smoking, the warm and companionable sessions given over to it, are not a vice or an indulgence, but rather a recovery: a recovery of simple *being,* from the desert wastes of *doing.* It is a return to the first and primal gift from God, who is *Being* itself, and in His love and for His glory, has created us, let us *be,* shared with us gift of *being.* Naturally we must occasionally *do* something, but that's usually where the trouble starts, as it did in Eden, and has continued since, until we become so foolish as to think we are saved by our own actions, our *works,* and God has once again to knock us off our latest high horse, as He did with Paul, and teach us to accept everything anew by sheer *grace.*

Of course, when I smoke my pipe, I *appear* to be doing something: I'm selecting my pipe, usually an old Irish Peterson. I'm filling it slowly, skillfully, and at just the right consistency, with tobacco that has been chosen with care, for its taste, its fragrance, its penumbra of delicate associations (*Deluxe Navy Rolls* to recall my nautical life, *Three Nuns* because it was commended by both C.S. Lewis and Seamus Heaney, *Troost Aromatic Cavendish* because the word *Troost* means comfort). I'm lighting the pipe, delighting in the sudden miraculous flare and energy of flame as it leaps from my battered brass Zippo. I'm drawing it gently, I'm letting the pipe itself, and the quality of its draw, settle my breathing into a rhythm proper for contemplation. And if I get to the right point of stillness, I do one other thing: I blow smoke rings. I blow them in honour of Tolkien, in honour of Bilbo and Frodo and Gandalf, I blow them for the sheer joy of summoning their form. Though no one actually "blows" a smoke ring. Were you to be so "active" as to blow or even gently exhale, the poor ring would be torn to shreds. You must attain complete stillness, no slightest breath must disturb the still air before you, and then you just make an O with your lips and pop the ring out of your mouth and watch it float and expand into the air for your private pleasure or the occasional amusement of your friends.

Stephen Crotts, *Second Joy*, woodcut

So when I smoke my pipe I am active to that degree, I am admittedly *doing* something, but I am only *active* in order to be *passive*. I do these little things in order, at last, to do nothing. And then, surprisingly, and by sheer grace, in that mellow smoky space, something of beauty is born, something for which there would have been no room if the pipe had not commanded me to relax. I put it like this once in a poem from my collection *Parable and Paradox*, a poem which, I am honoured to say, is read at the beginning of their sessions by my pipe-smoking friends in America, who form what they happily call The Brotherhood of the Briar:

SMOKE RINGS FROM MY PIPE

All the long day's weariness is done
I'm free at last to do just as I will,
Take out my pipe, admire the setting sun,
Practice the art of simply sitting still.
Thank God I have this briar bowl to fill,
I leave the world with all its hopeless hype,
Its pressures, and its ever-ringing till,
And let it go in smoke rings from my pipe.

The hustle and the bustle, these I shun,
The tasks that trouble and the cares that kill,
The false idea that there's a race to run,
The pushing of that weary stone uphill,
The wretched iPhone's all-insistent trill,
Wingers and whiners, each with their own gripe,
I pack them in tobacco leaves until
They're blown away in smoke rings from my pipe.

And then at last my real work is begun:
My chance to chant, to exercise the skill
Of summoning the muses, one by one,
To meet me in their temple, touch my quill,
(I have a pen but quills are better still)
And when the soul is full, the time is ripe,
Kindle the fire of poetry that will
Breathe and expand like smoke-rings from my pipe.

Envoi
Prince, I have done with grinding at the mill,
These petty-pelting tyrants aren't my type,
So lift me up and set me on a hill,
A free man blowing smoke rings from his pipe.

That poem came out in 2016, by which time I had been smoking pipes for forty years, but it was not the first time the muse, my smoky muse as I sometimes call her, had inspired me to celebrate the delicate and threatened art of pipe-smoking. My pipes have always accompanied my poetry, in that I was often smoking a meditative pipe when I put pen to paper, for I smoke when I compose, as Tennyson, Mark Twain, C.S. Lewis, and J.R.R. Tolkien all did. But it was when I came to write a poem about a country walk, in which I hoped to celebrate the four ancient "elements" of air, earth, water, and fire, that my pipe appeared for the first time *in* a poem, rather than simply sustaining and inspiring the poet. A rainy spring day amidst gusts of wind and on squelching muddy fields, took care of the first three elements, but what of fire? Here's how it came out in my poem "Out in the Elements," a poem written in Spenserian stanzas, from 2013's *The Singing Bowl:*

> As rain recedes, I pause to fill my pipe
> And kindle fire that flickers into light
> And lights the leaf all curled and cured and ripe
> Within a burr-starred bowl. How fierce and bright
> It glows against the cold. And I delight
> In taste and fragrance, watching whisps of grey
> And graceful smoke in their brief flight,
> As sun breaks from the clouds and lights my way
> I feel the fire that makes the light that makes the day.

I do indeed feel the fire that makes the light that makes the day, and there is something wonderful and paradoxical as you draw the smoke and the embers glow in the bowl of your pipe, to feel that for a moment you are holding fire itself cupped in your hands. I sometimes sense that, for me, that little blaze is the burning bush that God has sent to get me finally to turn aside, like Moses to the lit bush, "take off my shoes from off my feet," and listen to Him for a change, to remember that I stand on holy ground.

I have spoken of pipe smoking so far in its mode of solitary contemplation, but it is also an immensely companionable thing. And I speak not just of what Lewis celebrated in his essay on friendship, when he gives us a hint of what it must have been like when the Inklings settled into a pub after a long walk together, and took out their pipes for one of their "golden sessions":

> Those are the golden sessions; when four or five of us after a hard day's walking have come to our inn; when our slippers are on, our feet spread out towards the blaze and our drinks at our elbows; when the whole world, and something beyond the world, opens itself to our minds as we talk; and no one has any claim on or any responsibility for another, but all are freemen and

> equals as if we had first met an hour ago, while at the same time an Affection mellowed by the years enfolds us. Life—natural life—has no better gift to give. Who could have deserved it?[1]

For there is a further companionship in pipe-smoking, a fellowship with the past, a kind of communion of the saints, of ordinary saints, the pipe-smokers of former times, who form for me at least, a literary lineage. I have mentioned some of those writers already. Indeed, the next published poem of mine with a pipe in it was a celebration of Tolkien, the writer who inspired me to take up the pipe in the first place. It was occasioned by a wonderful photo of Tolkien by an oak tree with his pipe:

PATTERNS (TREE AND LEAF)

Tolkien is leaning back into an oak
Old, gnarled, distinct in bole and burr
As, from the burr and bowl of his old pipe,
Packed with tightly patterned shreds of leaf,
The smoke ascends in rings and wreathes of air
To catch the autumn light and meet such leaves
As circle through its wreathes and patter down
In patterns of their own to the rich ground.

Again he contemplates the tree of tales;
The roots of language and its rings of growth,
"The tongue and tale and teller all coeval"
And he becomes a pattern making patterns,
A tale telling tales and turning leaves,
From the print of thumb and finger on his pipe
To the print and press and pattern of his books
And all their prints and imprints in our minds,
Out to this grainy patterned photograph
Of "Tolkien, leaning back into an oak."

I will leave you with a final, yet unpublished poem. Conan-Doyle's hero Sherlock Holmes spoke of a "three pipe problem": a puzzle that needed the contemplation of three pipes to solve it. So I wondered if I might have a three pipe poem, and I wrote one in lockdown about how my enforced solitude was not solitude at all but an invitation to a richer deeper communion:

A THREE PIPE LOCKDOWN POEM

And so my solitude resumes
I settle down to light my pipe
And fill the air with fragrant fumes
And muse awhile till I am ripe
With mellowed verse, and empty time
Is ready to be filled with rhyme.

Ranged on my shelves in patient print
Old poets keep me company:
One phrase of theirs might be the hint,
The prompt for some new harmony;
Their echoes in my mind repeat
And their old metres keep the beat.

For in my mind their minstrelsy
Is somehow kindled and renewed,
As Andrew Marvel stands with me
in my "delicious solitude,"
I smoke a pipe with Tennyson
As Larkin nods to Betjeman.

Their echoes in my mind repeat,
Their cadences still fill my soul,
Call me to capture, to complete,
To make my broken verses whole,
To draw their courses where they run
And mould the many into one.

So help me, my old Peterson,
And let your incense still inspire,
Smoke sweetly till my task is done,
Your bowl aglow with friendly fire,
Until I bring, in true repose,
My three pipe poem to a close.

And I will bring this essay to a close by saying that when the smoke ascends from my pipe, it is always accompanied by a thankful grace, it is always a burnt offering: *Soli Deo Gloria.*

1 C.S. Lewis, *The Four Loves* (New York: Harcourt Brace & Company, 1960/1988), p. 71.

MUSEUMING

Looking to Love in All the Right Places

I remember the first time that I walked into the Metropolitan Museum of Art in New York City. I wanted to cry, not because of the aesthetic power of the art contained within the labyrinthian space, but because I felt absolutely overwhelmed. How was I supposed to see everything famous, much less forge some kind of life-altering, emotional connection with an artwork, all within the space of two-and-a-half hours?

Vincent van Gogh, *At Eternity's Gate*, lithograph

Sometimes, visiting an art museum can seem more like sprinting through an imaginary checklist. Van Gogh painting? Check. Raphael? Saw that. Rodin bronze? Got it. Picasso? Didn't understand it, but go ahead and cross it off. Oh, and take a picture so that I can post it online and let everyone know what I saw.

But what if we entered an art museum as an ordinary saint, looking to learn from the creative creatureliness of other image-bearers? After years of visiting art museums and leading others through them, I want to argue that these spaces can provide a unique opportunity for us to grow in our love for God, our neighbor, and this world that He made and sustains.

STUFF

Art museums are, obviously, full of *stuff.* A museum can contain hundreds, even thousands of paintings, sculptures, pottery, drawings, prints, and photographs, often alongside furniture, textiles, and other finely crafted objects. To visit an art museum is to encounter objects—things made of matter—not a set of disembodied ideas.

On a recent visit to the Metropolitan Museum of Art in New York City, I stood in front of a sculpture of the female pharaoh Hatshepsut carved sometime between 1479–1458 BCE. Even though the pharaoh was depicted in a kneeling pose she was still eight-and-a-half feet tall and absolutely towered over me. Her stiff, erect body, carved from dense, speckled red granite, dominated the space. Yet up close, I could see cracks and chips in the stone and the places where conservators had carefully restored missing sections with similarly-colored but still visible synthetic filler. The sculpture had an emphatic, authoritative presence, but it also bore evidence of its long history and of the attempt by Hatshepsut's own son, Thutmose III, to erase his mother's reign from Egyptian history. It was unequivocally and inescapably a made *thing,* an object that took up space and existed in time, made by now-unknown artists who bore the image of the Creator God even though they did not know Him.

I emphasize this point because Christianity in the West has been strongly influenced by Gnosticism, an ancient heresy that elevates the spiritual and dismisses the value of the physical world. We might be tempted to think that we should only enjoy art museums if we are contemplating

Large Kneeling Statue of Hatshepsut, ca. 1479–1458 BC, granite

the philosophical or theological meaning of the things that we view. Or, we might even wonder if art museums are a sign of cultural decadence. Perhaps we would be better off spending our time handing out evangelism tracts or listening to sacred music?

Yet as Christians we worship a God who took utter delight in making this material world. The creation narrative of Genesis 1 is filled with God's repeated affirmation that what He has made is very good. Furthermore, God's prohibition of idols in the Ten Commandments is not denial of the goodness of the material world. After all, He gives the Israelites specific, careful instructions on how to build first the tabernacle and then the temple. These places of worship are filled with handcrafted objects made from precious metals, fine textiles, and scented wood. The material world is not a hindrance or a shadow or a lesser reality because *this* is the world that Jesus promises to restore. "Look," He says, "I am making everything new" (Rev. 21:5 CSB).

So, when you visit an art museum, you need not be uncomfortable with the objects there. Instead, you can embrace the opportunity to marvel at so many objects purposefully crafted by other humans. Rather than immediately jumping to abstract questions of meaning, take time to appreciate the artwork as a thing. What do you see? Where do your eyes go? Does the artwork want you to come closer? To step back? To walk around it? Trace the gestural swoop of paint on an expressionist canvas? Imagine the artist's body, warm flesh and bone, standing where you are now, dabbing paint onto the surface. Even if we can't find an obvious human trace in the polished marble sculpture or crisp photograph, we can remind ourselves that it is still an object made by someone who was, fundamentally, the same as you: a breathing, feeling, thinking embodied soul.

STORIES

The objects in a museum are also part of a collection. This probably seems obvious, but museums do not snap into existence or materialize by chance. Someone—or more often many someones—selected, preserved, and organized the artworks. Sometimes a museum might house objects purchased by a single-minded collector, like the Isabella Stewart Gardner Museum in Boston. Other times, museums might focus on a particular period, like the Museum of Modern Art in New York, or a national history, like the Hunter Museum of American Art in Chattanooga, Tennessee. The largest art museums, like the Metropolitan Museum of Art, are encyclopedic collections, with artworks spanning centuries and the entire globe.

From these collections, museums can weave stories. Not everything that a museum owns is on display at the same time. Instead, curators select specific artifacts and decide how to organize them, making connections and crafting a particular narrative.

Traditionally, museums have been arranged chronologically. For example, at the Uffizi Gallery in Florence, Italy, we can walk through room after room of Italian paintings and sculptures from the fourteenth century through the seventeenth centuries, observing changes in style and medium. Stiff, tempera paint Madonnas with

Duccio di Buoninsegna, *Madonna and Child*, tempera and gold on wood

Filippino Lippi, *Madonna and Child*, tempera, oil, and gold on wood

egg-shaped heads against gilt gold backgrounds evolve into regal, full-bodied women, rendered in lush, glowing oil paint. The curatorial choices allow us to see how depictions of the same subject matter—Mary and the Christ child—have changed over time.

This story of artistic development can be attractive in its clarity. But some critics have pointed out that a selective chronological organization often encourages us to *oversimplify* history. By choosing to show some artworks and not others, curators can suggest that art develops in a linear fashion, where more illusionistic art evolves from and supersedes stylized icons. When at the Metropolitan Museum of Art, we might assume that Filippino Lippi's *Madonna and Child* (ca. 1483–1484) is better than Duccio's *Madonna and Child* (ca. 1290–1300), simply because Lippi's Christ child is more convincingly chubby and charming than Duccio's stiffer, seemingly weightless babe. The problem with this narrative of stylistic succession is that it obscures the rich texture and complexity of history. It encourages us to ignore the parts of the story that don't seem to fit in the predetermined trajectory.

But many museum curators today are telling more complicated stories. Through thoughtful juxtapositions, they direct our attention and encourage us to find surprising relationships. The Hunter Museum of American Art, for example, now includes a portrait of an anonymous Black woman—drawn on a piece of reclaimed barnwood—in a gallery of elegant paintings of White southern elites. The work's presence disrupts a nostalgic retelling of the past, forcing us to confront the erasure of Black women's labor in American history.

Or, at the Museum of Fine Arts Houston, curators have organized the contemporary art galleries by theme rather than chronology or country of origin. Visitors can see how artists from various cultures address community building, humor, or trauma in their work. A thematic structure helps us recognize similarities and particularites. How does the same theme take different forms according to a culture's specific needs or challenges?

When you visit a museum, learn from these curators and seek out complex, textured stories. As Christians, we recognize the storytelling impulse as part of our image-bearing. We know that we are part of God's great rescue story: Creation, Fall, Redemption, Restoration. But within this larger frame, the narratives contained in Scripture are hardly simplistic. Leaders like King David fail, the Hebrew prophet Elijah is sustained by a non-Jewish widow, and the Savior of the world is born to a poor woman from Nazareth.

So in the museum, too, look for stories and connections that surprise you. Read the labels, look across galleries, and weave together artworks that remind you of the seeming contradictions in history and the God who tenderly holds it all together. Learn to better love your neighbors—historical and present-day—by seeing how their artworks either echo or challenge your understanding of how the world works.

Anonymous (Spanish, ca. 16th century), *Pietà*, alabaster

SLOWNESS

Finally, visit an art museum in order to slow down. Rather than rushing to check off the famous artists from your list, allow yourself to spend time with a few artworks. Find a bench and stare. Draw what you see. Get close, step back, and jot down notes. You need not rush to unlock the artwork's meaning. Simply be curious about it as an object. Ask questions about the story it is a part of. What is it doing here? What has it done in the past?

Then, too, move slowly with artworks that arrest you in their seeming strangeness. Inevitably there will be an object that makes you raise an eyebrow, wrinkle your nose, or shrug your shoulders. Artworks made in unfamiliar cultures in response to an unfamiliar experience can humble us. But instead of feeling shame or frustration that we don't immediately understand a work, we can channel our discomfort into curiosity. Perhaps there is something in a Chinese landscape painting, an Islamic manuscript, or a Spanish Catholic devotional sculpture that eludes us. Perhaps the contemporary abstract painting or the crisply geometric boxes or the inexplicable pile of candy in the corner stymie us. This does not make them bad art or make us bad viewers.

Instead, embrace the long path of learning. We can be appropriately humbled in our not-knowing. And then, we can give these artworks time: time to learn more about our artist-neighbors and time to interrogate our own assumptions, fears, and desires. We may determine that we do not like a particular object, or we may even find it troubling and offensive. But moving through the museum as an ordinary saint with generous slowness—rather than tearing through as a critic on a mission—can enliven our imaginations and increase our empathy for our neighbors whose stories may be different than our own.

Art museums are not perfect places. Their histories and practices, particularly in relationship to the legacy of colonialism, should be thoughtfully interrogated. But they do offer ordinary saints an opportunity to practice looking with love. We can marvel at the material *thingness* of artworks, paying attention to how they impact our bodies and imagining an artist's body pulling the object into existence. We can seek out stories that help us better acknowledge and hold the world's complexity. And we can relish the slowness necessary to encounter even the objects that unsettle us. Secure in our Father's love for us as embodied souls, living in His story between redemption and restoration, and longing to share His love with our neighbor, we can step towards glory in even an art museum.

ROLLER SKATING

All Skate!

"If the good Lord intended us to walk, he wouldn't have invented roller skates."[1] Willie Wonka, not known as a theologian, makes a good point: God did in fact invent roller skates, indirectly. One day, one of his creative humans thought up the idea of fastening wheels to the platform of a shoe.[2]

It seems we've always been devising ways to sidestep our feet. Sometimes our lust for transit is in the name of progress, which is the case for planes, trains, and automobiles. Sometimes it's for pure fun. Ergo, roller skating.

When I casually mention to an unsuspecting adult that I seek out skating rinks on my travels, I notice a micro-expression of incredulity followed by a quip like, "Oh, I haven't skated since junior high."

I get it. Skating reminds us of the anxiety of staying upright in the most precarious situation, fearing sudden bone trauma, and feverishly avoiding embarrassment.

I experienced such vertigo as a junior high lad when a girl, much taller and new to our school, invited me to a skating party. Her parents picked me up in a green station wagon in which our thighs kept touching on the vinyl seat, and I didn't know what to talk about, staring at the back of her parents' mid-century heads, and I had to endure two hours of rolling anonymity and her adoring stares before the trip home could commence and I could return to my happy spot on the shag carpeting in front of the TV munching Oreos with milk while watching roller derby on WPIX Channel 11, New York.

In a word that would've come in handy in the 1970s, it was an "awkward" day.

These days, I relish the opportunity to lace up and hit the floor, weaving backwards to the music, my preferred form of locomotion. We all have our hobbies, some less trendy than others. Sometimes we find a tribe, as I have with skating. Sometimes a cool person puts our avocation on the map, and we feel vindicated.

Imagine my swagger when I thumbed through a *Red Bull* magazine and saw an article on a world-renowned, well-sponsored, professional roller skater called T-Stacks Frank. I recognized the name of his hometown skate center. Then it dawned on me, I had seen T-Stacks with my own eyes!

A month earlier, Becky and I were visiting Nashville as part of a study leave. She doesn't share my rolling passion, so I wished her a quiet evening at our cabin and drove over to Skate Center Smyrna, a working class suburb.

I noticed a diversity of ages and social-economic strata there, mostly white like me. It felt like Magic River Skateland in Lewisburg, Pennsylvania, where I honed my moves as a teenager.

Though rinks are social places, the regulars tend to keep to themselves. I was content with that, knowing I could talk to anyone if I pleased. Suddenly a middle-aged lady rolled up beside me, caught my eye, and made sure to get my name. She called herself "Mama Mary" and acted as the de-facto cheerleader to the locals. I could see the affection in her eyes. I told her she reminded me of my friend Leslie Bustard who occupies a similar post as chief Welcomer in my church.

I tapped a guy named Eric who was making me envious with his rolling spin moves. I asked him for some tips, and he was glad to oblige. He encouraged me to check out Rivergate in the north part of Nashville to witness some great skating. Ten days later, I drove forty-five minutes north to the rink, feeling a bit sheepish about the distance and time commitment for just a "little-old hobby of mine."

I could tell walking in from the parking lot that this was place had soul. The proportion of experienced skaters far outweighed the casual drop-ins and birthday celebrants. They were way above my pay grade. In situations like that, I feel like a kindergartner, but I'm also inspired to refine my craft. The music at Rivergate hooked me in: hip-hop and R&B, sometimes disco (my favorite). And unlike The Castle (my hometown rink), they had no restriction on backwards skating. I was one of the few white people in the room.

All around me, individual dancers melded into groups of three, four, or five, shuffling in unison. The center of the rink teemed with skaters rehearsing dance steps, a pulsating congregation of spirited friendship. Rising above them all like an NBA player on a high school court was T-Stacks Frank. He wore a baseball cap with tiny devil horns on it, pulled down low over his eyes, two chrome lip rings catching the colored chaser lights above him.

His full-body engagement, rhythmic acumen, and effortless spins, all while navigating scads of other bodies, were nothing short of mesmerizing. I had no idea he was a Big Deal until I read the article in *The Red Bulletin.*[3] I must admit to a surge of personal vindication for my juvenile hobby!

What is roller skating, anyhow? If Harold Hill, *The Music Man,* were here, he'd tell you squarely: skating is merely *sustained walking.* The sustain bit is what keeps people on the floor because a crowd of people walking in a counter-clockwise circle on a large dance floor would be boring and silly. But you add some wheels, well-amped music, and spectacular lighting, and voila! A new avenue of human enjoyment is ignited.

But does it glorify God? My question is, how can it not?

When my family moved to conservative Lancaster County, my children would sometimes attend homeschool Christian music skating "parties." I always felt like I should hold back from enjoying myself too much because dancing, as we all know, is a sign of utter worldliness. Though I never truly cut loose, I'd swing my arms a bit and keep the beat, generating a few comments (to my wife, not me): "Tom's really good, isn't he?"

Enjoyment. Didn't God make us to enjoy not just a relationship with Him but with all that He's made? And hasn't He created us with the capacity to re-create such whimsical and "unnecessary" endeavors such as roller skating?

If we take the Bible's overall message seriously, the answer is a resounding yes.

Mr. Wonka's theology is off-base because it denies the sub-creator aspect of our humanity. God didn't have to invent roller skating. He left that up to us, along with theoretical mathematics, bridge construction, and antibiotic treatments.

And that, my friend, glorifies God as much as when the sun rises and the people talk and the slime molds do whatever they do in God's good earth.

Besides the fun, numerous health benefits come from roller skating. On several skating rink web sites I've seen an infographic that is clearly meant as a marketing tool for their industry.[4] Still, I can't find anything about it that isn't true by my experience:

- Skating for just 30 minutes produces a heart rate of at least 148 beats per minute
- The average person can burn up to 600 calories with just one hour of vigorous roller skating at 10 miles per hour
- Roller skating causes 50% less stress to joints than running

Beyond the exercise, skating is safer than most other vigorous activities like basketball and bicycling. It always amazes me how many people do not get hurt at a typical public skate. Somehow, the movement of all the bodies puts individual skaters on self-protective alert, leading to a high degree of social care. It's this social dimension of skating that I'm most taken with as I mature. (Notice I didn't say "get older.")

On another trip to Raleigh, I experienced United Skates of America. Ahh, that name! The rink, featured in a 2019 documentary produced by John Legend,[5] is an example of how skating builds community, especially among African-Americans.

Roller skating is an all-age, nonalcoholic night out. On that score, it sure beats the dance club scene in generating healthy culture. It's also a context to ply one's moves, meet new people, and have fun in a climate-controlled setting, usually. On may way through St. Louis, Missouri, I made it a point to experience a weather-dependent skating rink in Dellwood, near Ferguson. Built by the local recreation center, the glassy smooth, outdoor rink is flanked by terraced seating and a DJ's table.

I skated with two retired men there, both Black, who affirmed that the rink is an oasis for their neighborhood.

No doubt, skating is not for everyone. It takes thousands of counter-clockwise laps to develop a second nature on wheels. Comfort with the fore-and-aft axis takes time, as does the crossover leg turn. Thanks to a whimsical God, in His providence, I developed those skills and many more before I even began to call Him my Father.

When I did enter into a relationship with God through faith in Jesus Christ, I questioned skating's worth. I didn't hang up my skates, but I wondered, "How can this activity glorify Him?" I was being influenced by pietistic teachings of Christian ethics that spent more time on gray areas than on the deeper concerns of the Bible such as justice, love, and mercy.

My concerns were put to rest by one unplanned comment my college minister made to me during a time when young Christians in our group were hidebound from enjoying everyday pleasures out of an honest desire to please God. Pondering this, Joe turned to me and said, "I don't walk around each day worrying about if I'm glorifying God. I just live." I realized then, I want to be like Joe: just live with a lust for life because God is my Father.

Soon after that, at a skating party hosted by the Fellowship of Christian Athletes, the DJ must have gotten tired of playing our stacks of Christian rock LPs and instead threw on "Start Me Up" by the Rolling Stones. At first, I felt risqué about dance-skating to such an aggressive tune. But it was just too funky to pass up, so I let loose and boogied down. I felt free. I enjoyed myself. I put on a show. I glorified God.

I glorified God in two ways: first, in the general sense that any human endeavor does—it points back to the Creator who made humans to do all sorts of things they couldn't do if they themselves weren't first created. Second, I remembered why skating gave me such joy. In that instance I chose to honor God by having fun.

If God intended us to walk, then He must've intended us to walk on wheels too.

1 "Willy Wonka & the Chocolate Factory," Wikipedia, July 30, 2022, https://en.wikipedia.org/wiki/Willy_Wonka_%26_the_Chocolate_Factory.

2 "Roller Skating," Wikipedia, July 12, 2022, https://en.wikipedia.org/wiki/Roller_skating.

3 Abby Lee Hood, "Roller King," Red Bull, October 24, 2021, https://www.redbull.com/int-en/theredbulletin/roller-king-t-stacks-frank.

4 Lynette Annaker, "Roller Skating Infographic!—It's All in the Facts," *Roller Skating International,* May 28, 2015, https://www.rollerskating.com/blog/roller+skating+infographic+its+all+in+the+facts/4.

5 "*United Skates,*" IMDB, https://www.imdb.com/title/tt4009728/.

KNITTING
To Knit is to Join

Knitting yarn is a thread formed from fleece, or fiber spun and wound on a frame to form a skein. A skein is a web of threads that may be later wound into a ball for knitting a new garment, avoiding snarls and tangles. Loving hearts are knitted, joined in affection and relationship. The yarn of family, familiarity, and trust binds us in close-woven friendships, kin-ships. ("Yarn" is also what we call a wild or loosely connected narrative.)

I started knitting early, as a youngster in Toronto during World War II, when the men in our Canadian armed forces were on the front lines dealing with severe winter cold. Groups of women in our church, perhaps accustomed to meeting for a book group or a Scripture study, switched functions and gathered by the fireplace in the Sunday school room with their baskets of woolen yarn. To knit socks.

So, at the age of ten, I joined the Senior Sisters Knitting Circle in which my mother was a member. The elderly ladies taught me how to knit a woolen cap, turn the heel in a sock, join multiple snatches of leftover colored yarn to make scarves. We also knitted the old-fashioned hot-water bottle covers that guard the toes from the scalding heat. I still have the pattern for that, with a hole at the top for the open spout and one at the bottom for the hanging loop.

My knitting life has continued, now these more than eighty years on. (I sense I am both knitter, and knitted one, in the swift and skillful hands of the Creator.)

Here's how it happens. When one knitting project is completed, say, a new sweater for one of my great-grandchildren (because they have grown so fast out of the previous one), I dive into my knitting drawer for a pattern. Some of my old, printed pattern books have been used so often the pages are worn and tattered (like me!). The models in the illustrations are striking artificial poses, with hilarious hairstyles. But the garments they are modeling, the patterns of which I have often used in the past, are basic enough, malleable enough to allow for creative changes, yet still attractive enough for a new century.

THE KNITTING

First, it's the yarn that beckons, fleece
buttery with lanolin from the just shorn sheep,
a woolly proof against wind and rain.
Combed, carded, spun, it becomes a skein of
possibility. For color, you might dunk it in a hot,
vegetable stew of petals, leaves, bark, seeds—
until it rises from the vat like an animal, and offers
its beautiful, material self into your hands.

It was the habit of my New Zealand
aunt Lucy, for whom I was named, to gather
fleeces (damaged, and therefore affordable),
from the local farmers' black sheep. She would
card the fibers and whirl them on her spinning
wheel into knitting wool. One year, she
mailed across the ocean ten pounds of dense,
dark wool, wound into skeins for me to knit
into a suit. Later, when the suit was no longer
fashionable, I ripped it out, and re-purposed it—
ample material for sweaters, socks, caps—
like the way we sometimes need to switch
directions in our lives, developing original
patterns, designs never seen before.

For most of my adult life I've loved buying woolen yarn skeined in the Hebrides or Aran Islands. In my knitting drawer I've hoarded books of patterns for what are called "Fisherman" knits, with intertwining cables, bobbles, spirals, artful knit and purl combinations, seed stitches. Because the Irish wool itself is seldom washed before being knitted it is full of lanolin from the sheep's skins. Thanks to that residue, the lovely, rich, traditionally-patterned garments are waterproof, and almost windproof, to boot. Every region in these islands has its own traditional patterns. The garments wear like iron and last a lifetime and can even be handed down the generations!

I estimate that I've knitted at least one hundred of these fisherman sweaters and cardigans, with button holes and artful bone or leather buttons, to give away to friends. I used to tell a prospective customer/friend, "You pay for the yarn and I'll knit you the sweater." It brought me a lot of joyful satisfaction to know who I was knitting for! And praying for, as I worked.

I once wrote an article for a magazine, "Knitting a Sweater and a Life," about how tricky it is to get it right, using a new pattern, ripping out the mistakes, starting over. My prayer was and is that in the end, my life, like the sweater, will be both beautiful and serviceable for God to take and use.

Now, when an elderly church member is in hospital or assisted living and is unable to come to church, knitters in the congregation like me will work on a prayer shawl. We use washable, synthetic yarn. The pattern is simple: Cast on sixty-three stitches. Knit three and purl three, alternating them throughout the length of the shawl, about four to five feet long, to be worn over the shoulders on chilly days. We love to think they sense our love, and God's love, warming them. I think of it as "trinitarian" knitting, and for me it is a meditative way to bring comfort to some lonely, elderly friend. The practice is a form of soul work.

KNITTING IN THE WILD
Douglas Fir Campground, October 2012

The pale bits—twigs, fibers,
pine needles—sun-struck,
fall through the lazy air
as if yearning to be embodied in
my knitting, like gold flecks woven into
a ceremonial robe.

Then, surprise—a new marvel!
Like a parachutist, a very small beetle
lands on the greeny stitch I have just
passed from left needle to right;
the creature's burnished carapace
mirrors precisely the loop of glowing,
silky yarn he has chosen.

When this shawl ends up
warming someone's shoulders,
will she sense the unexpected—
this glance, this gleam,
this life spark?

SHAWL
from *Angels Everywhere*

Early. I sit by the window.
The sun lays his bright cloak
across my shoulders.

All winter long I add
to daylight's warmth, knitting
prayer shawls for shut-ins—
knit three, purl three—
a kind of woolly, trinitarian
meditation, but nothing
as golden as this.
Nothing as warming to the heart.

Because it's almost impossible for me as a knitter to know exactly how much yarn to buy for a new project, I end up having to estimate how much is needed, and then some, just to make sure the weight and the dye-lot is a match so I don't have to go back to my friendly yarn store and say, "Hey, I'm going to run out of yarn and need more for this sweater." They may look through their masses of yarns stacked high on shelves and tell me, regretfully, "Sorry, we're out of that. We could order more, but remember, it may be a different dye lot, and it could take months." I go ahead and order more, and, inevitably there *is* wool left over after the sweater is finished. My sewing basket continually overflows with lovely, redundant yarn. This collection is known as a "stash." Like all knitters, I have stashes of lovely, virgin wool that was a bit more than I needed. It lies in a basket, glowing, waiting.

Sometimes I ask God to rescue me from the stash of old age. I say, "Here I am. Use me. Don't put me aside. Knit me into a fresh, new garment."

KNITTING THE FIELDS
from *Angels Everywhere*

Spring, and the Skagit's new-plowed fields
are tapestried chocolate brown, their soil warm
and richly gleaming after rain, and sun,
and rain again. Row on furrowed row across
our fertile valley the farmers guide their combines,
over-turning the soil, patterning it for planting.

John at the wheel, we drive the roads that
transect this vital land. He steers. I knit a sweater
for a friend, an interior landscape of
variegated yarn that grows under my needles,
its serried rows almost the same rich color as

the furrows in the Spring sun. I knit a stitch
of red barn, purl another, dark as the wing of
a hawk overhead, then a knot the gray of a
fence post, a fleck the pale color of sheep.
Under my fingers the textures of the season
grow this garment into what I hope will be,
by Fall, rich and warm as earth under noon sun.

Breezy Brookshire,
Knitting (above and
previous), pencil

RETAIL
Filthy Lucre

How does one glorify God as a bookseller? Well, beyond the obvious—have a pure heart, put God first, show some biblical discernment, don't be a jerk—booksellers glorify God by selling books.

Every day a retailer does many things, from paying bills, managing staff, evaluating inventory, ordering new merchandise, and—if one is a real retailer and not a faceless, automated online selling platform—talking with the actual humans that we call customers. I am sure other shop-owners selling other products in helpful ways have this experience, but there is something about bookselling that brings to the fore big questions about things that really matter. A customer wants a book on marriage, on depression, on politics, or prayer, and we are off to the races.[1] We are asked daily for guidance and usually for a small bit of comradery and encouragement. Most booksellers have seen it all, and we wonder often what we've gotten ourselves into as we offer a listening ear and provide resources to help. We booksellers are part pastor, part bartender.

As many tasks as there are in a day for a retailer, our central vocation—shaped by a disposition for teaching and mentoring others, perhaps—is selling. The Bible is clear that there is no sacred/secular dualism[2], no dichotomy between the human activities God cares about (what some might call spiritual or church-related or theological) and those God cares less about (like, say, the mundane concerns of ordinary material life). All of creaturely life was called "good" by God at creation and, although it is distorted by sin and idolatries, Christ is, as Abraham Kuyper put it, reclaiming and restoring "every square inch" of His creation.[3]

There is no shame in any legitimate work, and I give God glory when I do it well.[4] Sure, selling theological books (as I sometimes do) may seem more obviously religious, and talking with customers with tender care about matters of the heart (as I often do) may make it seem like a ministry, an easy place to give God praise. But the call of God echoes down from first century Corinthian homes and markets to twenty-first century shops and online stores: "Whatever you do, whether you eat or drink, do all to the glory of God" (1 Cor. 10:31). Paul gives the new followers of Jesus instructions about working out their faith in ordinary, embodied practices that honor God, not only in communal worship and witness and charitable service but in the concrete stuff of mundane life—eating, drinking, buying, selling. For the bookseller this implies much but comes down to this: we glorify God by running a business that serves customers by selling stuff that is helpful and good.

There is in the church, and in some streams of Western culture, an embarrassment about money and, to some extent, business.[5] *Filthy lucre,* the early English Tyndale Bible called it. It is understandable—wealth is almost always seen in the Bible as a threat to faith, and Mammon is one of the chief idols about which Jesus warned. Open-handedness, especially to the poor, is a central pillar of a Christian social ethic. From the law to the prophets, from the wisdom literature to the Gospels, from the stories of Acts to the teaching of the Epistles, generosity, work for public justice, and resistance to what we moderns call materialism is consistent and compelling. "Give to all who asks of you," our Master declared (Luke 6:30). No wonder shopkeepers and financiers have been held in suspicion in some parts of the church; no wonder it is complicated to be biblically directed and redemptive in the way we think about selling. But this is not the place to work out a full-orbed and coherent theory of Christian economics that would inform a faithful approach to Christians in the business of retail. My point here is simple and two-fold: those of us with any amount of money, and certainly those who work exchanging it, must grapple

Ned Bustard, Detail from *Dog-Earred* (above and previous), linocut

regularly with the teachings of the Bible on these matters and, somehow, we must forge a positive and faithful perspective that allows us to see God's ways as integral to the business. We must sense God's presence, and be directed by God, in the very ordinary practices that makes up the daily grind of running a retail shop.

Add to our anxieties about money the popularly assumed (but unbiblical) sacred/secular dualism that suggests that typical, human activities such as work are "worldly," and therefore less important than more seemingly spiritual activities for ordinary saints, and we end up with a curious quandary. We think business and retail and selling is somehow debased, unseemly. And we are to glorify God *there?*

In my situation, I must glorify God not only by selling religious books and praying with customers or giving away free merchandise to the needy, but I must run our business and do our routine selling in a manner that would be pleasing to God and bear witness to the ways of Christ's kingdom. We don't justify our "secular" retail work by glorying in the seemingly spiritual components—the religious content of the books, our ministry with our customers, our charitable giving. It is too easy to suggest that we glorify God by slapping some spiritual veneer on our seemingly secular work, giving God praise for *those* aspects of the job.

Businesses (actually networks of businesses) are part of the cultural development God intends. The ones I'm most interested in here, the other enterprises that relate to my own calling as a bookseller—paper and ink manufacturers and printers and book binderies and publishers and their workers (such as writers, editors, graphic designers, publicists, reviewers, sales representatives, order takers, accountants, wholesalers, distributors, not to mention the vital USPS and other such delivery services)—are all a part of a web of service that gets books into our bookstore and, eventually (with our help), into your hands. If I am to glorify God in the actual reality of retail, I must say from the start that I do not do it alone. Our team at the shop, our UPS and FedEx guys, our banker, the company that sends out our online newsletter, and the local municipality that plows our street (but not our parking lot, sadly)—not to mention, obviously, our often fiercely loyal customers near and far—

Ned Bustard, Detail from *Cuppa Books*, linocut

make up the matrix for our bookstore's embodied worship service of God each day.[6]

It's easy to say a prayer for a vendor when placing an order; with God's help we can be gracious to customers who are late in their payments. What retailer doesn't take joy and thank God for a customer who is well-served and appreciative? Thanks be to God for those opportunities to shave a bit off the price to help a customer on a fixed income. Especially in the work of bookselling there are daily joys about books and literature and Christian growth and deepening insight, and I have no doubt that God smiles over much of this lovely and rewarding livelihood.

Yet, yet. There are moments, it seems to me, when we are called upon to be clear about who we serve. Glorifying God as an ordinary saint in the world of business means dancing a complicated dance, walking on the razor's edge, doing a balancing act between the idealism of a transforming vision of what God can do in and through our work, for our customers, places, towns, and regional economic ecologies, and the mundane and often tedious duties of "how the sausage gets made."[7] We serve God in the here and now, in the real work, attentive and earnest, offered over to our neighbors for their flourishing, even as we offer our days to God. But we long for the renewal and restoration that only God can bring. This is the sort of thing that inspires me as I wonder how an ordinary saint working in retail-land might comport himself, finding a worldly sort of holiness amidst the clammer of customers and their credit cards. In one of the most lovely and inspiring brief writings on this, a chapter in the extraordinary book *The Call: Finding and Fulfilling God's Purpose for Your Life*, Os Guinness says that even drudgery, offered up for God, can create "patches of Godlight."[8]

Take off your shoes in Aisle Eight, at Table Nine, at cash register Three. It is holy ground.

There is a marvelous passage in the second chapter of Haggai, a moving promise of a time when the temple would be rebuilt, when after exile and loss and destruction, there would be a spiritual visitation empowering the people to rebuild. "The gold is mine and the silver is mine," God reminds them, claiming His ownership of the very materiality of their labor. It was going to end well, God promised, and there would be peace in that place due to their diligence in attending to God's gracious presence in their good efforts. "Be brave and work," God commands, "and in this place, I will give peace" (Hag. 2:1–9). May it be so with you ordinary saints who work in business, especially in small shops, serving as you sell. As do you the work, He will bring His peace.

1 See the weekly Hearts & Minds BookNotes blog (http://www.heartsandmindsbooks.com/booknotes) for reviews or announcements of the many books I recommend. For mostly like-minded suggestions on a variety of topics by exceptional scholars, writers, and friends, see *A Book for Hearts & Minds: What You Should Read & Why—A Festschrift Honoring The Work of Hearts & Minds Books*, edited by Ned Bustard (Baltimore, MD: Square Halo Books, 2017).

2 The book that best explores the roots and implications of a non-biblical dualism and counters it with a robust, wholistic Christian worldview is *The Transforming Vision: Shaping a Christian World View,* by Brian J. Walsh and J. Richard Middleton (Downers Grove, IL: InterVarsity Press Academic, 1984.) Although very different in tone and approach, recall *Practice of the Presence,* the famous story of Brother Lawrence, the Parisian monk who in the late 1600s wanted to learn to pray and did so by doing the dishes (and sensing God's presence while shopping in the local marketplace). Try the vivid, new translation by Carmen Acevedo Butcher (Minneapolis, MN: Broadleaf Books, 2022).

3 Kuyper first uttered his famous lines in a speech at the 1880 opening of the Free University of Amsterdam, proclaiming, "There's not a square inch in the whole domain of human existence over which Christ, who is Lord over all, does not exclaim, 'Mine'!" This "all of life redeemed" worldview is most succinctly spelled out in his 1898 Stone Lectures, delivered at Princeton Theological Seminary and published as *Lectures on Calvinism* (Grand Rapids, MI: Eerdmans, 1943). For a fabulous and thorough study and update of these seminal lectures, see *Calvinism for a Secular Age: A Twenty-First-Century Reading of Abraham Kuyper's Stone Lectures,* edited by Jessica Joustra and Robert Joustra (Downers Grove, IL: InterVarsity Press Academic, 2022).

4 Happily, in recent years, there has been a renaissance in thinking and writing Christianly about work. Perhaps the best serious book is *Every Good Endeavor: Connecting Your Work to God's Work,* by Timothy Keller and Katherine Leary Alsdorf (New York: Penguin Books, 2013). For a punchy, brief reflection on making a difference in the workplace see *Work That Makes a Difference,* by Daniel M. Doriani (Phillipsburg, NJ: P&R, 2021). Dorothy Sayers famously insisted that the goal of Christian work is, at least, to do good work. See her still-relevant remarks in the chapter "Good Work" in *Letters to a Diminished Church: Passionate Arguments for the Relevance of Christian Doctrine* (Nashville, TN: Thomas Nelson, 2004).

5 There is a plethora of books that wisely explore the dangers and blessings of wealth in the Bible. The most comprehensive is *Money and Possessions* by Walter Brueggemann (Louisville, KY: Westminster John Knox Press, 2016). Don't miss *Christians in an Age of Wealth: A Biblical Theology of Stewardship* by Craig L. Blomberg (Grand Rapids, MI: Zondervan, 2013). Excellent advice thoughtfully offered is in *Practicing the King's Economy: Honoring Jesus in How We Work, Earn, Spend, Save, and Give* by Michael Rhodes and Robby Holt, with Brian Fikkert (Grand Rapids, MI: Baker Books, 2018).

6 Three well known leaders from church history who each wrote directly about our social interdependence are Martin Luther, John Calvin, and Martin Luther King, Jr. Of course, don't forget the famous John Donne line, "No Man Is an Island," taken from his *Devotions Upon Emergent Occasions,* "Meditation 17" (New York: Vintage Spiritual Classics, 1999, orig. publ. 1624).

7 One of the lovely recent books about cultivating a sense of place is *The Power of Place: Choosing Stability in a Rootless Age* by Daniel Grothe (Nashville, TN: Nelson Books, 2021). See also the work of the fabulous urban pastor Léonce Crump in *Renovate: Changing Who You Are By Loving Where You Are* (Colorado Spring, CO: Multnomah Books, 2016). To realize how local enterprises help the local economy more than out-of-town online sites, study *How to Resist Amazon and Why: Local Economies, Data Privacy, Fair Labor, Independent Books and a People-Powered Future* by Danny Caine (Portland, OR: Microcosm Publishing, 2021). For a riveting exploration of how online sales and fulfillment warehouses effect various communities and sectors in American culture, see *Fulfillment: Winning and Losing in One-Click America,* by Alec MacGillis (New York: Farrar, Straus, and Giroux, 2021).

8 Os Guinness, *The Call: Finding and Fulfilling God's Purpose for Your Life* (Nashville, TN: Thomas Nelson, 2008).

9 Again, see the remarkably Biblical and practical wisdom for economic practices in Rhodes, Holt, and Fikkert, *Practicing the King's Economy.* For a short, hard-hitting and deeply theological study, see Michelle A. Gonzalez's fascinating book *Shopping* (Minneapolis, MN: Fortress Press, 2010).

10 Please enjoy the exceptional, short reflection "The Flash of a Fish Knife," in which Calvin Seerveld writes, "My father is in full-time service for the Lord, prophet, priest, and king in the fish business" (*Comment Magazine,* August 1, 2005, https://comment.org/the-flash-of-a-fish-knife/).

Hey, hey you—wait up! I dash out the back door of the store, down the brick sidewalk to our parking lot, wanting to catch up with the customer before he gets to his car. "I just thought of this," I shout, waving another book in the air. I press it into his hands, half-apologizing for chasing him down and half-laughing, knowing (if I read him correctly) that he will be delighted to hear about one more title that is just right for his particular need. A bookseller wanting to connect a particular reader with a particular title can be a force of nature and, well, if there is one more thing to show, one more thing to say, I dash out, inviting my customer to hold up. *You don't want to miss this.*

And so, dear reader, I'm chasing you down, inviting you to not yet turn that page. There is one more thing.

Many who have read this retailer's rumination on glorifying God as an ordinary saint working both behind the scenes and on the store floor, selling books with a holy sense of calling and a high view of business, may think that it is fine, interesting, even, to see how a retailer reflects on some of the ways to serve well in his particular field. Without getting into the details of serving people well, I've shared a holistic kingdom vision where work can be holy ground, where businesses matter, and where we can honor God in many ways, including in the mundane tasks found at ordinary job sites. I hope you, too, lean into a deeply Christian vision for your workplace, wherever it is.

But, wait: while thinking faithfully about selling merchandise we must necessarily flip the coin over to the other side that is inextricably linked to selling—buying. Allow me to invite you to the same sort of deeply rooted, Christianly conceived, spiritually shaped vision of the nature of glorifying God when buying stuff.[9]

This could be a topic for an entire book, given both the delights of good things to purchase at this stage in history and the obligations to do justice as we spend our money, engage in commerce, and vote for the kind of enterprises with which we desire to do business. I will say only this: shop wisely, intentionally, to God's glory, deepening those bonds of interdependence. Skip the bland chain stores and avoid the faceless online behemoths that are not healthy for a real economy or a healthy commonwealth. We honor God as we live into the new ways of being that discipleship brings. Surely this means glorifying God as ordinary saints in the marketplace, buying with joy what we need from caring merchants,[10] practicing the presence of God as we do, living into that promise that the ordinary stuff of daily life will shout: holy unto the Lord.

DRACULA
Vampire-Hunting Saints

I first read Bram Stoker's *Dracula* when I was twenty years old. Like many, I came to the book knowing of its title character primarily by reputation—as the suave, larger-than-life blood-sucking villain embodied by Bela Lugosi, Christopher Lee, Frank Langella, or Gary Oldman. What I actually read surprised me. The basic storyline was not wholly unexpected: after a few initial chapters in Transylvania, the narrative switches to England, where a series of characters gradually come together to fight the infamous Count Dracula, culminating with a showdown back at his castle.

But a few elements surprised me. I did not expect the multiple narrators, nor the fact that piecing together their stories is itself a major part of the plot. I did not expect just how many characters would end up playing a part in hunting down the title vampire. And I certainly did not expect to read a book thoroughly imbued in Christian language and biblical imagery. I loved the novel more than I thought I would, and what I discovered over years of rereading and thinking through this text is that all these unanticipated elements tie together to present a vivid picture of the church's role in the world.

I suspect I'm not alone; few people come into *Dracula* expecting any theological content, even though, as one critic has pointed it out, it may be "the most religiously saturated popular novel of its day."[1] In its early history, the novel was read mostly as entertainment (because it's entertaining!), so many of its deeper features went unnoticed. From the 1930s onward, though copies continued to sell, the Dracula of the text became eclipsed by the iconic Dracula of the films, all of which depart significantly from their source material.

For decades, meanwhile, literary scholars largely ignored its Christian content focusing on other aspects of a text that truly is quite complex and can be interpreted from may angles. But its Christian content isn't accidental. Over fifteen years prior to *Dracula,* Stoker's first book, *Under the Sunset,* was a collection of children's stories tinged with Christian allegory. At around the same time, he was writing poetry based on Scripture. About a decade after *Dracula* was written, Stoker penned an essay entitled "The Censorship of Fiction," in which he argued that the goal of fiction writing was, essentially, an expansion of Christ's use of parables in storytelling: "The highest of all teachers and moralists, Christ Himself, did not disdain [fiction] as a method or opportunity of carrying great truth. But He seemed to hold it as His chosen means of seeking to instill truth. What is a parable but a novel in little?"[2]

In other words, from the beginning to the end of his career, Bram Stoker's writings mark him as a man thoroughly invested in writing with an explicit Christian agenda in mind. And this is true of *Dracula,* whose title villain is clearly an anti-Christ figure: "everything that Christ is meant to be, Dracula either inverts or perverts."[3] The vampire hunter Van Helsing remarks about the Count that "[o]ur enemy is not merely spiritual."[4] This comment notes that he certainly is an *embodied* figure, but it also presupposes the fact that Dracula *is* a spiritual enemy as well. Accustomed as we are to cinematic and televised versions of Dracula that depict him as a brooding, sexy antihero, a tragic figure, or even a flawed protagonist, Stoker's original is a malevolent and monstrous villain,[5] and a danger both physical and spiritual to those he pursues and those who end up pursuing him.

It's that second group, the vampire *hunters,* who interest me here, although I'm one of the few. From the earliest days of celluloid adaptations, many of the side characters got axed (and the others altered substantially). Francis Ford Coppola's 1992 version was the first to keep the whole team, but in the process, as I'll observe, his film jettisons much of what makes them interesting to me.

Exactly how many of characters make the team is a matter of some debate, but it's clearly a sizable number. The Dutch polymath Abraham Van Helsing becomes the de facto leader of the group, and he is followed closely by his British protégé John Seward. Seward brings along his friends, the aristocratic Arthur Holmwood, Lord Godalming, and the Texan entrepreneur Quincey Morris. They are joined by the solicitor Jonathan Harker, who first encountered Dracula at Transylvanian castle. In addition to the five men, two women play major roles. Lucy Westenra, the unrequited love of Seward and Morris and the eventual fiancée of Arthur Holmwood, is one of Dracula's first victims in England. Her friend Mina Murray eventually marries Jonathan Harker and becomes an invaluable resource in tracking down the count in the end.

The prevailing view among filmmakers seems to be that there are too many characters, and so they tend to omit or consolidate them. Literary critics often take a similar stance and regard them as generic and interchangeable. They are often seen as dull vestiges of Stoker's Victorian morality at play, overshadowed in the narrative by their supernatural adversary. Christopher Craft famously nicknamed them the "Crew of Light," a handy epithet, though he is one of many to interpret them in a morally subversive way.[6] That is, many interpreters believe that the plot of *Dracula* undercuts the moral claims of its heroes, most of whom are boring and more or less interchangeable.

But this reading, I would contend, is at odds both with Stoker's stated intentions and with an honest reading of the text. As his corpus of writing demonstrates and his work like "The Censorship of Fiction" shows, Stoker was deeply interested in communicating both moral and doctrinal concerns in his works. The tendency of both popular culture and literary criticism to prefer the alluring and transgressive Dracula to his opponents says more about our culture than it does about the original novel. And it has caused readers to miss a key feature of the vampire hunters: the extent to which they function as a church.

If Dracula is undoubtedly an anti-Christ figure, a natural question to ask is whether the book includes a *Christ* figure. The answer to this is both yes and no. I believe that the vampire hunters together form a collective body of Christ—that is, they make up a church.

Scripture frequently refers to the church as Christ's body. Paul writes in Romans 12:5 that "we, though many, are one body in Christ, and individually members one of another." Elsewhere, he maintains, "For just as the body is one and has many members, and all the members of the body, though many, are one body, so it is with Christ. . . . As it is, there are many parts, *yet one body*" (1 Cor. 12:12, 20, emphasis added). The individual members of the church together form the main means by which people across the world incarnationally experience Christ following His ascension.

This dynamic is present in the Crew of Light. While their number is contested, if we include all five men and the two women, we come to the theologically symbolic number seven.[7] The conflict with Dracula draws them together for the purpose of religious, spiritual warfare. Their leader, Van Helsing, administers the sacrament,[8] along with more or less preaching.[9] The vampire hunters worship and often pray together. Indeed, the final defeat of Dracula climaxes with a moment when "with one impulse the men sank on their knees and a deep and earnest 'Amen' broke from all."[10]

And as with Paul's insistence that the church is one body with members performing different functions, so too do the members

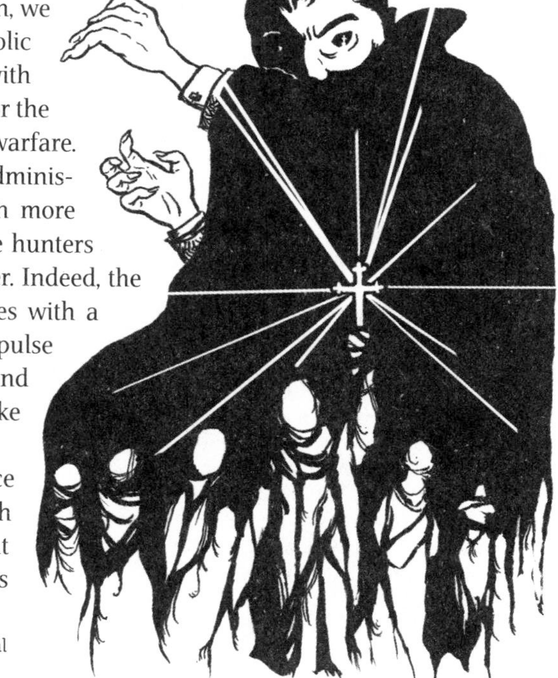

Will Kelly, *The Count*, ink and digital

of the Crew of Light. Van Helsing recognizes the threat and makes the plans. Seward uses his own medical and psychological knowledge as a disciple of Van Helsing. Lucy provides important information before her death. Mina provides moral leadership, gathers together the narrators' accounts to make sense of them, and uses her astonishing memory to coordinate their travel. Arthur Holmwood's wealth funds their activities, and he joins Quincey Morris, Jonathan Harker, and the other men in the active hunting.

Apart from Arthur and Lucy, none of the Crew are aristocrats. They are middle-class wage-earners (Mina included) who—at first incredulously and reluctantly—take on the call to defeat a powerful spiritual opponent. Far from his glorified pop culture portrayal, Dracula in Stoker's novel is diabolical, a being who parasitically feeds on victims, manipulating or violently assaulting them. *Dracula* the book is indeed a good versus evil tale. Not simplistically, of course—even the print version of the Count does have a certain magnetism, and the heroes are not allegories or flawless exemplars. Each member of the Crew must overcome faults or personal sins in order to contribute fully to the task at hand.

In other words, *Dracula* is populated by ordinary saints. Unlike many contemporary readers who go into the text preparing to identify with the vampire, I see myself in the imperfect, doubting, fearful, yet ultimately triumphant members of the Crew of Light. They muddle through to victory in a battle for souls, which is what Christ's church, however haltingly, has always been called to do. Or, as Van Helsing puts it, "It may be that we are chosen instruments of His good pleasure, and that we ascend to His bidding as that other through stripes and shame; through tears and blood; through doubts and fears, and all that makes the difference between God and man."[11]

1 Christopher Herbert, "Vampire Religion," *Representations,* Vol. 79, No. 1 (2002), p. 101.

2 Bram Stoker, "The Censorship of Fiction," reprinted in *Dracula,* ed. Maurice Hindle (London: Penguin, 2003), p. 426.

3 Clive Leatherdale, *Dracula: The Novel and the Legend* (Wellingborough: Aquarian, 1985), p. 176.

4 Bram Stoker, *Dracula,* ed. Maurice Hindle (London: Penguin, 2003), p. 265.

5 See Geoffrey Reiter, "Dracula Takes the Pulse of Culture," *Christ and Pop Culture,* accessed August 18, 2022, https://christandpopculture.com/capc-mag-volume-1/dracula-takes-the-pulse-of-culture/.

6 Christopher Craft, "'Kiss Me with Those Red Lips': Gender and Inversion in Bram Stoker's Dracula," *Representations,* No. 8 (1984), pp. 107–133.

7 The women tend not to be included in most counts, especially Lucy, who is superficial and flighty throughout much of the text. But her courage and insights as her death approaches make her an invaluable member of the group, and once her posthumous vampirism has been exorcized, she is depicted as being spiritually healed. (Cf. Stoker, *Dracula,* 232).

8 Stoker, *Dracula,* pp. 224, 317. This is a bit controversial because Van Helsing is not a formally ordained priest and uses the Host in ways no Catholic would (if he even is Catholic). But there is little evidence that Stoker himself was Catholic, and his understanding of church seems to be more ecumenical. The point here is that Van Helsing performs a clerical function.

9 Stoker, p. 316.

10 Stoker, p. 401.

11 Stoker, p. 316.

PSYCHOANALYSIS

I Sing a Song of the Saints of God

When I received a calling to be a psychoanalyst, I wasn't as old as Sarah,[1] but I wasn't a spring chicken either. I had been an artist all my life and the new career filled me with excitement, anticipation, and fear. The Reverend McAteer describes a calling in the following way:

> A vocation calling is a very vulnerable moment. It often comes in the silence of the heart. It is persistent. It is a desire. It is a longing, a yearning. It seeks to be fulfilled. There is excitement, uncertainty and sometimes fear in experiencing a sense that in God's plan for you, He is calling you to walk with Him in a most intimate and personal way. Yet in a way marked by a life of outreach to others. No one else can respond to your call. Only you. It is only giving yourself completely to God that one can taste the sweetness of a unique relationship with God.[2]

My whole life changed in a blink of the eye, a huge God imprint. I went through four years of rigorous study that included faith-based training in psychoanalytic theories, immediate residency in the clinic, and my own psychoanalysis twice a week. In the analysis, I mainly grappled with my relationship with my mother, who had gone through the trauma of World War II in Poland, and how this was transmitted onto me. I experienced much healing and recovery. I emerged a full-fledged psychoanalyst.

What is psychoanalysis? Psychoanalysis, like the experience of faith and the creative process, recognizes and involves deep and overarching themes such as love, the meaning of life, relationships, desires, identity, and the search for something transcendent and *numinous*—the experience of divinity, or the holy, or "the other." Ann Ulanov writes of the numinous as follows:

> As analysts we know such moments that quicken our blood, or make our breathing hasten as if we are running to greet some ineffable presence. . . .

> Each of us may describe those moments with Self somewhat differently—sometimes including different body experiences of energy or excitement, a watchful stillness, or feeling plugged in, or even ignited—but we share the sense of something there, pushing, pulling, or absorbing.[3]

Ulanov is here naming a sacred and otherworldly experience that happens in the therapy room. Some describe it as the analytic third. I call it God, where separateness is transcended. In the hours and hours of talking and listening, looking into each other's eyes and souls, we become connected with our patients in a way that can only be described as mysterious . . . numinous.

In working with my patients, I have seen that "The glory of God is man fully alive,"[4] and I have been confronted with aspects of my own humanity that I would rather not see. As I sit with my clients, I know the experience described in those oft-quoted lines of William Blake: "Hold Infinity in the palm of your hand / And Eternity in an hour" (or, for me, fifty minutes).

I held eternity in an hour many times while sitting with my patients. I continue to be awestruck and humbled by the beauty and courage of human life—the struggle and suffering, the joy and pain. I am humbled by this sacred work that allows me to be intimately involved in the lives of others.

Erik Erikson describes the encounter between a mother and her baby as numinous. It is a ritualized encounter that is sacred and transcendent. A similar sacredness and transcendence occur during the ritualized encounter between an analyst and analysand. Every time I am in a session with a patient we sit in the same chairs as before; our eyes meet, we talk, but it is a special kind of talk, one that is numinous, hallowed. When I am with a patient, I am aware that the space we are in together is sacred space, that we are on holy ground. As I experience firsthand the lives of my patients, I can at times hear the divine voice, feel the divine hand, perceive the divine love. As a photographer I created the series "Masks."[5] I was fascinated by human faces, they were mystery, as at the time I didn't know who was behind them. After I became a Christian, I saw the faces I had photographed as revealing the image of God in which all are made. When I became a psychoanalyst, I continued to see God in the faces of my patients, as described by Adam Gaynor in *Images of God*:

> The face is a mirror in which God appears, a mirror of the soul that bears the imprint of the invisible God. Perhaps there is no better way to have a vision of God than by looking in the eyes of our fellow human beings. In the gleam of joy, the wince of pain, the gaze of desire, there dwells the image of the imageless God.[6]

Krystyna Sanderson, *Cynthia II*, silver-gelatin photograph

What is the goal of analysis? I believe the goal of analysis is the same as the goal of life itself: to become the best we can and to be fully alive. To quote W.D. Winnicott, "Oh God, may I be alive when I die."[7] The goal of analysis is also to find our true self. Melanie Klein writes in *Love, Guilt and Reparation*[8] that there is in human life a powerful force for love and a drive for reparation. We deeply want to believe that goodness exists. As analysis progresses, reparation occurs, guilt is lessened, and trust in oneself and in others is increased. We understand in our hearts what it means to love and to be loved.

When M. Scott Peck opened his book *The Road Less Traveled* with the statement, "Life is difficult,"[9] he was addressing not only the fact that life is filled with difficulty and suffering but also by implication the importance of accepting that that is so. Carl Jung believed that anybody could endure suffering well if he or she finds meaning in their suffering. What the human being cannot endure, Jung claimed, is meaningless suffering. The sufferer who does not understand what they are going through assumes that they are being punished for some real or imagined misdeed. Jung went further, saying that meaninglessness is equivalent to illness, and that meaning makes many things endurable, perhaps everything.

The psychoanalyst is a healer, but a prerequisite is that the psychoanalyst must be wounded to be effective. Jung maintains that "Only the wounded physician heals."[10] For me, Jesus Christ is the Wounded Healer. I, as a sinner in need of salvation, forgiveness, and healing, a wounded healer myself, have become a conduit of the Wounded Healer. One might ask, "Why would anybody in their right mind voluntarily expose themselves to another person's pain, trauma, and misery and find it rewarding?" The answer is that there is a mystery in the way we become connected with our clients and experience life together, in both sorrow and joy. It has become a path to the mystical and divine.

Being present to the suffering of another is a sacred work. God is present in suffering. He is with us in our pain. He suffered himself. Suffering is God's invitation to a deepen our encounter with Him. In the Christian metaphor I may be a Simon, assisting my patient in carrying their cross, which is too heavy for them to bear alone.

Witnessing human suffering in my psychoanalytic practice has softened my judgmental attitude toward the emotional troubles of myself and others. In his book *Life Together*, Dietrich Bonhoeffer writes to this point:

> Anybody who lives beneath the Cross and who has discerned in the Cross of Jesus the utter wickedness of all men and of his own heart will find there is no sin that can ever be alien to him. Anybody who has once been horrified by the dreadfulness of his own sin that nailed Jesus to the Cross will no longer be horrified by even the rankest sins of a brother.[11]

Within our woundedness lies the numinous, the awareness of "the other," of divinity, of the holy. Hence, our suffering is relevant to our spiritual search, often the beginning of it. C.S. Lewis writes, "God whispers to us in our pleasures, speaks in our conscience, but shouts in our pain."[12] The good news is that Christ can bring us from suffering into joy, from the darkness into light, from death to life, from anxiety to peace, from fear to love, from our helpless poverty into the limitless kindness of God, to God's undeserved grace, God's sheer loveliness, God's awesome beauty.

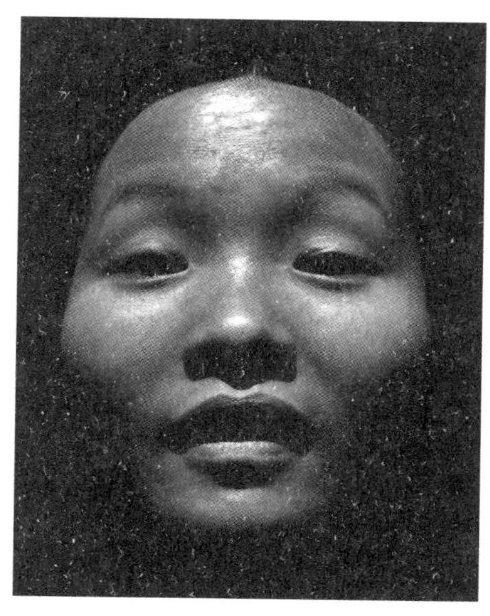

Phu III, silver-gelatin photograph

Let's move from the sacred life to an ordinary, everyday life of this saint: during the pandemic I moved the office to my apartment and more specifically to my bedroom. I arranged "my office" at one side of the bedroom with shelves full of books behind, a bright lamp beside me, and a window to my left. On Zoom it looked like a real office, though unbeknownst to my patients the bed was situated at the other side of the room. Who says that Zoom is not intimate? (And what would Sigmund Freud say about my seeing patients in my bedroom?) As I lost my office, I brought a corn plant to my "new office" in the bedroom and continued the ritual of watering the plant as an analogy of my work with my clients.

Zoom brought a dimension to the sessions that I had not been prepared for—namely, being able for the first time to peek into my patients' natural environments. I saw patients in their beds with their laptops propped up on the stacks of pillows. I conducted sessions with cats strolling in front of the screen. In one session I saw a dog wistfully gazing through a window. In another, a dog lovingly licked the face of my client who is battling cancer. I did a session with a mother holding her newborn baby in her arms. Another time children darted across the room, prompting bursts of laughter from the children, the client, and me. A patient who had long remained in a codependent relationship with her parents moved out after several sessions and got her own apartment. I got to be an eyewitness who saw her depressed in her parents' home and beaming with happiness in her own.

Psychoanalysis, whether through in-person or Zoom sessions, is a ritual of my consciousness and unconsciousness meeting my client's consciousness and unconsciousness. It is a miraculous, numinous event that Jung describes in the following way: "The meeting of two personalities is like the contact of two chemical substances: if there is any reaction, both are transformed."[13]

I'm grateful to God for entrusting me with this sacred work in the lives of others. I'm awestruck and deeply moved for that amount of confidence in me. As an ordinary saint, I'm singing a song with other saints, both ordinary and extraordinary, to the glory of God:

> I sing a song of the saints of God,
> patient and brave and true,
> who toiled and fought and lived and died
> for the Lord they loved and knew.
> And one was a doctor, and one was a queen,
> and one was a shepherdess on the green:
> they were all of them saints of God, and I mean,
> God helping, to be one too.[14]

1 Genesis 17:16
2 Dianna Weyers, my friend who was a saint, gave me a page from a Roman Catholic magazine with this quote in it about fifteen years ago. She died and I didn't get the reference. I will get it when I join her.
3 Ann Ulanov, "Countertransference and the Self," *Journal of Jungian Theory and Practice 1*, no. 1 (1999): p. 3.
4 Saint Irenaeus (ca. AD 130–202), a Greek bishop.
5 Krystyna Baker, *Masks* (Lubbock: Texas Tech Press, 1981).
6 Adam Gaynor, *Images of God* (New York: Hazelden, 1999), 3.
7 Joyce McDougall, *Donald Winnicott the Man: Reflections and Recollections* (London: Karnac Books, 2003), p. 43.
8 Melanie Klein, *Love, Guilt and Reparation.* (New York: The Free Press, 1984).
9 M. Scott Peck, *The Road Less Traveled* (New York: Simon and Schuster, 1978), p. 15.
10 C.G. Jung, *The Practice of Psychotherapy* (Princeton: Princeton University Press, 1966), p. 20.
11 Dietrich Bonhoeffer, *Life Together* (San Francisco: Harper Collins, 1954), p. 118.
12 C.S. Lewis, *The Problem of Pain* (San Francisco: Harper Collins, 1996), p. 91.
13 C.G. Jung, *Modern Man in Search of a Soul* (New York: A Harvest Book, 1933), p. 49.
14 *The Hymnal 1982*, "I Sing a Song of the Saints of God" (New York: The Church Pension Fund, 1985), p. 293.

DRAWING

What is a Drawing?

In my mind, I make a distinction between drawings and sketches. Most people keep sketchbooks (most people who do that kind of thing, anyway). I tend to keep drawingbooks, not sketchbooks. I'm not knocking the sketchbooks, I've used them myself; I just want to make distinctions. In my mind, sketches are quick, disposable things that are in the service of something else. Maybe the artist is working out a problem, making preliminaries for a larger work, or maybe just killing time. Who knows? The point is that drawings are something else altogether. They are far more than simple attempts to make a picture—some flowers, a ship, or a bowl of fruit or something. Drawings are far more perilous than that: they come from somewhere inside the artist that is not always clear to him. They have the ability to clarify what is obscure and to obfuscate what, on the surface, seems clear. Drawings are windows, mirrors, pictures. God, in speaking through the prophet, Hosea, says, "I have used similitudes" (Hos. 12:10 KJV). Whatever else this passage may mean, it at least means that God also sometimes uses pictures to speak.

Most of us recognize that there are books that we can read and reread many times, each time gaining from the experience. There are many films that bear up to multiple viewings and deep reflection. We all know of music that becomes rich-

Matthew Clark, *The Wrath of God*, ink

Matthew Clark, *The Home Economy*, linocut

er to us the more intimately we know it. The thing that elevates these things—that makes a book literature, a movie film or a tune music—is art. This is not news to anyone. However, what most people do not realize is that art works on the artist as well as the viewer. There is a sense in which the artwork is more than the sum of the parts that the artist puts into it. Powerful drawings can be as revelatory to the artist who made them as much as they are to anyone else.

I recall speaking to a friend who is in possession of a drawing of mine. You see, I made a drawing on linoleum for him to cut out and print. He had taken a very long time to make this print and I had not seen the drawing at all while he was working on it. Once he had finally finished the print and shown it to me, I told him that seeing that drawing come back to me after he had been working on it for so long was like seeing a child after having sent him out to live in the world on his own. He comes back looking similar, but with more experience. This is one way of looking at a drawing. It is a thing that takes on a life of its own quite apart from the artist who made it.

Many of my drawings take a very long time to make. I labor over them. I talk to them, and I listen to what they say back to me. There is a constant dialogue going on between me and the drawing (if I'm doing it right). Here's the way it works: the guy doing the drawing (me) starts off with some harebrained scheme for an image and starts making marks. Then the drawing starts to take shape. *Starts* to take shape. It's important at this point that I step back and look at this protean mess I've made and try to see what is happening. What does the drawing need to be complete? What is happening—apart from my intentions—with the drawing? Are there new directions that are being suggested by the confluence of lines and colors? Ideally, I pay attention to all of these things—I listen to the drawing.

The same friend from above recently looked over a series of drawings that I had made several years ago. These drawings were of a very personal nature; I had made them in reaction to a great personal tragedy. He was quiet as he looked through the dozen or so images. As we went through them again together, he started making some comments, but really more than comments, he started asking a lot of questions. He was seeing these drawings for the first time and so had no preconceived notions of what they were "about." As I talked and tried to answer his questions, he would at times disagree and point to other drawings in the series that perhaps contradicted what I was telling him. This surprised me. What I discovered was that these drawings were functioning and coalescing in ways that I did not foresee or intend.

A colleague once told me about his father who was a music critic. His father told him that when trying to understand a certain piece of music, the musician is the last person you want to talk to! He said that musicians rarely understand where their music comes from or what it is doing. I don't know how true this is, or if it was hyperbole. But I do know that when I get distance from my drawings and I look at them through other people's eyes, I begin to understand that I don't always understand what's going on in my artwork.

Matthew Clark, *Covenant with Abraham*, etching

Matthew Clark, *Self Portrait*, etching

Drawings beget drawings. Good drawings are fertile things; they suggest, whisper to the artist new directions that he had not considered before. They aren't preparatory for anything else, they are complete in themselves. And yet, this is not entirely true. They are complete like a man and a woman are complete in a marriage; they desire to add to their completeness or to reproduce themselves. New drawings in the future will be in conversation with old drawings from the past; they will inform each other and interpret each other. They will also work on the artist and change him. He will love his drawings. Not in the sense that he thinks they look incredible or that they are some achievement in artistic virtuosity, but in the sense that a piece of him has been put into them and that piece has taken on a life of its own.

It is a profound joy to look at a drawing that I have made and to see it as a thing that stands apart from me, to be able to look at it and think about it and discover new things that I did not know I had put into it. The very best of drawings continue to speak long after the pencil has been put down and the artist has moved on to something else. At the beginning of this essay, I asked what a drawing is. It is an object made by an artist that exists apart from the artist and in some ways apart from his intentions. It takes pieces from the artist and uses them to make something new that communicates with and confounds its viewers. A drawing is a mystery.

BROKENNESS

To Be the Bad Man

And the one who falls on this stone will be broken to pieces;
and when it falls on anyone, it will crush him. (Matthew 21:44)

Self-knowledge is a terrible thing. Well, I suppose it needn't always be. Jesus' self-knowledge must have been quite pleasant, even if it did include the knowledge of the shattering of His person on the cross. I think it must have been pleasant because He would know that He did not deserve those things, that they were not coming upon Him as a result of His own wretchedness. He alone could hold His head high and say, "I am a worthy son of the King of Glory." But for the rest of us: well, self-knowledge is a terrible thing when the self is terrible.

I didn't always think of myself as wretched. In fact, for quite a long time (even after my conversion), I thought of myself quite positively. Sure, I was a sinner in need of God's grace, but I had received that grace. Yes, I still stumbled from time to time, but my heart was fundamentally right with God. I was a child of the Kingdom and an heir of Glory: that trumped everything else. It was easy to affirm the most damning statements of Scripture about fallen humanity by seeing how true they were of myself before grace. I knew I was still a sinner, but I moved past that quickly. I could see the sin of another and say that I was no better, but I sure *felt* better.

I couldn't continue forever in this illusion, however: no one can. A crisis is coming, and it's coming in the form of a rock. A stone, actually. A stone rejected by the construction workers as unsuitable for the work, but that then turns out to be the key piece to lock in the whole foundation. This rock struck the clay feet of the kingdoms of the earth, destroying them, then grew into a mountain that has filled the whole world (Dan. 2:31–35). So, you see, you really can't avoid it. I certainly couldn't. I was just walking along, sinning as happily as only a Christian can, and then there's this massive stone. And, it turns out, there are only two ways that encounter can go: you can fall on the stone and get broken to pieces, or it can fall on you and crush you.

Which of these two is better? Well, I'll remind you that this same rock crushed Satan's head (Gen. 3:15). We're given the chance to cast ourselves on this rock before it crushes us. What's broken may be mended, but what is crushed is forever rejected.

So, this is where self-knowledge comes alive: where the knowledge hits the road, if you will. Because I looked upon that rock in all its perfection, in all its transcendent beauty and wondrous majesty, and I despaired. In a surface polished like obsidian, I saw myself truly at last. When the Scriptures talk about the desperate wickedness in the heart of a man, they aren't saying that my heart was only—or even primarily—wicked before the grace of God found me. Allow me to tell you what I saw.

My heart is full of desires too large to be contained, and so my heart is constantly breaking, cracking, and sagging under a weight it was never meant to bear. I cannot be happy because I will always move the finish line of happiness. There is no "much" so much that I would not want more, no place of rest I could call final because I will always press on. These desires are not only too big for my heart, they are more than my strength could ever accomplish. I long to be a god when I am not even strong enough to be a man.

That's another point: weakness. I had once thought myself to be a person of discipline and strong character. That's not what I saw in the gleaming surface of that rock. I am wildly undisciplined, bound to a weakness of will that handicaps my every effort to do or attain to anything meaningful. I give up so easily, even when it matters most.

Now, what would a wretch be without paradox? Being weak, I nevertheless thought myself strong. I could never manage to shake the belief, however much I tried to school my heart to humility, that I was worthy of power and wealth and wisdom and might and honor and glory and blessing (Rev. 5:12). And if I was worthy of them, then the onus was on God to account for why I didn't get them, and the attainment of them was met not with wondrous gratitude but with a cry of "finally!"

I was also—am also, for none of this is over—deeply frustrated with the fact that everybody else around me also seemed to think that they were worthy of these things, and that in their pursuit of them interfered with my own attaining of them. Their wealth and power and honor somehow took away from mine—as if there wasn't wealth enough for countless kingdoms in this world.

Beneath all of this, at a layer so darkened that the conscious mind can scarcely see it, is a whole nest of insecurities. In exactly those places where I think I am strong, I am afraid (or rather convicted) that I am not. And so I am afraid that I will be revealed to be actually weak, worthy of nothing but shame, hatred, spite, and rejection. So insecure am I that I don't even trust the ones I love the most to see me clearly, because I am afraid that if they did, they wouldn't love me. Their love is contingent upon their not knowing the truth about me, and so I must keep up appearances. These insecurities stoke up all of my previous obsessions to a fevered pitch: I fight all the harder to possess what I cannot reach and couldn't hold if I did; I lash out all the more desperately against the world, others, and myself in my frustration at the withholding of the glories and blessings I feel I deserve.

I am, fundamentally, not *free*, and this is what irks me most. I cannot reach what I want, have what I want, *be* who I want. And in all of my thrashing about, I only entangle myself more deeply in the cords that bind me, reducing my freedom more and more until all hope of rescue is lost. Even the vision of God is no remedy, for I am a man of unclean lips and I live among a people of unclean lips: what would be the good to me of seeing the Lord of Glory (Isa. 6:5)? Would He not be my very destruction?

Self-knowledge is a terrible judgment, but it is also a terrible grace.

In the moment of encounter with that rock, I was given the grace to cast myself upon it. It is only this that separates the saints of God from the damned of hell: we recognize that we have no hope but to be dashed against the rock. As Hwin the horse says to Aslan: "You're so beautiful. You may eat me if you like. I'd sooner be eaten by you than fed by anyone else."[1] Or as Job says: "Though he slay me, yet will I trust in him" (Job 13:15 KJV). And, even more amazingly for a man who has never heard of the resurrection:

> I know that my Redeemer lives,
> and at the last he will stand upon the earth.
> And after my skin has been thus destroyed,
> yet in my flesh I shall see God,
> whom I shall see for myself,
> and my eyes shall behold, and not another. (Job 19:25–27)

Here is the important thing: our brokenness is not something we can fix or have fixed in this life. The proud, selfish, petty child who fell upon that rock walks among you still. And so what I am *not* doing in this reflection is showing you how to overcome your brokenness so that you may glorify God. We cannot overcome or escape our brokenness in this life.

Nevertheless, we are summoned to praise, indeed, even to glorify God. That means that we must somehow find a way to glorify God *in* our brokenness, not in spite of it. I think that means that we have to lean into it and take possession of it.

Leaning into brokenness doesn't mean that we ever stop treating it as an evil and a blemish on God's world, for that would not glorify God. Rather, because the horizon we steer toward is the glorification of God, God's glory and what is conducive to God's glory will control how we think of, react to, and in general *manage* our brokenness. This means two things.

First, we inhabit our brokenness. This we do when we sit with the sorrow of it, the offense of it, the injustice of it. As we daily call to mind our sins and unworthiness and cleanse the feet of Jesus with the tears of our hearts, we declare to others and (more importantly) to ourselves that we are tragically broken, and that any good that comes out of us is small consolation to the great evil we are.

Second, we hand our brokenness over to God. It may not be much of a crown, but *all* our crowns are meant to be cast at His feet. We offer God our brokenness to make of it what He will: it is the cost of entry for receiving the forgiveness Christ offers, because this forgiveness is both free and costly. It is free because we have done nothing to earn it or to even deserve that it be offered to us; but it is costly because it requires that we let go of the broken pieces of ourselves we have been clinging to for so long, desperately hoping we could glue them back together.

God takes this brokenness, and begins to do a new work. In His hands it changes, becomes not an obstacle to His glory but the very site where it will be revealed: "My strength is made perfect in weakness" (2 Cor. 12:9 KJV). And so it becomes increasingly His: it is now a work of God, and can only be rightly interpreted in light of all He is doing. Only when we decenter our brokenness from our being and cast it out beyond the small confines of our ruined kingdoms can it be reforged into a new whole that will ground our new being in Christ. Then our greatest shame will become our greatest glory.

But when our greatest glory erupts from the center of our shame, who can boast? Instead, whenever our glory streams forth, we will praise not our own good sense in submitting to the mercy of God but rather the mercy that so relentlessly pursued us and that was, alone of all the beings in the world, not ashamed of our shame, and that deigned to work it into something worthy. When we glorify God for His glory in giving us glory, then he becomes in us truly all in all.

1 C.S. Lewis, *The Horse and His Boy* (New York: HarperTrophy, 1982), p. 201.

BONE BROTH

More Than Leftovers

We ate a lovely farm-raised chicken for dinner last night, and now it's time to take what could be seen as trash and to transform it into something that makes you close your eyes and sigh when you taste it. I pour all the left over bits into my Instant Pot and turn it on for two hours. It's sticky and cold and, if I'm honest, gross. But it's real. It's the bones of an animal and it won't let you forget it. Yet if I'm going to eat it, I'm going to give it the honor of using every last bit of what it has to offer.

It fills the house with a pungent, earthy smell that my husband barely tolerates. It travels up our stairs and fills the second floor with its miasmic presence, and my children whine: "Are you making broth again? It stinks, Mama!" I make a mess straining out the soft bones into a colander, along with the flotsam of pieces that swirl around, and then I pour the broth into jars. Glistening drips of fatty juice fall over onto the counter no matter how careful I am. The hot golden liquid slides off to one side, while I start the real work of transforming plain bone broth into something extraordinary.

I'm an Enneagram 4, so my brain is never just making broth. In my mind, I'm with all the women throughout time who have made something out of seemingly nothing in order to nourish their families. I'm standing with the apothecaries and healers of old who mixed up tinctures and concoctions to heal their communities. For me, it's never simply a matter of feeding people; it's always about giving them life. It can feel silly at times, the way that my imagination runs away with me. If I think only in practical terms, I'm just saving our family money and using up what we have. In prosaic terms, it's just me cooking—doing something that a myriad of women do every day.

But I think it's okay that I make it more than a utilitarian task. Perhaps it's even *supposed* to be more than mere food preparation. For some of us, it may be that we rationalize away the enchanting parts of our life because we are afraid to be seen as childish or flighty or, God forbid, "weird." But what if that's precisely the point? What if God put strangeness into the world on purpose and that feeding and eating are part of the gloriously weird part of being creatures?

God makes plants that give us things to eat: sometimes from their leaves, sometimes from flowers, sometimes from the roots. We make tea to drink from certain plants. Other plants we have to peel and to grind and dry and cure in order to make them palatable to the human digestive system. These things are weird and strange and, seen rightly, downright fantastic—which, as I see it, also describes fermentation, aging cheese, and the brewing of beer. It's all full of mystery and wonder and discovery and delight. And maybe that's a little part of the way that God meant for us to experience His glory in our day today.

In my case, I experience that glory when I take plain broth and make it into what I call "Super Duty Broth." That's what I write on the lids of all the containers that I stash in our freezer after I'm done. When one of us in the family is sick or feeling worn out, or if a friend needs something deeply nourishing, I pull out the Super Duty Broth, and I feel like Father Christmas from *The Lion, the Witch and the Wardrobe,*

Phaedra Taylor,
Broth Wreath,
watercolor and ink

handing out magical healing cordials and vials of comfort for body, heart and mind.

I should also say that my Super Duty Broth needs a few extra things in order to take it from good to incredible, and it's all, well—it's all a bit primal. First, I rough chop garlic, onion, ginger, and turmeric with the peels on and I transfer them to my cast iron pan in order to sauté them. I then add lemon grass from my garden, which I've cut into sticks. I pound the thick stalks to release the fresh, bright-smelling liquid, and throw them into the mix. I add chopped kaffir lime leaves and stir all the aromatics around while they heat up and begin to sizzle. To the untrained eye, the whole thing looks like something that a toddler would make when playing kitchen outside with sticks and leaves and clumps of gooey mud. Nothing about it is pretty or tidy. But the smell fills the house and I begin to feel like some kind of fairytale creature, concocting things out of roots and berries that have been foraged in the woods—the untamed, wild, enchanted woods, that is.

I pour the warm broth over the aromatics and add dried fish flakes, fish sauce, and tamari for a rich umami flavor. I then place a big piece of kombu seaweed on top and I wait for it all to come to a simmer. I can't let it boil or the kombu will make it taste bitter, so I have to stand and watch the big pot as it slowly heats up. I stir it frequently, and the mess of herbs and vegetables begins to bubble up and pile over each other. Every single ingredient adds a specific healing element to the broth. Kombu is rich in minerals, high in iodine, iron, and calcium, in addition to vitamins A and C. All the aromatics contribute to the broth's immunity-supporting powers and serve likewise to lower inflammation levels in our body. Bone broth alone is high in collagen, minerals, amino acids, and so much more. It's also *really* delicious.

After I take out the kombu, now reduced to a big floppy sheet of rubbery seaweed, I let the broth simmer for twenty-five minutes and then strain it thoroughly before putting it into jars. I also add a spoonful of miso to each jar after it's cooled a bit. Miso is a healthy superfood, containing a live probiotic, so it shouldn't be cooked but just stirred in at the end. The miso breaks apart into a thousand tiny particles that swirl around like some kind of food glitter.

When I'm finished, eight to ten jars of beautifully rich broth sit on my counter, and I feel properly enchanted. It's a trash-to-treasure story that happens every time in my kitchen. I will usually pour some into a mug and drink it hot and feel the burst of savory, salty flavor in my mouth and then the warm, comforting liquid sliding all the way down into my chest. I smell it and I think of the magnificence of this world that God has made: full of things that He put here for healing and beauty and life, every single thing with purpose and meaning.

God could, of course, have made our food in the form of a gray cube, but He didn't—thank God. And by making us in His image, He made us to delight, as He does, in the beautiful, multifaceted things of creation. He chose to give us the gift of being able to make foods and drinks of a myriad sorts and to nourish ourselves with these things. He made us to create things like beef bulgogi, Thai green curry, spinach quiche, corn tortillas, chai with milk, and yogurt. And smoked salmon. And chocolate. And, yes, bone broth, too.

When I wonder if I might be getting overly excited about making broth, I remember this observation from Robert Farrar Capon, author of the famous book about food and God, *The Supper of the Lamb*. He says:

> Why do we marry, why take friends and lovers, why give ourselves to music, painting, chemistry, or cooking? Out of simple delight in the resident goodness of creation, of course; but out of more than that, too. Half of earth's gorgeousness lies hidden in the glimpsed city it longs to become.[1]

This observation on our creaturehood is similar to another that N.T. Wright makes in his book *Surprised by Hope*. He writes:

> What you do in the present—by painting, preaching, singing, sewing, praying, teaching, building hospitals, digging wells, campaigning for justice, writing poems, caring for the needy, loving your neighbor as yourself—will last into God's future. These activities are not simply ways of making the present life a little less beastly, a little more bearable, until the day when we leave it behind altogether. They are part of what we may call building for God's kingdom.[2]

So maybe my delight is not just about this moment, but also about the new creation peeking through the veil of space-time as we know it and being made more real in this world, even "just" in my kitchen, with my soup-pot full of weeds and roots and bones. This bone broth work can also be new creation work. And if that is so, then praise be to the God who made us able to dip our toe into His kingdom while we simmer the leftovers from last night's dinner. What a gloriously tasty gift.

1 Robert Farrar Capon, *The Supper of the Lamb: A Culinary Reflection* (New York: Modern Library, 1967), p. 189.

2 N.T. Wright, *Surprised by Hope: Rethinking Heaven, the Resurrection, and the Mission of the Church* (New York: HarperCollins, 2008), p. 193.

KNOWING
The Marvelous Process

"You need to know yourself," said the oracle at Delphi and Socrates.[1] What could that mean, and why know who you are? Can't you just be and live happily ever after? Then Jean Calvin upped the ancient Greek ante: "If you don't know yourself, you can't know God either."[2]

Good night! It sounds serious. And suppose we took the biblical hint in Genesis seriously, where the Hebrew text says, "Now Adam *knew* Eve his wife, and she conceived and bore Cain" (4:1, emphasis added). Is "knowing," biblically understood, something like human sexual intercourse?!

What is "knowing" all about anyhow?

ORDINARY KNOWING

Knowing—*an understanding grasp of something*—normally follows "learning," which is a marvelous process. Most objects in God's world are given to be discoverable; things are by nature objectly revelational. So when we learn about a new subject we investigate what is there and take note of the configured whole (usually called a "Gestalt").

We gather in sights and sounds as we learn about and become acquainted with, for example, fish—their swimming movements, their enemies, how to catch them, whether or not they are edible. We do this learning, becoming acquainted with fish, as a whole person who remains subjective—our individual make-ups and idiosyncratic histories, and whether we are hungry, tired, jealous, irritable, thoughtless, or happy at the time, all enter into our conscious attempt to understand fish, or whatever.

Daily ordinary knowing, you could say, is intuited, tentative, on-going, helter-skelter dealing with a welter of prima facie phenomena. The whole-bodied You takes things in at face value. Our early knowing of some thing may be mistaken, have blind spots, and be incomplete. A more experienced knower of salt-water fish is aware that weakfish swim mid-depth in bay water, while flounders inhabit the sandy bottom; so you need to weight your baited fishing line differently if you wish to catch a few. And you best put your eel pots in dirty, garbage-filled watery spots since that is the favourite hangout for eels, which can be smoked into delicious hors d'oeuvres.

So human learning is time-consuming, and is often a troubled searching for clues that need to be detected and remembered if our level of knowing whatever is to become developed, more detailed and sure.

It turns out there are different kinds of ordinary knowing in daily life too.

I once walked closely behind a young Sierra Leonean boy in Africa through a tall bank of thick reeds to go wash clothes in a nearby brook of running water; he stopped every so often to listen for the silent slither of snakes, while North American-educated I stood still and heard absolutely nothing. Some people seem to know (and others do not) when it's time to get married or to decline another beer. A lot of our ordinary, everyday knowing is not particularly thought through or argued, and one kind of knowing does not always bolster the other kinds. If you fall off a dock into water over your head and don't know how to swim, it doesn't help much to be fluent in biblical Hebrew and Greek. And if you run a red light, it will not give you much credit with the police officer who pulled you over if you know the date Jackie Robinson first played baseball for the Dodgers at Ebbets Field in New York City.

I wonder, is some knowing more important than other kinds of knowing? Or does it simply depend upon the circumstances? It seems like having the proper kind of knowledge for the different vicissitudes of our human living is worth considering. What should parents teach their children? Because children subconsciously pick up knowledge that can subtly bolster or inflict trauma on them throughout their lives. What's the worth of schooled learning? Because schools are indeed the best places to make mistakes, since intelligent and compassionate teachers are even paid money to correct your inaccurate knowledge. And has unknowing—stupidity—increased with the rise of technological gadgetry in our secularized culture? Are the "hard knocks" of ignorant experience still necessary or worthwhile for a person's quality of life in the long run?

COMPLICATED KNOWING

Beyond ordinary knowing we find other, more complex forms of knowing. *Scientific knowing* tends to want to make sure that what we know is actually so. Scientific knowing tries to avoid the historical variability of ordinary knowing. Scientific professionals, it seems, have to reduce what we undergo in daily life to get at certain specific, specialized functions of Gestalten.

The cardiologist treats you as a malfunctioning heart. He prescribes medicine and carefully checks your pumping organ for microscopic faults, but he may not know whether or not you have enough money to pay for the treatment. The biologist runs multiple tests on the drinking water strictly to find out if it is safe to swallow. Space engineers don't roughly guess on speed and distance but have to make untold mathematical calculations dealing with mass, trajectory, and timing in order to land astronauts on the earth's moon instead of setting them adrift in empty space. Some people trust scientific knowing as a final arbiter on many human matters, but I question whether its abstracting gifts are able to direct us to a culture of peaceable living in the earthworld.

Special imaginative knowing is a modified form of ordinary knowing too. You can imagine you are a tree with roots and leafy branches in which birds build nests, or you might stretch your vocabulary with crossword puzzles, or play chess or Scrabble just for the exhilarating fun of it. You can make-believe you are an important person, or that you've been given just one wish in the world which will be granted, no questions asked—and what now is your one and only wish? That is, imaginative knowledge can enrich our lives with possibilities and provide a relaxing diversion from everyday knowing troubles that normally demand practical answers.

When imaginative knowledge is trained to produce artworks, it can illuminate a delightful world of unexplored nuances and secrets: Shakesperean drama can describe the excruciating evil of Iago's deceit or an Ursula LeGuin novel can invite readers into the comforting sanity and security of a tree forest. A Phrygian modal constellation of tones (Genevan Psalm 51) can cry out with deep sadness in words that still a person's remorse. The softly brown-blackened darkness, with its dozen colored underlays, of Rembrandt's last self-portraits hints at tribulation weathered within a trust that shalom is still possible. A well-danced tango can exhibit a dashing erotic lust that reveals the all-consuming clout and brevity of sexual pleasure. Poems with a sprung rhythm hold and express a joyful exuberance which tends to mimic the last five lyrics in the book of Psalms. Artistic knowing can open a huge reservoir of important creatural matters that can massively disturb (or enrich) our worldly existence.

SELF-KNOWLEDGE AND KNOWING GOD

Philosophical knowledge is dangerous if we believe it can give us the truth with certainty. What we humans need is wisdom, not theoretical or gnostic certainty. And here it is appropriate to discuss self-knowledge and knowing God—the two knowings Jean Calvin said are intimately related.

Of course we humans tend to hide what is unlovely about ourselves. We are ready to admire our selves and celebrate our abilities and good features. That's who I am, we would say somewhat proudly: careful thinker, well-intentioned, sensitive to others' feelings, good at my job, a capable mature person. But it can take an honest friend to make us recognize our shortcomings and native faults.

Here the Bible can be helpful: only humble people can know who they are at heart, because we humans are by nature vain. We are mortals dependent upon the mere breath of air that we are given on loan for a little while (James 4:13–16). We are created to be children of God—the God who showed up on Earth as Jesus Christ and who rules world history by the Holy Spirit. We are called to be self-giving caregivers, communally doing what God wants done. Accepting and living that challenging reality is true self-knowledge. If we don't accept it, we can't know who we really are; we will remain at loose ends, up for grabs.

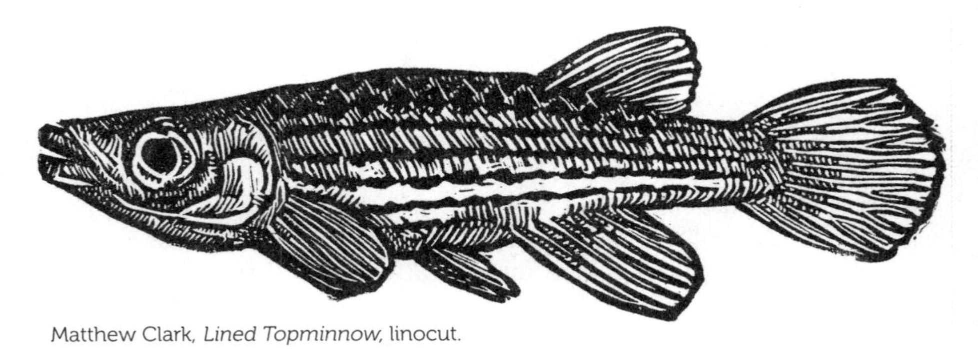

Matthew Clark, *Lined Topminnow,* linocut.

Knowing God settles things down. But knowing *about* God, as if God is an eternal unchanging Being with communicable and incommunicable attributes that we can pin down, wrongly treats God like an ordinary object of scrutiny. The God revealed in the biblical Scriptures is an almighty Creator *Person* (not a philosophical "Being") whose Word and Doings are utterly trustworthy, and whose promise to give His children everlasting life is sure. We know God when we hear and obey God's word, accepting and doing what God self-graciously and generously gives us: edifying peace (shalom) in love that surpasses understanding (Ps. 139, Phil. 4:4–7). Knowing God is not a matter of objective comprehension so much as an assurance, with grateful acceptance, of God's love shown in Jesus Christ's deeds mediated to us by the Holy Spirit.[3]

And that's where Adam and Eve's sexual intercourse comes in. Good sexual intercourse, I believe, is an action of mutual trusting love filled with intimate full-bodied joy: through it, two lovers become one with each other. Their identities remain intact, but they develop a deeper awareness of one another's glory increasing as promising, committed, fellow creatures in God's world.

Our knowledge of anything needs to be touched by that kind of gentle exciting investigative union—kinship, really—between the knower and the known that breathes wonderment and shalom. Otherwise we compromise; we lose the full meaning of ordinary creatural human knowing. When we know fish as fascinating miraculous animals worthy of attention, or we know God as the inscrutable merciful Lord of the universe who *talks to us!* (in the Bible) and even listens to our prayerful laments, we see the world as the inspiring place it is. And we understand ourselves as the knowable creatures we actually are. And while sound human knowing has a completed, restful moment to it, good knowing remains humbly and thankfully explorative.

1 Xenophon, *Memorabilia,* Book IV, ii, 24–29.

2 John Calvin, *Institutes of the Christian Religion,* Book I, i–vii; Book II, i, 1–3; Book II, ii, 18–21; Book III, ii, 14–15.

3 See I John 2:3–6, 4:7–9; Colossians 2:2.

GRAYING

Mirror, Mirror, on the Wall

“My curls are gorgeous and unique.” That’s daily affirmation number ten in a list of twelve on a website called Luxy Hair Co. “I can handle taking care of my hair,” announces affirmation number seven. “I am looking forward to wash day because that is my self-care time,” says number eight.[1] It is possible, claims Luxy Hair Co., to “manifest” great hair through positive thinking, but mostly, as you will see if you scroll around the website, by buying expensive, high-end hair extensions. For anywhere from sixty to five hundred dollars you could potentially walk out of your front door looking like the rich and famous, or like Eve before she had to leave the garden. I was curious enough, I hate to admit, to click on a long video about how to install—is that the word?—ten or twelve extra helpings of hair by means of heavy-duty, specially designed clips. The woman in the video had lovely tresses already. After the extensions were in, and she flipped the whole “do” around, I was suddenly overcome by the absurdity of my own life. Seriously? Wash day is my “self-care” time? That is almost as big a lie as “I can handle taking care of my hair.”

Jean Charles François/François Boucher, *Head of a Woman,* engraving

I could handle it before, but to say I can handle it now is as truthful as a lovely new box of hair extensions. The trouble is that in two short terrible years, my hair has gone from being how I knew it to being the hair of a stranger, and the resulting emotional tumult has been hard to keep up with. What am I talking about? Hormonal changes—that’s what it’s called when you step over the threshold of being young to wondering whether or not you should lie down and die from the sheer hassle of age and infirmity—came home to me in the era of Covid. I went rapidly, in one interminable year, from being a "put together" person to a venomous harridan.[2] I have entered the passage of life characterized by graying frizz. I am a sagging wreck of a person with a bigger middle. I am losing both my mind and my hair in clumps. And this, the internet tells me, is supposed to be a time of unusual "empowerment," of "becoming who I really am in middle age," of "not caring anymore what anyone else thinks"—to summarize a plurality of google searches on "menopause hair."

It might be helpful for me to concede that as a baby, while cute in every sense, I was bald. I lacked hair. Eventually, to the relief of all my good family, thick dark brown—and this is the crucial point to keep in mind—straight hair appeared. Straight dark brown hair that, apart from two terrible adolescent miscalculations that resulted in artificially perpetrated curls, meant that my sense of myself through my teens, twenties, and thirties was contextualized by a short, basically chic inverted bob. For those that don't spend a lot of time learning the names of various hairstyles, an inverted bob means that the back is cut shorter than the front and that bangs are basically held in contempt. You can easily tuck the longer strands of hair behind your ears. You rarely have to use a blow-dryer. "Wash day" is actually every day. And the only time you ever spray your hair with anything is when you're invited out to dinner at dusk in a high wind.

Or maybe not you—I think we're still talking about me. The lush dark luster of my hair—so I thought—gave my short stature some character, élan even. The sleekness of my bob made me feel like I had my act together. And, as motherhood overtook me and one child was added to another until the number came to six, as my weight and my energy ebbed and flowed like the inexorable tide, my sense of myself was constantly sustained by that short cut. The trouble, as you may have guessed, is that I didn't know this about myself. The problem with hair is that it is ubiquitous, like blood and skin. Until it isn't there, one isn't sufficiently grateful. Until it isn't there in the way one expects, one doesn't even know that one had a sense of self at all.

Christopher Lasch, writing about the vanity of Andy Warhol, and the narcissistic turn of American culture in the 70s, quotes Warhol (I'm skipping the horrible bit about Warhol's awful pimple): "I have to look into the mirror for some more clues. Nothing is missing. It's all there. The affectless gaze ... The bored languor, the wasted pallor ... The graying lips"—and this is the essential bit—"The shaggy silver-white hair, soft and metallic ..."[3] He looks at himself hoping that the reflection will tell him who he is. That, at least, is why I stand there, measuring not just my appearance, but the state of my own soul.

Lasch, still talking about Warhol, dryly understates the point: "The sense of security provided by the mirror proves fleeting. Each new confrontation with the mirror brings new risks. Warhol confesses that he is 'still obsessed with the idea of looking into the mirror and seeing no one, nothing.'"[4] Is that what Eve would have felt, trying to pull herself together after her flight from the garden? Wondering whether to pin up her long curls, or leave them down?

Is it what Saint James means in his brisk, curt admonishment to beleaguered, exiled Christians to stop staring at themselves in the mirror, imagining they won't walk out the door, patting their pockets for their keys, and immediately forget their own reflection (James 1:23)? Is it a taunt? Or a sermon? The human reflected back to herself is so elusive. If only I could, just for a second, catch hold of myself by what I look like, maybe then I could be happy.

My husband, in defense of his own sanity, took the valiant step of wresting some of the food out of the mouths of my monstrously big "babes" (the oldest is twenty and the youngest eleven) so that, quarterly, I can languish under the bright lights of the salon being ministered to by someone clever named Melinda. The money pays first for me to cope with the curls. Every time I am reinstructed in the way of delicately coiling a strand of hair and applying a very gentle, diffused heat—after masses of product—so that the strand will hold its shape. Having never had to do this in my whole life, I am very bad at it. Second, the money pays for the introduction of a lighter caramel brown, so that the gray is softened. It's there, but less obvious. The lighter bits of hair, and holding my chin out so that it doesn't sag so much, causes people to say, "But you look so young!" when they find out the ages and number of my children.

Gustave Courbet, *Jo, the Beautiful Irish Girl*, oil on canvas

It isn't about the self-care—who doesn't adore spending piles of money on complicated product and situations and, after two hours, emerging still hating herself—it's about having to learn how to be a different kind of person. God, all those long years ago, made a man and a woman in His own image, male and female created He them. But they didn't like it very much, so they chucked it all and were thrown out of that perfect place He had made for them to live. I like to imagine that when they went away from God, it was their own sense of who they were that took such a terrible blow. From then on all the clothes fit badly. The hair had to be combed and cut and fashioned into complicated designs, like those bizarre eighteenth-century concoctions that involved an actual tiny ship being woven into a wig and then powdered and perched on the head of some poor, corseted aristocratic female. I suppose the ship motif made it easier to figure out whose heads deserved to be cut off in the Great Terror.

As I get older, I am deeply unhappy to discover that my hair is not only getting grayer but worse, coarser every single day. Other women with white or gray hair seem to be able to achieve the sleek look. Nary a hair out of place, they look just as chic and put together as I used to feel. How do they do that? Am I going to have to cut my hair into one of those tight, stiff-curled elderly confections and wear a net over it when the wind sweeps up? How much more time and money is it going to take for me to feel "good about myself" (which, I am constantly told, is "so important in middle age")?

"Love," points out Saint Paul, who tradition tells us was actually bald as well as being short, near-sighted, and not a very arresting public speaker, "never ends" (1 Cor. 13:8). He is talking about the kind of love that God has for the creature, the person He brings alive by faith. Whoever that creature is—Eve, me, hopefully you—is invited (and James says this too, but is so brusque about it) to give up "childish ways" (1 Cor. 13:11), to admit that the look into the mirror is so excessively dim that it cannot satisfy the longing for self-knowledge. Only looking at God can do that. Looking at Him, you can begin to know "in part," that is, enough to carry you past all your dissatisfaction. Later—and this is the line that is so astonishing—I shall "know fully" even as *"I have been fully known"* (1 Cor. 13:12). Hair or no hair, memory or no memory, mirror or no mirror, God knows the number of hairs that you ever had, as well as their shape and color. He is keeping in heaven for you, just to riff on another writer of the Bible, by His own divine power, an inheritance that is unfadingly perfect (1 Pet. 1:4). It is Himself, of course, but I rather hope that it will include not fake hair-extensions and piles of empty bottles of product, but a gloriously effortless updo with a ship woven in.

1 "Manifest Healthy Hair with these 12 Positive Affirmations," Luxy Hair Co., https://www.luxyhair.com/blogs/hair-blog/manifest-healthy-hair

2 This is just my own name for myself, one that I stole from a funny YouTube clip while glowering irascibly at myself in the mirror one wintery gray dawn.

3 Christopher Lasch, *The Culture of Narcissism: American Life in an Age of Diminishing Expectations,* (New York: Norton & Company, 1979, p. 93. Kindle Edition.

4 Ibid.

CHICKENS

The Joy of . . . Chickens

Standing beneath the wall she appraised its height. She stared with one eye, then the other, calculating as a gleam shot from her brain. She crouched, sprang, and landed on the narrow ledge, nearly diving off the other side. She settled. Smug. A ball of black fluff only hours old.

This plastic storage bin was totally inadequate. It would do for a couple more days, then what? These six babies!

Three years ago my four hens died due to various causes and I spent each of the following seasons trying to decide if replacing them was worth the effort. Plowing through drifts of snow to reach their house. Hanging a lightbulb above their waterer when the temps dropped far below freezing. Scraping and hauling their droppings from their house to the compost pile. Finding my sugar snap peas stripped after a free-range trip to the garden. Calling, calling, searching, searching, crying, giving them up as lost forever until they nonchalantly appeared from under the hostas.

I had named them after women authors and Jane was my favorite. She was a friendly Red Star who laid a coffee brown egg nearly every day. Eudora was next, a sweet silver-laced Wyandotte. There was, of course, an Annie and a Charlotte. The four followed me around the yard—flying, if it can be called that, in their awkward chickenly way, tumbling at my feet, scrambling to see where I was going and what adventures I had in store for them.

This year I finally decided, yes, it was worth it. The desert years of Covid, and a change of policy at the Iowa hatchery where I order my chicks convinced me to start again. The last time I ordered, the minimum number was twenty-five chicks, and I had to Craigslist them down to our community's limit, which was four. This year, to my delight, I only needed to order six. I poured over their catalog and googled Buff Orpingtons, Blue egg-layers, and chickens with feathery crowns, trying to decide which six I wanted. My husband insisted I get a White Polish with a fluffy white topknot to match my head of curly hair, so I could be like a dog owner who resembles her pooch. I couldn't think fast enough for a crack back and there aren't many bald-headed chickens. Later I found an amusing species, the Naked Neck Turken and suggested its feath-

Matthew Clark, *Cream Legbar Among the Ferns,* linocut.

erless neck reminded me of his bald head. They are nice but ugly.

In the hours after a chick is first hatched it takes a skillful expert to determine their sex. Those determinations are 95% accurate. Not bad odds. I eagerly paid extra to get females in anticipation of all the eggs they would soon lay. Since roosters disturb the peace at all hours, they are frowned upon by neighbors and therefore by law are not allowed into our community. Even the writer of Proverbs understood this about roosters, having penned an ancient observation: *"If anyone loudly blesses their neighbor early in the morning, it will be taken as a curse"* (Prov. 27:14 NIV). However, there are some communities that allow an overnight male visitation once a week. Exercising conjugal rights, I guess. I was surprised by how joyful I felt choosing a variety of girls.

All this ordering was accomplished in late January after hours of research comparing egg colors, friendliness, and hardiness down to below zero temperatures. I purchased supplies. Chick mash, grit (little bits of sand needed to help digest food), chicken probiotic water treatment packets, and shavings. On my way to checkout at Tractor Supply a clerk caught me heading out with a big bag of gloriously scented cedar shavings. He jerked me to a halt and asked if I wanted to kill my chicks? Well, of course not, duh. I was informed that the strong scent of cedar can harm the respiratory tracts of chickens to the point of causing death. Uh oh. I thought I knew everything. He pointed me to a large bag of clean white shavings. At home, I dug out the heat lamp, set up the plastic storage bin, scattered shavings, and settled in to wait for my little darlings to arrive at the post office.

Matthew Clark, *Leghorn Rooster,* linocut.

About two weeks before the shipping, without warning, I woke to a headline: "H5N1 Avian Flu Spreading Across Flocks in the US." In May there was this: "The Worst Outbreak of Avian Flu in Seven Years Fades." By then thirty-six million turkeys and chickens had died or been slaughtered to stop the spread of the disease. While waiting to hear about my order, a call came in from the hatchery telling me that some of the chicks I had ordered were wiped out. I had to replace them with the surviving breeds still available. So there went the White Polish hen with the jolly head feathers. The new delivery date was May 15. I settled in to wait once again.

As I sit beside their upgraded temporary cage in the garage I'm getting a chicken education once again. I've been through this before, but it feels new. When they are awake there is a constant gentle peeping. Too small to perch, they sleep lying down, their heads laid out on the shavings like dead birds. Awake, they do all the chickeny things they were created to do. Without classes or mentoring in poultry behavior, they eat, drink, peck at one another's beady little eyes, and vigorously scratch as the shavings fly out the back. Mysteriously, one suddenly darts across the enclosure and dashes back as if possessed. Another finds herself lost in the desert of a box about twenty-four inches from her sisters. Her peeps change to pathetic shrieks until I lift her to the middle of her mates, dropping her into the warmth of the circle. Without cause one flockmate targets another with deliberate spite. Her tiny wings beating, legs churning, rising two inches off the floor, she lands on her sister's head and gives a vicious peck, causing her to freak out with cries of "I'm being killed, I'm being killed." Chickens are sinful creatures from birth.

Today I am questioning the 95% accuracy of the expert chicken sexer person. One of my little Wyandottes and a Black Star are behaving in a very aggressive roosterly manner, charging one another, chest bumping, necks out-stretched, staring one another down. I don't know. Perhaps these two "girls"—Pecorino and Fontina—are not hens after all? Yes, I've named them all after cheeses. For obvious reasons I chose to forgo "Stinking Bishop," an English goat cheese—there are other cheeses that seem more appropriate to gentle hens. And so we have Feta, Brie, Velveeta, and—the one exception—Buttercup, because she was a fluffy yellow baby chick.

It's easy to anthropomorphize animals. It is also easy for me, as a Christian, to spiritualize "my life with chickens." It could be told as a metaphor—a journey through a view of creation, fall, and redemption with chickens as my guide.

Something like this: born into a perfect world with all that's needed to be happy honorable chickens, they are tempted to practice aggression and greed even though they have all their needs met right there in their chicken universe. They have a keeper who loves and cares for them, who gets up early to water and feed them. She makes sure they are clean and warm even though they poop all over their world. Although they do not care one whit for their keeper who provides them with all they need to thrive, they would as soon peck her hand bloody one moment, and in the next sit calmly on her palm, content to close their eyes as she tenderly strokes their heads.

There's no harm in thinking that as a very small inadequate comparison, Jesus loves us regardless of our sin and failure as I love my chickens in spite of their greedy attitudes. But it isn't necessary to justify the ordinary pleasure of caring for a flock of hens who will surprise me with a beautiful clutch of cinnamon, rust, and latte colored eggs on most days of the year.

In this I find the joy of God and holiness in the everyday. Hens that race back and forth in their pen greeting me with loud squawks, behaving in a chickenly manner just as God created them to be. The very act of caring for them, cleaning their nest boxes, and spreading sweet-smelling shavings brings glory to God and joy to my life. That's enough. It is how God made them. It is how God made me.

Now, excuse me, I must see to changing the water in their jar which has been stood upon and dribbled with excrement, and the trough below has been industriously plugged with wet, scratched-up shavings.

LIMITATIONS

The Back-Up Plan

One night after band practice, when I was seventeen, my left wrist began to ache. I played bass at my downtown church plant and guitar in a punk band with two other girls; I was pretty sure I'd spend my adulthood living in a van, playing shows in a series of bars that smelled like peanut shells and sweat. (Some of my friends were already doing this, and I thought they were unbearably cool.)

That year, when a guidance counselor asked me to fill out a questionnaire on potential career paths, I wrote "Musician" on the first line but left the other three blank.

"Maybe you should consider a back-up plan?" she asked.

On the second line, I wrote "Tattoo artist."

I'd known Jesus for only a year by then, but I'd known music for nearly ten: I'd painstakingly settled every egg I owned into that basket. Music was my way into friendships and, later, into the life of my small church; writing songs gave me the language I needed to make sense of the world as it blustered and raged around me. So when I first noticed the pain in my wrist—an electric buzz between the bones after a long rehearsal—I ignored it.

Not this, I thought. *Nope.*

But one night the pain wouldn't abate. No matter how I moved my wrist or how forcefully I willed the pain to recede, it blazed on. I couldn't sleep; I couldn't get comfortable. I knew, but did not want to know, exactly what that pain meant.

. . .

My pastor recently described the love of God as "kind and severe," and that is how I knew it that year as the pain went from occasional to constant, from uncomfortable to needling, persistent, intense. On a good day I felt it only in my wrists; on the worst days it thrummed from my collarbone to my fingertips, pooling in my elbows and wrists. Wearing wrist braces helped a little, so at my doctor's suggestion, I buried a pair under my studded cuffs and spiked bracelets and wore them day and night.

For a long time, I had no obvious diagnosis: my symptoms acted like carpal tunnel, but not quite. Like tendonitis, but different. My parents took me to specialists and to a physical therapist who eventually diagnosed me with thoracic outlet syndrome—a repetitive stress injury which is in fact like carpal tunnel, except the nerves are compressed not in the wrists but between the collarbone and top ribs. While all that was happening, I attended homecoming in a thrift-store dress and fairy wings and was cast, wrist braces and all, as Benvolio in my school's production of *Romeo and Juliet.* That spring, I graduated high school.

Sometimes it was hard not to feel bitter about the severity of this. Here I was, a young, ought-to-be-healthy girl, with my whole life ahead of me—right? But I could not sleep on my side or open a jar or type my own college entrance essays. Every week I spent an hour with Ned the physical therapist, who did things like "reset muscles" and rearrange, with his fingers and a whole lot of pressure, my top rib and my collarbone. In the aftermath of those appointments, I went through a lot of ice and ibuprofen.

When I started physical therapy, I agreed to set my guitars aside for a while and give my hands time to heal, but at first all I could think about was "when I can play again." I was still a musician, I thought—just a musician on pause. I might have to make some adjustments to the way I held my guitar or how often I played, but I'd get back to it eventually. I had to. I didn't have a back-up plan.

But during one appointment Ned told me that I should prepare for the possibility that I might not play again. This moment required something else—not a willingness to pause, but a willingness to stop completely and wait until God gave me a new direction. At first I could see only the gaping wound that sacrifice would leave, the severance of my soul from so much of who I thought I was. But by then I was beginning to see how swiftly the Lord rushed in to fill those empty spaces, and I understood: He wasn't putting these limits around me because He loved subtraction—He was clearing space, making room for better things. He was preparing me to receive more of Himself (Phil. 3:7–9).

So, I let go. I quit my bands, sold my bass and both my electric guitars, and donated my amps and mics to my church. All I kept was an acoustic guitar, which I buried behind the laundry in the back of my closet—a memento of sorts that I didn't plan on playing ever again, because I didn't want to keep my fingers crossed. I didn't want to hope that God might change His mind.

It sounds dramatic to say "and then I had to figure out who I was"—I know. But after that I *did* have to figure out who I was, because I genuinely didn't know. For all those formative years of middle school and high school, I'd been a musician—the girl who played a grungy cover of "These Boots Are Made for Walking" at the school talent show and who dyed her hair a new color each month in keeping with her angsty MTV image.

With music went the hair dye, as well as several friendships. Even the boy I'd been dating for a year and a half—our relationship buckled under this shift, and that fall I found myself single and sharing a rented house with five other Christian girls, wearing my dad's old wool sweaters and considering a degree in creative writing, my hair mouse brown for the first time since seventh grade. It was a time of remaking.

. . .

Auguste Rodin, *Study of a Hand*, cast plaster

In the years since it happened, I have told this story so many times, and every few tellings I see something new in it. As I tell the story this time, I am struck by this: when the Lord calls us away from some good thing, He is giving us an assurance of His love—a reminder that we are His children, beloved and pursued. "Endure hardship as discipline," the author of Hebrews writes. "God is treating you as his children. For what children are not disciplined by their father?" (12:7 NIV). Or, as Proverbs 3:12 says, "The Lord reproves him whom he loves, as a father the son in whom he delights." Though accepting this discipline means accepting the limits of not belonging to anyone else—not even ourselves—the boundaries our Father places around us are a sign of His love and affection.

The world I'd spent my first seventeen years living in said that I should be limitless, unfettered by anyone else's expectations, able to be whoever I wanted to be. But certain flowers need trellises, twine, and trimming before they can thrive, and through the limits God placed around me at the very beginning of my Christian life, He cut back the spindly leaves and trained me up a trellis so the sunlight could reach me. The process wasn't pleasant; it hurt, and I cried and lost my temper a lot. But the growth that came afterward proved He was right: the limits He placed around me were severe, but by pruning back the sprawling vines, He allowed me to grow strong roots.

But this is where the gardening metaphor breaks down: God met me in the physical pain of that year with the tenderness one shows not to an untended vine but to a lost and suffering child, for that is exactly what I was. He did not ask what I had done or what had been done to me but simply enfolded my hand in His own and brought me home. He gave me a room in His house and clean clothes; He made me a meal and scooted my chair up close to His. He adopted me as His daughter and promised that one day all He possesses will be mine (Rom. 8:14–17).

His kindness still bewilders me. Why should we—who threw all God's good gifts in our packs and struck off to spend them on our own pleasures—be received at God's table as beloved children? Our only way in is through Jesus, who accepted the limits of a physical body, with its frustrating tendency to get hurt and its inability to occupy more than one place at a time (Col. 1:15–22). Before the Incarnation, nothing limited Him—not time or space or sin or death. He could go anywhere, know everything, do anything, yet He accepted the limits of living in the feeblest, most helpless of human forms and entered our world as a baby (Phil. 2:5–8).

God clearly does not despise limitations. To Him, they seem to be synonymous with love.

. . .

This is a story with an asterisk at the end. My hands did heal; I did play the guitar again, though not the bass—that was gone for good. I married a man who was there for the whole thing and learned to write new songs, songs that were more open and hospitable and less angry. I even played in a band briefly and occasionally lead worship at our church.

But every five years or so, I wake up with my collarbone blazing. It comes on slowly, a twinge here and there over the course of a few days, and my first thought when I wake up aching is always panic: *It's happening again.* I'm a mother of four—I bake and write and garden, and I need my hands for all of those things. I want to braid my daughters' hair and shuffle cards and chop rhubarb; I don't want to do this again.

But when that panic subsides, I remember: God was good to me that first time, so good. By asking me to lay down this thing I loved, He broadened and deepened my heart and taught me to love better, more lasting things. Those limits, it turns out, weren't a wound but a salve; they were a tangible, every-moment reminder of His love.

And so these mornings are no longer filled with frightening unknowns. I know what comes next and it is love—the steady, unchangeable affection of a Father who knows His daughter's needs before she does. Maybe I've forgotten how abundant His love is, how free, and I need reminding; maybe I wandered too far from the house, and He's calling me to come back home. So far the pain has never lasted long—a week or two at most. But I'm learning to feel, in that sudden ache, the gentle pressure of my Father's hands as He gathers me back into His arms.

MUPPETS

The Eucatastrophe of Muppetdom

One of the most transformative cultural moments of my young life—though I didn't know it at the time—involved a fuzzy frog in a man-made swamp.

In the opening moments of a movie I watched countless times as a child, the credits flicker onto the screen over a helicopter shot of a swamp drenched in morning sun. We're still far enough away that only the trees are visible, but the camera dips closer, zooming into the midst of the woods, down to the swamp surface. The green water is still, the Spanish moss curling from the trees at the fringe of the frame.

At first, we don't know where our eyes should go. But as the camera moves across the surface of the water, a small green figure becomes visible, sitting upright on a log, singing a simple melody and steadily plunking out the accompaniment on a banjo.

"Why are there so many songs about rainbows? And what's on the other side?" he asks. "Rainbows are visions, but only illusions. Rainbows have nothing to hide."

The song rolls on to its conclusion, with words so wistful and lovely, they haunt me still: "Have you been half asleep, and have you heard voices? I've heard them calling my name. Is it the sweet song that calls the young sailor? The voices are one and the same. Someday we'll find it, the rainbow connection, the lovers, the dreamers, and me."

That moment with Kermit the Frog remains embedded in my consciousness, for it did what all exceptional moments of cultural progress do: they "expand the horizons of possibility," as Andy Crouch writes in his book *Culture Making*. These moments add something significant to the culture in a way that makes innovation possible by begetting other cultural breakthroughs, which beget other cultural breakthroughs, and so on through the years. For me, expanding my personal horizons of possibility went something like this:

If a frog puppet can play a banjo in a swamp and make me feel like I can take on the world, then anything is possible.

There have been many other Muppet moments throughout my life, several of which I've been fortunate to share with my own two boys, now ages fourteen and twelve. I'll readily admit that the Muppets—from their breakthrough into popular culture on *Sesame Street* in the 1960s through the present—with their zany comedic non-sequiturs, verbal wit, physical comedy, and moments of unapologetic earnestness, check a lot of boxes for me. All the boxes, pretty much. But what I have come to realize as I've rounded the corner from youth to middle age, is that there is much else about the Muppets that allows them to speak so loudly to me as a follower of Christ.

To say that the Muppets have framed my view of orthopraxy—correct conduct —might be overstating it, but not by much. Without doubt, the Muppets have given me a lens on a well-lived life that reflects the gospel in more ways than I would have suspected a few decades ago. Yes, they're art made right, but they also present life lived right, both in the characters on the screen, and the performers just out of frame, standing on tip-toes, arms outstretched high overhead. Muppetdom inhabits a little cosmos in which the gospel values of wonder and innocence, joy and community, and laughter and rest, are incarnate, albeit in the furry bodies of puppets.

I'll be the first to admit that these are not values exclusive to Christianity, and that Jim Henson did not espouse orthodox Christian belief. There are also themes within Muppetdom that veer outside of the gospel. But I firmly believe that all truth is God's truth, and that within many pieces of popular entertainment, there are signs aplenty which can point a discerning viewer to the gospel.[1] So, in the same way that *Finding Nemo's* touching depiction of sacrifical parenting presents a profound reminder of God's love for His children, so does Henson's work bring to the world a winsome picture of what I'll call humbly call the "eucatastrophe of Muppetdom."

Eucatastrophe, as coined by J.R.R. Tolkien in his essay "On Fairy-Stories," is a moment in a story which contains a redemptive turn—a sudden, unexpected snatching out of the jaws of sorrow and defeat, as depicted when the Riders of Rohan suddenly appear to reinforce Gondor at Helm's Deep. Tolkien elaborates on his concept, calling it "a sudden and miraculous grace: never to be counted on to recur," adding that eucatastrophe "does not deny the existence of . . . sorrow and failure: the possibility of these is necessary to the joy of deliverance; it denies . . . universal final defeat . . . giving a fleeting glimpse of Joy, Joy beyond the walls of the world."[2]

I've come to believe that eucatastrophe wears many faces within Muppetdom. First, I'd like to begin with the suspension of disbelief. I'm not sure it's possible for anyone to engage with the Muppets—or puppets in general, for that matter—without accepting the terms of the engagement. A Muppet, as envisioned by Jim Henson in its infancy in the mid-1950s, was as simple a creature as could be imagined: a hand puppet made—in the case of Kermit—from an old turquoise felt coat belonging to Henson's mother, with two halved Ping Pong balls inked with slashed circles for eyes.

But on the hand of Henson, the puppet becomes something more. It comes to life, in a manner of speaking, so fully and completely that there are numerous filmed exchanges between human and Muppet in which the human seems to forget there's a Henson attached to the frog. I've marveled at the way that whenever Henson appeared as a guest on a talk show, the host would start by interviewing Henson, but then, as Henson brought the puppet to life—without any interest in presenting himself as a ventriloquist—the host would begin to address the puppet principally. At first, it's part of the act, a sort of "oh, this is cute, I'm talking to the puppet," but then, there's a moment where you can see the host genuinely forget that the puppet on Henson's arm possesses no life of its own. It's remarkable. There's a willing suspension of disbelief which naturally occurs in such exchanges.

Why is this suspension of disbelief so important, and how does it relate to the gospel? It's crucial to discuss what this involves, and what it does not involve. Willing suspension of disbelief is *not* blind faith, a head-in-the-sand misdirection of attention so as not to face unpleasant reality. No, when we supend our disbelief we know exactly what's going on, but we choose to disregard the actual facts of the case in favor of the reality presented through the fictive universe.

In the case of novels, we are fully aware when reading, say, *The Return of the King,* that the Shire does not physically exist in the world we inhabit. Further, not only do we hold its "non-existence" in our heads when we flip through the final chapter of the novel, "Haven's Gray," we are also aware that we're holding thin sheets of processed wood pulp which have been printed on a large press which lays ink down on the pages to correspond with the twenty-six symbols assigned to the English alphabet. But, though we intellectually know all of this to be true, we suspend all of these "truths" when reading "Haven's Gray" because we are swept up in the power and vividness of Tolkien's writing, the connection to the characters, and the flow of the narrative which has brought us to this point.

All of this is important to consider because it explains what Jesus might be referring to when He rebukes the disciples for starting to dismiss the children who are brought to Him: "Don't push these children away. Don't ever get between them and me. These children are at the very

Jonny Jimison, *Jim,* ink

center of life in the kingdom. Mark this: Unless you accept God's kingdom in the simplicity of a child, you'll never get in" (Mark 10:13–15 MSG). When we consider the principles at work in willingly suspending disbelief, we begin to understand what Jesus means when he says to "accept God's kingdom in the simplicity of a child."

Whole sermons have been written about this passage, so I'll leave it at this: believe. As illustrated through dozens of Jesus' parables, the qualities of the kingdom of God are so upside-down in the face of the world in which we live, that only one who is fully aware of the nature of the world, with all of its wrenching, grinding venom and cruel warping of truth, and who has *chosen to suspend his disbelief in the face of a narrative as captivating as the kingdom narrative,* can fully accept it. That's why suspension of disbelief matters.

Yes, Henson worked tirelessly to create an immersive, fully-realized world in many of his works, especially the 1982 film *The Dark Crystal.* But even so, being pulled into the conflict facing Jen and creations such as the Gelflings, Skeksis, Mystics, and Garthim necessitates a suspension of disbelief. And the suspension of disbelief is the soil from which wonder can grow.

"As I try to zero in on what's important for the Muppets," Henson is quoted as saying, "I think it's a sense of innocence, naivete—you know, the experience of a simple person meeting life."[3] Wonder is a natural consequence of innocence, and flourishes of wonder resulting from innocence are splashed all over the Muppet canon. The four-season run of *Fraggle Rock* is perhaps the finest example of this wonder, as seen through the species of Fraggles who live below the workshop of an inventor and his long-suffering dog, Sprocket. In the first episode, Gobo's uncle Matt ventures up from the Fraggle cave-world to explore what he calls "Outer Space," but is actually our human world. In each episode, he sends a postcard to his nephew recounting another human custom in a slightly confused way. Each of Traveling Matt's adventures serve to transpose our everyday lives into a new key, forcing us to see the seemingly mundane or routine as wondrous by showing them to us differently.

In addition to Traveling Matt's adventures, the five principal Fraggles—Gobo, Mokey, Wembley, Boober, and Red—approach their everyday lives with a spontaneity and joy that's invigorating. After all, the show's theme song begins with the line, "Dance your cares away, worry's for another day." Rather than advocating an abdication of responsibility, the Fraggle ethos centers on blithe, communal living which cares for others in equality to one's self and takes time to marvel at soap bubbles, shiny rocks, and of course, music of all kinds. This sort of focus on the wonder of the everyday makes each trip to Fraggle Rock a reminder that the world we live in is crammed full of wondrous creations meant to remind us of the hand of its Creator.

My other personal emissary of wonder is that hose-nosed weirdo, Gonzo. In Gonzo's very first on-screen appearance in the first episode of *The Muppet Show,* he makes the brash pronouncement, "Tonight, ladies and gentleman, I will eat this rubber tire to the music of 'The Flight of the Bumblebee.' " It does not go well, as you'd imagine. But Gonzo, like so many of the Muppets, is far from a one-note character. To the credit of his creator and performer Dave Goelz, he traveled far from his daredevil, performance artist origins to become a wide-eyed dreamer whose exuberant whoops and earnest desire to pull back the curtain on the world and see what lies behind it are consistently inspiring.

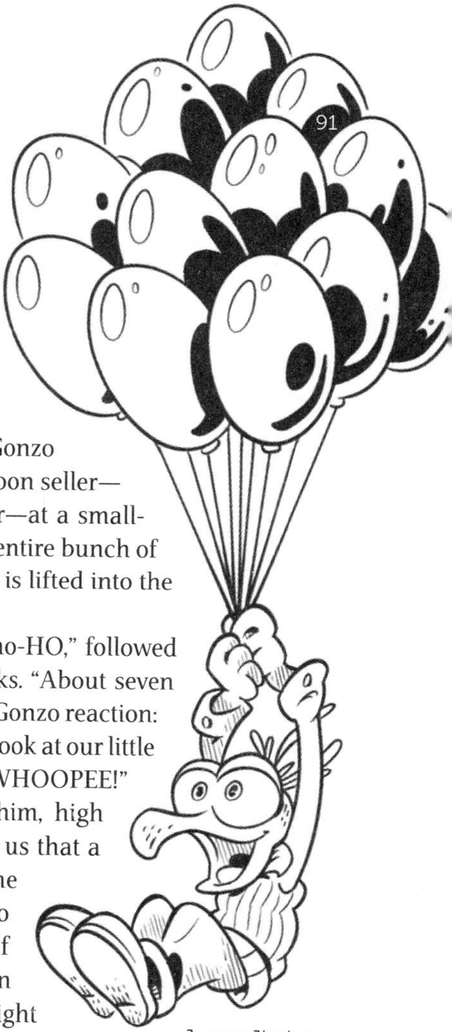

In a memorable scene from *The Muppet Movie,* Gonzo and his chicken-girlfriend Camilla approach a balloon seller—who happens to be played by comic Richard Pryor—at a small-town fair. After Pryor encourages Gonzo to buy the entire bunch of balloons, the handoff goes wrong, and soon, Gonzo is lifted into the air, held captive by a fistful of helium balloons.

His response is at first a manic "Whoa-ho-ho-ho-HO," followed by a joke ("Gonzo, what are you doing?" Kermit asks. "About seven knots" is Gonzo's reply), and then the quintessential Gonzo reaction: "Here I am, floating in space! This is the place to be. Look at our little car down there," he says. "It's like flying. It is flying! WHOOPEE!"

By placing Gonzo, and the camera tracking him, high above the scenery below, the movie again reminds us that a perspective change can help us fully experience the world the way it is created. "Look up," it's as if Gonzo is urging us, "Every atom of the universe is magic, if we choose to notice." As Michael Card expresses in his song, "There is a joy in the journey / There's a light we can love on the way / There is a wonder and wildness to life / And freedom for those who obey." [4]

Jonny Jimison, *Gonzo,* ink

Knowing that the world around us is made good at its core, and will be redeemed someday, allows us to drink in its wonders. And these fuzzy, wide-eyed puppets help us to see this. This, I believe, is a result of the principle of anthropomorphism, which attributes all the characteristics of humans to these oddly-shaped creatures. How else to explain Miss Piggy's tenacity, vanity, and unexpected tenderness toward her dear "Kermey," or the earnest, eager-to-please insecurity of Fozzie Bear? Once these characters encounter the world as our avatars, we're drawn into their world, and experience it as they do, which cracks open the door for profound realizations about our own world.

These anthropomorphic puppets—and their talented performers—accomplish what C.S. Lewis described in his essay "Sometimes Fairy Stories May Say Best What›s to be Said":

> Supposing that by casting all these things into an imaginary world, stripping them of their stained-glass and Sunday School associations, one could make them for the first time appear in their real potency? Could one not thus steal past those watchful dragons? I thought one could.[5]

In their own way, these Muppets steal past our own watchful dragons of cynicism, familiarity, and cold analytical observation so we can dance our own cares away.

The Muppet world is vast and, as mentioned earlier, not consistently in keeping with the tenets the gospel. But within its boundaries are countless opportunities to consider the concepts of wonder, innocence, joy, laughter, spontaneity, and play—all of which have the potential, if taken in regular doses, to provide the sort of eucatastrophic experience which Tolkien describes as "a sudden and miraculous grace."

How is this world one of grace? I'd suggest that in a culture like ours, which regularly presents images of selfishness, greed, injustice, and scarcity, traveling to a world which presents regular opportunities to consider these subversive gospel values is its own form of grace.

Whether in a sketch from the 1970s *The Muppet Show,* an episode of *Fraggle Rock,* a sequence of breathtaking originality from *The Dark Crystal,* or one of the Muppet films, old or new, to watch the Muppets is to encounter a vision of "sudden and miraculous grace." It's not a salvific grace, per say, but it is a familiar ringing of the kingdom bells in our everyday existence, and Muppetdom takes its place among scores of other artistic melodies which remind us of the truth, goodness, and beauty of the gospel story.

And we dance to its music.

1 As John Piper puts it, "I ... give thanks that believers may learn many of God's truths from unbelievers and see them rightly and thus desire God more and delight in God more because of those truths, so that unbelievers become, unwittingly, the means of our worship." This is the sort of circumstance which serves as a foundation for this essay.

2 J.R.R. Tolkien, "On Fairy-Stories," from *Tree and Leaf* (London: HarperCollins, 1964), p. 69.

3 Brian Jay Jones, *Jim Henson: The Biography* (New York: Ballantine Books, 2016).

4 Michael Card, "Joy in the Journey," from *Joy in the Journey: 10 Years of Greatest Hits,* Sparrow Records, 2006.

5 C.S. Lewis, "Sometimes Fairy Stories May Say Best What's to be Said," from *On Stories: And Other Essays on Literature* (New York: HarperCollins, 1982, orig. publ. 1966), p. 70.

PLAYLISTS
In the Mix

When my friends and I go on our annual vacation, everyone has a "director" role: Director of Relaxation, Content, Housing, Hydration, Cuisine, or Coffee and Aesthetics. Sometimes these roles change, depending on which friends are able to make it that year, the spot we're traveling to, the activities we have in mind. But regardless, my title is Director of Music. It is my job to curate the correct musical experience for every aspect of the trip. This involves a few key factors: I must anticipate what each day will look like, how long it will take to get to our different destinations, and the musical tastes of everyone on the trip. There needs to be a mix of throwbacks that will get everyone excited and new songs that I think everyone will enjoy. Beach Day playlists are very different from Road Trip playlists, which in turn are different from the Getting Ready to Go Out to Dinner playlist. There is nothing like the feeling of satisfaction I feel when a playlist is a hit with the group.

I would like to say that my love of playlists was something that I cultivated on my own, a passion that I discovered, but that is not the case. It was conditioned into me. My dad is the original playlist king, making mixtapes for me, that later turned to burned CDs, all before the invention of Spotify or Apple Music. These mixes worked their way into the deep spaces of my being, influencing how I feel music should go together. For example, because of my first mixtape presented to me before I could walk, the only way one can listen to "Yellow Submarine" by The Beatles is if it is played after "Under the Sea" from *The Little Mermaid.* (I don't make the rules. That's just how you must listen to those two tracks.)

My dad marked each important life moment with a burned CD that he had curated for the family's enjoyment. My sisters and I always looked forward to the summer mix that Dad ceremoniously brought out to the car at the beginning of the season and the vacation CD that he burned in anticipation for whatever road trip we were going on. Each Christmas had its own sound, a mix of new seasonal tracks sprinkled with previous hits. These playlists were so naturally ingrained into our family culture that I thought the soundtracks for *The Big Chill* and *That Thing You Do* just happened to be mixtapes my dad had made for the car. It wasn't until

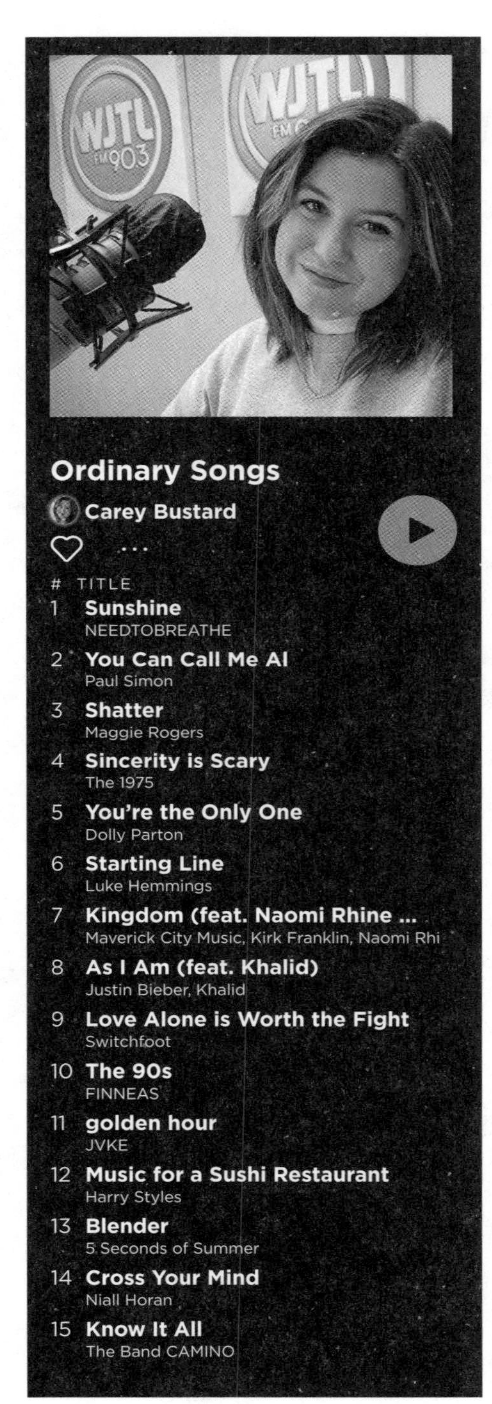

I was older that I realized these were actually the tunes of major motion pictures. In middle school and high school, the baton was passed to me and my friends. I discovered some of my favorite songs through mixes I was gifted that expanded my horizons. Whenever I hear The Shins, I always think about Death Cab for Cutie and The National. "Calendar Girl" by Stars should always be played in proximity to "The District Sleeps Alone Tonight" by The Postal Service.

The beauty of these mixes, both physical and electronic, is the marriage between sharing something you love and something you think your listener will love. The best ones require a certain amount of vulnerability, creativity, and care. These characteristics are innate in our identity as image bearers. Playlist making can be an act of creation and celebration. It is participating in creating something new and also celebrating the art of another. In his essay about instruments in *It Was Good: Making Music to the Glory of God,* Gregg Strawbridge wrote about how we have sovereignty over creating tools for sound and how that expresses "more of the reality God made in the soundscape."[1] As I combine sounds, genres, and artists into a narrative arc in a playlist, I am participating in enriching creation and celebrating those who already have created in this new soundscape. Strawbridge goes on to say, "We show the *imago dei* as we make sounds which aim to musically recreate. Through such musical *work,* we *glorify* (add weightiness to) creation and the Creator, our rightful dominion is a cultivation which produces new fruits. These fruits require the work of human hands."[2] Though he is talking about the use of instruments in work and worship, this idea can be applied to playlist making as well. I am producing new fruit in my combination of songs, in a creative way that introduces new meaning or interpretation to the track. This requires my brain as well as what my hands can produce.

It also requires my ears. I have to listen, not passively, but with intentionality and a desire to discover and grow. Mark Chambers talks about listening—specifically listening broadly—and about how if we stay within one genre, artist, or album, and do not stretch ourselves beyond it, we box ourselves in. This could ultimately make us unable to truly parse out our own feelings and aesthetic habits. Chambers goes on to say,

> This is important because of the ability of music to act as a vehicle of discovery. We do not normally speak of music, or think of it, as a means of discovering something that can have a profound impact on the way in which we perceive the world around us. More commonly we think of music as something that should make us feel a certain way, an emotional stimulant or narcotic, or even to reinforce certain of our own habitual aesthetic preferences.[3]

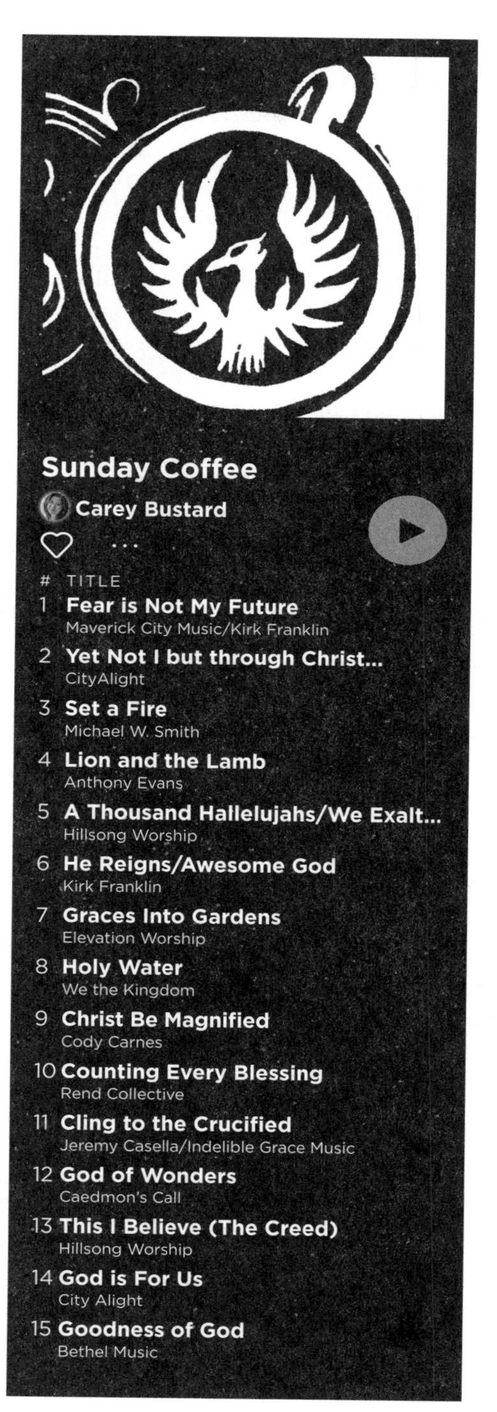

In order to know myself, I have to listen. In order to know my friends and be able to produce something that will speak to them, I have to listen. In order to know God better, I have to listen. If we only consume music in one way, we box ourselves in, not gifting ourselves the ability to learn and grow. This impoverishes our delight in music, because music is never to be enjoyed in a vacuum and is always moving and blossoming from other music and genres beyond itself. As jazz works best when the musicians listen and respond to one another, so too we discover that the moving song within the Trinity is one of call and response.

God the Father, God the Son, and God the Holy Spirit, dancing together in holy communion and harmony, bring glory to one another in the unique goodness each person provides to that relationship. Music, according to my dad, "offers a rather particular way of experiencing an aspect of who God is." We are given the opportunity to experience different layers of emotion, thought, and discovery. He goes on to say, "When we share the experience of hearing music, singing music, playing music, or writing music, we are brought closer to each other in a harmony that vaguely resembles Trinitarian harmony."[4] Creating and experiencing playlists can be another way of echoing this Trinitarian harmony. Playlists serve the person they have been created for or shared with; they serve the songs, which have been arranged in an order that allows them to become something greater; and they serve me as I use my creativity to shape them.

During the beginnings of 2020's Covid quarantine my sisters and I created playlists together. Each day we would send a song that we felt went with whatever theme we were working on at that time. At the end of the month, we would have a specially curated playlist of songs that were just for each other. I got to experience the music that was bringing them joy and helping them through pain, and they introduced me to music I didn't know. I was able to share the same experience with them. We kept up the practice for two years, each day sending each other songs, keeping in constant contact as we couldn't be together in person. The playlist was serving as our means of daily connection. In a similar way, there are times when a friend will send me a song and ask for a playlist with a related vibe. It is in service like this that we are all able to be in harmony with each other in a very particular way.

I was listening to Paul Simon one day and had to stop everything I was doing to create a playlist highlighting Simon's "Obvious Child" from *The Rhythm of the Saints* followed immediately by One Direction's "Girl Almighty" from the album *Four*. Those songs needed to be in conversation with one another and my soul would not rest until they were. In a similar way, when Shawn Mendes and Justin Bieber came out with their song "Monster" in 2020, I was inspired to find songs that I felt were also monster-like in theme and musical expression—for example: "Night Crawling" by Miley Cyrus (featuring Billy Idol), "N.F.F. (No Fake Friends)," by Jaguar Twin, and "Therefore I Am," by Billie Eilish. Both these playlists are celebrations of the art one artist has created and how it is in conversation with those who have gone before them and who will come after. Songs have a historical connection with one another similar to the one a painting from the Renaissance might have with a painting from Surrealism because the curator has placed them side by side. Another example is a playlist featuring my favorite songs from the 1980s and recent songs that have similar sonic feelings. I encourage you to listen to "Head Over Heels" by Tears for Fears with "TOOTIMETOOTIMETOOTIME" by The 1975. It is like when you select a wine to go with a meal because the label says it pairs well with steak.

This act of creating a musical dinner party is one way my creativity flows best. I don't professionally produce music myself, but being able to celebrate others and their creations brings me joy. To create a narrative arc—sonically, lyrically, thematically—feels like my way to participate in the ways God has gifted musicians, producers, songwriters, promotors, managers. It is in service to the creativity that God has granted to me. Music is all about creating opportunities for relationships, as Strawbridge reminds us, in addition to simply being for the sake of being.[5] All of these work together to create that Trinitarian dance between serving the listeners, the tracks, and my own interests. These work in tandem to point us to the ways God is in relationship with Himself.

Jesus gives us the ultimate example of sharing music with friends. After sharing the Lord's Supper with His disciples, He sang a hymn with them

(Matt. 26:30). The hymn was probably one of the psalms. Jesus quotes often from the psalms, most famously before going to the cross and while on the cross. The entirety of the Book of Psalms is like a full playlist. It grows. It arcs. There are sets of Psalms for sadness, pain, celebration. Psalms expressing confidence and wisdom. Psalms to remind the listener of history. The Book of Psalms ends with the ultimate expression of musicality:

> Praise the LORD!
> Praise God in his sanctuary;
> praise him in his mighty heavens!
> Praise him for his mighty deeds;
> praise him according to his excellent greatness!
> Praise him with trumpet sound;
> praise him with lute and harp!
> Praise him with tambourine and dance;
> praise him with strings and pipe!
> Praise him with sounding cymbals;
> praise him with loud clashing cymbals!
> Let everything that has breath praise the LORD!
> Praise the LORD! (Psalm 150)

1 Gregg Strawbridge, "Instruments Are Good," from *It Was Good: Making Music to the Glory of God*, ed. by Ned Bustard (Baltimore, MD: Square Halo Books, 2013), pp. 256–257.
2 Ibid.
3 Mark Chambers, "Listening Between the Lines," from *It Was Good: Making Music to the Glory of God*, ed. by Ned Bustard (Baltimore, MD: Square Halo Books, 2013), p. 145.
4 Ned Bustard, "Making Music Soli Deo Gloria," from *It Was Good: Making Music to the Glory of God*, ed. by Ned Bustard (Baltimore, MD: Square Halo Books, 2013), pp. 7–8.
5 Strawbridge, "Instruments Are Good," p. 247

JUGGLING

Joyful, Joyful, We Juggle for Thee

When I tell people that I juggle for a living, I wish I could also get into their heads and hear the livestream of their thoughts. Judging by the looks on their faces, they are either impressed or they feel sorry for me—I am unable to tell the difference. What I do know is what they say after I tell them. And there are two questions I get far more than any others. The first is, "How did you get into that?" The second is, "Can you juggle chainsaws?" I'll answer those questions in reverse. To the chainsaws, the answer is yes, and I still have most of my fingers left.

To the former question, when I was in the fifth grade, I found out that my best friend, Tim, could juggle three balls. I had to learn, and I made him show me the basic steps. Within two weeks, I was juggling three balls with relative ease.

For reasons that still elude me, I was hooked. I wanted to keep juggling. I wanted to learn more. There was something about juggling that called out my name and I had to figure out how to juggle longer, better, and with more objects. I proceeded to search for every book I could find about juggling (this was before YouTube). I hauled my short stack of books home from the library and devoured every page of titles such as *The Joy of Juggling*[1] and *Juggling with Finesse*.[2] I admired the photographs of the great circus performers, the comedy jugglers, and the technical jugglers (if you're wondering, the former two focus on performing while the latter focus on raw juggling skills). I discovered that juggling has been around for at least five thousand years—depictions of jugglers have been found on the walls of ancient Egyptian tombs. I also learned that juggling has a lot to do with *joy*. I observed pure joy in the faces of the performers in the books. For me this sense of joy extended beyond the books.

A 5th century B.C. oil flask depicting a juggler.

I personally felt joy when I juggled anything. In juggling, I could temporarily suspend the perception of the law of gravity. It was like a superpower. I could toss objects in various repetitive patterns that were ascetically pleasing to my eyes and mind. I had discovered something that brought me a sense of accomplishment for sure, but more importantly, it brought me joy.

By the time I reached high school, I had developed my skills to the point where I could juggle machetes, balance ladders on my forehead, and juggle up to six rings. I found other jugglers in my city and we met weekly for informal practice sessions. That is also where I learned about the wider juggling community around the world. Our juggling club would travel together to various regional and national festivals where I was able to see and meet the great jugglers of the world—like the ones I saw in those books years before.

I then earned a spot in my high school talent night. What I remember from that night was that the crowd loved the juggling. I was a bit surprised in fact. I had mostly kept this talent to myself for several years. But when I expressed it in front of a captive audience, I saw that it brought joy to them. The joy I experienced internally from juggling was now something that I could pass on—an external joy that others could experience as well.

That show was my big break. There were people in the audience who saw my act and subsequently reached out to me to perform for more shows and events. The past twenty-five years of my life have now been a string of shows that apparently bring joy to others, and people in each audience then call upon me to bring joy to their next event. I consider myself blessed to have a vocation that I enjoy and that is centered around an idea of childlike playfulness. It is a vocation that I would consider utterly ordinary (tossing and catching stuff).

The line from Eric Liddell's character in the film *Chariots of Fire* is not lost on me as I reflect on my vocation of ordinariness: "[God] made me fast, and when I run I feel his pleasure."[3] God gave me to be a juggler, and when I juggle, I feel his pleasure. In juggling, whether alone or for others, I experience a sort of communion with God Himself. "You make known to me the path of life; in your presence there is fullness of joy; at your right hand are pleasures forevermore" (Ps. 16:11). I think juggling somehow reflects the image of God. For example, at the heart of juggling is the idea of creating order out of chaos. Without the pattern, without the successful toss and catch, there is chaos. Juggling is the attempt to maintain repetitive patterns of objects in flight, like the movements of celestial beings. Then there is something called "passing," which is when jugglers juggle together. They labor as one to create a communion of toss patterns that are impossible to achieve as a solo act.

There is a medieval tale about a juggler called "Our Lady's Tumbler" (also known as "The Juggler of Notre Dame"—Tomie dePaola wrote a rendition of the tale in his classic 1978 children's book *The Clown of God*).[4] The original legend comes from a thirteenth-century French poem that was soon thereafter used as a Latin exemplum (a sermon illustration). In that period, much like today, pastors would consult collections of exempla to find anecdotes and stories to aid their preaching. Not surprisingly, this story about the juggler appeared in a collection of exempla under the categorical heading, "Joy."[5]

A thirteenth-century illumination from *Our Lady's Tumbler*.

The story goes something like this: a simple juggler lives the nomadic life of traveling from village to village, performing street shows for anyone who will watch and throw money. The juggler is good at his craft and overall tries to live a virtuous life, though he never considers himself extraordinarily spiritual or holy. As he ages, he becomes weaker and less proficient at his juggling skills, which makes it difficult for him to make a living out of his craft. One day, when he is distressed and feeling useless, he spots a monastery on a hill. He figures that he could become a monk and offer something of use with whatever he has left of his life. But when he joins the monastery, he looks around and discovers that all the other monks have "useful" skills that serve the monastery's objectives and mission. Some monks cooked the food as chefs, some copied the Scriptures as scribes, and some led the chants during vespers. So the juggler perceived himself to be as useless in the monastery as he was outside of it. He felt he had nothing to offer at first.

But then an idea came to him. What if he offered all he had? And what he had was a little bit of his juggling skills left. So at night, when no one was looking, he would sneak into the chapel that housed the statue of the virgin mother. He would then perform his juggling before the statue of Mary. This continues until one night, the other monks get word of his secret shows. They peer through the keyhole with disgust as they witness a juggler disgracing the holy chapel with a lowly busking show. But before they can burst in and reprimand him, the juggling monk falls to the ground from exhaustion (in some versions of the story, he dies). He had poured out all he had in his act of worship. And in a miraculous Pygmalion-like moment, the statue of Mary comes to life. She bends down and blesses the performer, wiping him with a cloth. The fellow monks then marvel at the miracle, falls to their knees, and declare, "Blessed are the simple, for they shall see God."[6]

This narrative provides us with a character who acts as a stand-in for all those who are ordinary and who lay what little they have upon the altar of worship unto the Lord. Jugglers bear His image in the mundane tasks of the manipulation of objects, the ordering of things into patterns, and the playfulness of tossing and catching things. But everyone is a juggler in a sense, trying to bring order out of chaos, just like our Lord does.

When I was in college, I spent a semester studying abroad in Jerusalem. During my time there, a war broke out between the Israelis and the Palestinians.[7] A principal of a small school in Bethlehem heard about my juggling show and invited me to come perform for the students at his primary school. He picked me up in Jerusalem and drove me to his school. On the way, we visited a village that had been ransacked by war activity the night before. People were still sweeping up glass in the street from rocket fire damage. We continued on to the school, where I juggled for the children. It was a normal show for me—I did my tricks, told my jokes, and tried to bring the kids a joyful experience. But what I heard from the principal after my show was different than any other show I had ever done. He said to me, "Thank you so much for coming today. You brought joy and smiles to their faces. The kids really needed that, because lately during recess, they've been playing funeral."

That was the first time I had heard those two words together in a sentence: *playing funeral.* But that was the effect of war upon their minds and hearts. What they saw in their streets at home is what they imitated in their play at recess. My juggling show did not heal them or fix all their pains, but apparently it brought a dim light for just a moment on that particular day. And that was enough for me to know that God is in the juggling. His joy is in the playfulness.

1 Dave Finnigan, *The Joy of Juggling* (Jugglebug, 1993).

2 Kit Summers

3 The scriptwriter for *Chariots of Fire,* Colin Welland, should technically be credited with the quote. He himself said in a letter to an inquiry about the quote that he came up with it. But he believed that it reflected how Eric Liddell felt. For more information, including a link to an image of Welland's signed statement about the quote, see https://www.veritesport.org/?page=welland.

4 Tomie dePaola, *The Clown of God* (San Diego, CA: Harcourt Brace, 1978).

5 Jan M. Ziolkowski, *The Juggler of Notre Dame and the Medievalizing of Modernity, Volume 1: The Middle Ages* (Cambridge, UK: Open Book Publishers, 2018), pp. 23, 55–59.

6 France, Anatole. 2018. *The Juggler of Our Lady.* Illustrated by Malatesta. Translated by Jan M. Ziolkowski. Facsimile reproduction of original 1906 edition published by F. Ferroud in Paris. Nansha, China: Everbest Printing.

7 This war came to be known as The Second Intifada.

STORYTELLING
Chirping in the Distance

> He has made everything beautiful in its time. Also, he has put eternity into man's heart, yet so that he cannot find out what God has done from the beginning to the end. (Ecclesiastes 3:11)

Narrative is everywhere. There are the grand stories, called "metanarratives" that we use to describe our collective history and progress of our world (or at least our cultural corner of it). Some of these "metanarratives" have taken a battering of late, being dismantled and deconstructed by different social and cultural theorists. These critics have asked things like "Whose history? Whose culture?" and said things like "What you call facts, theories, and informed consensus are simply established conventions with their own blind spots, biases, and prejudices."

However . . . not so fast! Perhaps what some are now calling "the narrative turn" offers a way out from under all this rubble of deconstructed "metanarrative." Academics, sociologists, ethnographers, knowledge constructors, and critical theorists of many stripes are using storytelling as a way of framing their ideas.

Why, you ask? Well, the chastened theorists and practitioners in a variety of fields suggest that a narrative approach seems to offer a more nuanced and circumspect approach to describing theory. Some see in this approach a nod to the previously unacknowledged hidden biases and powerplays lurking in neutral, dispassionate language and abstract propositional statements. When someone puts their ideas in story form (these theorists and practitioners suggest), they frame a theoretic statement or proposition in more modest terms. This anecdotal approach also reminds people of our personal involvement in what we know and describe. It lets the listener or reader know that we, too, have a dog in the fight.

But this approach isn't limited to the classroom, textbook, or keynote speech: the emphasis on narrative is trickling down into other parts of our culture as well.

Some theorists and practitioners in the fields of psychology and also talk about the central role that story plays in our lives. According to them, we construct our very sense of personal identity in narrative terms. A place in a story tells who we are and offers reasons (or excuses) for why we do what we do. Some counsellors, therapists, and pastors propose that we might change for the better if we work with someone on "changing that story."

Marketing is also in on the game. Whether you are marketing a product, a service, or a user experience, part of your success will depend on how well you (and your team) listen to your intended customer—and to the customer's story.

In some cases, you and your sales team will even brainstorm and construct an "ideal customer" for your product. In order to sketch out this future customer you might create a back story to somehow give them that third dimension. You and your team may ask, "What is it about this individual and their story that makes them 'need' our product, service, or experience?"

Or, perhaps, you might tell a story that helps the customer to see that a) they are the hero of your story, and b) buying your stuff is the only reasonable thing to do.

Maybe you want to be storyteller of the more traditional kind. You are an aspiring novelist or screenwriter. There are plenty of books that will inform and instruct you on archetypal story patterns, scene breakdowns, plot points, and emotional beats. You too can walk the hero's journey and learn to see it as the grand template behind many stories in many cultures.

There are even those who will break down for you what happens at a neural level when a reader is entranced and carried along by a successful story. Did you know that a story makes parts of the brain light up? That is not all: a good storyteller can add plot beats and sudden twists that will raise the cortisone and/or serotonin levels for the reader, or at some point pump him full of endorphins. Some of these chemical changes will have him riding an emotional rollercoaster as he reads.

We are all involved in different ways in the world of story. In fact, I believe it was the anthropologist Gregory Bateson who said somewhere (don't ask me where) that one of the things distinguishing the human animal from all the others was the sentence "That reminds me of a story."

Now, having said a few things about storytelling in general, I'd like to tell you a few stories of my own.

THE HIMALAYAS

Just over a year ago, for reasons that are still not entirely clear to me, I downloaded several rather academic papers on the ecosystem in the Himalayas. I concentrated on papers that dealt with the abundant variety of songbirds. I learned about the conditions that allowed some of these birds to flourish and thrive. I also learned about the systemic changes that were threatening the continued existence of some of the bird species. I also discovered a thing or two about intergenerational song transmission. As I recall, it has something to do with larger skull cavities on the mom's side of things.

It was not long (no, it really wasn't) before I was on my computer, cruising for examples of different varieties of birdsong you might find in the regions of the Himalayas. I found plenty of video clips posted by everyone from amateur enthusiasts to research institutions. The people posting offered lots of sonically pristine feathered sound bites to be listened to, savored, and possibly even sampled for a sort of digital "recollection in tranquility."

By the time I had finished my excursion into all things Himalayan, airborne, and melodic, I had bookmarked several places for a return visit and even signed up for a couple of mailing lists.

While I was thinking about the relative ease of access to all those videos and sound samples of birdsong from that part of the world I mentioned to someone how different it all was for me about twenty-five years ago. One very early morning I had gone out with my two daughters and a cassette recorder to a local nature center to try and capture bird song for inclusion in a mixed media artistic collaboration with painter Gaylen Stewart. When I mentioned these marked differences in experience to my friend, he replied, "Ah . . . but the memories!"

CROSSING THE BOUNDARIES

Gaylen Stewart is a practicing painter, mixed media artist, who also teaches and lectures about his work and ideas in a wide variety of contexts. He and I would cross paths regularly in the early to mid-1990s at places like the Cornerstone Festival in Peoria, Illinois. Given our shared interest in mixed media, performance, and collaboration it was not long before we began to explore the possibility of working on a project together. We set about pooling some combinations of images, sounds, texts, and spoken word performance. The resulting gallery installation was called "Crossing the Boundaries." It featured fifteen of his paintings, flanked by wall mounted portable CD players. The CDs in play featured my spoken poetry read over sound beds of musical loops. As our general theme explored fragile interlocking natural systems, Gaylen's paintings and mixed media collages incorporated imagery from the worlds of birds, insects, and flowers. Sometimes his collages also took words or lines out of my poems and wove them into the painted surfaces.

My poetry touched on different aspects of our shared theme, sometimes building metaphoric webs and layers from fragments of other more prosaic sources. Working with sound loops allowed me to combine musical passages composed in the studio with excerpts of my own homemade recordings of bird song.

As I said, on one occasion I went out with my two daughters, Emma (then nine) and Rebecca (six) and a portable cassette recorder. We drove out at the crack of dawn to the local nature center.

I wish I had made a recording of the two girls earnestly explaining to the baffled looking park ranger what it was we were hoping to accomplish on that somewhat grey overcast morning.

I do know that somewhere deeply buried among all the cassettes marked "Work" is the one where the soft but persistent threads of bird song are suddenly eclipsed by a flurry of excited whispering from Rebecca as she spotted a baby deer and its mother moving through the trees in front of us.

The day was a success. My older daughter had a clipboard and kept a meticulous tally of all the sounds we captured ("chirping ... general chirping... chirping in the distance"). Our trip to the nature center was supplemented with a quick walk through a local exotic pet and wild bird store with the cassette recorder running, and then we adjourned for an executive debrief over croissants and hot chocolate in a nearby coffee shop.

THE FOREST AND THE TREES

Eventually the mixed media collaborative show was completed. The original installation of Gaylen's paintings and my sound loops and poetry traveled to a number of US galleries, and the project mutated and lived on in CD form, PowerPoint lectures in different parts of the world, and descriptive articles published here and there.

So do stories like these have spiritual meaning? I am happy enough that, for many of us, the ghost stories of "Sacred" and "Secular' no longer haunt our imagination and conscience. I, for one, am also happy if parts of our brains glow a bit from time to time, or the right kinds of chemicals are released into our system at the right kind of moment. These things for me are all windows and doorways into God's glory. I am certain that God delights in our capacity for storytelling, even as God delights in sometimes changing our stories.

I have no doubt that God also delights in the freshly woven chorus of birdsong rising from the depths of the forest each morning. However, I would also like to think that God stands beside me as I gaze wistfully over a plastic case full of old cassettes, wishing that I could lay my hands on the one with the little girl whispering.

NAPPING
A Foretaste of Eternity

> I love a good nap. Sometimes it's the only thing getting me out of bed in the morning.—George Costanza[1]

As I write, it's midsummer, which next to winter, spring, and fall, is my favorite season for napping. A summer afternoon nap is one of my favorite pastimes in the whole world. Each July, we spend a few weeks vacationing in simple waterfront cottages in upstate New York, where, even on the hottest days, we can keep windows open to catch the lake breezes. Each afternoon, immediately following lunch, I carry a library book (which I will not actually read) and a cold beverage (which I will not actually drink) to the little bedroom. I slip my hot skin under a cool cotton sheet and fall asleep, listening to the drone of a strong fan ruffling the curtains.

This vacation ritual began when our four children were small nappers themselves. If we were lucky, the kids would tucker out for a long afternoon nap right in the middle of the hottest part of the day. When the heat and activity had drained us of our purpose, we'd tuck them away, their pink cheeks pressed to the pillow or the playpen, into darkened bedrooms, fans gasping out rattly air. My husband and I would move our naptime outdoors in a variation on the theme. Once they'd given in to sleep, we'd tiptoe around the floors outside their bedroom doors, slipping into our bathing suits, picking up our pillows, books, and cold iced drinks to spend the afternoon reading in the sun. Reading happened, but usually only for a few moments before our day's activity—pushing swings and lifeguarding swimming babies—caught up with us.

And it turns out we were on to something. Scientific data points to several productive benefits of daily naps, including improved performance in reaction time, logical reasoning, memory, learning, and emotional regulation.[2] Anecdotal evidence from some of the world's most influential leaders highlights the benefit of a daily nap.

Sara Mednick, a professor of cognitive science at the University of California at Irvine and author of *Take a Nap! Change Your Life* assures us that "Napping is not what lazy people do. It's what people who are really effective and creative and self-regulating and conscientious do. Those are the type of people who nap."[3] She shares Winston Churchill's advice:

> You must sleep some time between lunch and dinner, and no half-way measures. Take off your clothes and get into bed. That's what I always do. Don't think you will be doing less work because you sleep during the day. That's a foolish notion held by people who have no imagination.

Artists and creatives also report benefitting from a daily nap.

A few years ago, I asked one of my favorite artists, Jim Janknegt, to share a "day-in-the-life" post with readers on my blog. I'd followed his work for years and felt drawn to his steady commitment to not only make art but also to live generatively in his home, family, church, and community. Of all the wisdom he shared, this might be my favorite:

> After lunch, I take a nap. Naps are civilized. The world doesn't come to an end if you take time for a nap. After the nap, more work.[4]

If daily naps offer value during ordinary seasons of work and rest, what about extraordinary seasons of our lives, particularly those marked by suffering? Napping during stages of grieving, illness, or recovery from trauma may be one of the deepest graces available to us, particularly for those in communities with long histories of suffering.

In the book *Rest Is Resistance,* Trica Hersey, author and founder of the Nap Ministry, offers a "call to action and manifesto for those who are sleep deprived, searching for justice, and longing to be liberated from the oppressive grip of Grind Culture." Her ministry aims to create awareness of sleep deprivation as a justice issue.[5] The performance artist, writer, activist, and theologian offers site-specific installations for public napping. Beneath the shade of a tent with big letters (not unlike a white revival tent), COME NAP[6], she invites the community to rest together.

As the self-described Nap Bishop, Hersey offers a combination of both soothing and rousing exhortations such as "Rest is a meticulous love practice. Practice daily"[7] and my personal favorite: "Lay yo ass down."[8]

While I cannot fully understand the oppressive weight generations of Black women and men carry, I have experienced seasons of deep grief and healing that required relentless napping. My napping survival strategy when my children were young was not only because of the sheer physical labor of that season of life but also due to repeated experiences of postpartum depression. I did not understand it then, but I can only look back at my early twenty-something self now, kiss my exhausted forehead, and whisper, "Sleep, darling. Napping is not weakness, but strength."

Vincent van Gogh, *The Siesta (after Millet)*, oil on canvas

Throughout the years, depression has returned on occasion and required more sleep. As I parent and offer care to a young adult suffering from major depression, I find that naps come for me again as a daily respite even when I'm not the one suffering from illness this time. In these seasons, naps don't feel like the sensory refreshment of those summer afternoons on the lake. They often feel like falling into a soft ditch on the side of a dusty path with no end in sight. On these afternoons, I awake groggy and heavy, blinking into the late afternoon light and wondering how there can still be so many hours left in the day.

Sometimes sleep devolves into inertia, a dulling of the senses, and loathing the remaining day. In these moments, naps remain a gift that our shame or ingratitude turns into something else.[9] As the temptation for gluttony does not negate the good gift of food, oversleeping or sloth (Prov. 19:15) does not negate the good gift of naps. I find that even napping is too much work when sloth shows up. I settle for rest*less* grasping for news and entertainment to numb my senses.

Benedict speaks to this daily routine of care in the Little Rule, a holistic way of life for the first monastic communities. Among other practices, the Rule of Saint Benedict gave specific instructions for his monks to nap after lunch.[10] This practice became part of the monastic way of life still practiced today. "Siesta" comes from the Latin word sext, or the "sixth hour" of the day, which falls around noon. If you're familiar with the fixed monastic hours of prayer, the word sext will sound familiar as the midday prayer of monks.[11] Understanding the correlation between siesta and sext begs the question: might our naps be a form of prayer?

It's believed that napping was a central part of Greco-Roman life, but it wasn't until Saint Benedict that napping became "codified" and an official part of the monk's rule of life. The industrial revolution heavily influences our current system of sleep. Till Roenneberg, professor of chronobiology at the University of Munich, reminds us of the origins of the eight-hour rule of sleep most of us take for granted as the only acceptable time for rest:

> Capitalists in the old days told us that we should do 12 to 16 hours of work for them, and then have eight hours to do what we like, so they wanted us to sleep efficiently in a certain window—that's where the idea of consolidated sleep comes from.[12]

Cue Nap Bishop Tricia Hersey's insistence that napping disrupts the economic systems that would treat human beings like labor-producing machines. When asked what happens when she isn't able to fall asleep during her daily rest time, she said: "If I nap, I do; if I don't, I've disrupted capitalism for 30 minutes."[13]

Sandro Botticelli, *Venus and Mars* (detail), tempera on panel

While God neither slumbers nor sleeps (Ps. 121:3–4), Scripture affirms the goodness of connecting sleep and labor. In the same Psalm that declares sleep a gift to the Lord's "beloved," Solomon warns against the vanity of "anxious toil" and roots us in the surest foundation for our labors: "Unless the LORD builds the house, those who build it labor in vain" (Ps. 127:1–2). You can almost hear Tricia Hersey's "Lay yo ass down" as a rousing *amen!*

From the beginning, the Creator established rhythms of work and rest into the DNA of the cosmos. Somehow in eternity, our need for sleep will change into something presumably even more glorious than my summer afternoon lakeside naps (Rev. 21:25). Still, while we exist in these human bodies, we follow the footsteps of the God-man Jesus, who invites us to the kind of counterintuitive rest He repeatedly modeled in His years on earth. The Lord of the Sabbath knew how to take a nap.

Through the gaze of millennia, we might find Jesus' habit of rest endearing, but in the daily minutia as well as the extraordinary seasons of crisis in our own lives, our perspective is more likely to side with the storm-tossed disciples in the Gospel of Mark (Mark 4:35–41). Much like the indignant and terrified disciples yanking the pillow out from under Jesus' head, I often scorn God's way of rest.

With our own experiences of feeling lost in the stormy seas of this capricious world, it's easy to relate to the words of the displeased disciples and hard to understand Jesus' response. We turn again to a monk, this time from the early twentieth century, for insight:

> And then they turn to Christ and do what we very often do with God: we look at God in time of stress and tragedy, and we are indignant that He is so peaceful. The story in the Gospel underlines it by saying that Christ was sleeping with His head on a pillow—the final insult. They are dying and He is comfortable. This is exactly what we feel about God so often. How dare He be blissful, how dare He be so comfortable when I am in trouble? And the disciples do exactly what we do so very often. Instead of coming to God and saying "You are peace, you are the Lord, say a word and my servant will be healed, say a word and things will come right," they shake Him out of His sleep and say, "Don't you care that we are perishing?" In other words, "If you can do nothing, at least don't sleep. If you can do nothing better, then at least die in anguish with us." Christ reacts, He gets up and says, "Men of little faith!" and brushing them aside, He turns towards the storm and, projecting His inner stillness, His harmony and peace on the storm, He says, "Be still, be quiet" and everything is quiet again.[14]

Perhaps when we choose the simple practice of a daily nap, we can rewrite the story in Mark. We can choose the inner stillness of Jesus instead of being scandalized by sleep. In the face of anxious toil and accumulation, and instead of mindlessly numbing of our senses, we can take a nap. We place the responsibility on the One who invites our weary, heavy-laden selves (Matt. 11:28–30). into rest to put us upright again, returning, restored, to our work (Ps. 3:5).

In this way, we worship the God who naps in capsizing boats, following in the footsteps of His Father, who takes days off even though the spinning universe depends on His attention. In every season, naps are a means of grace. They are a gift from the Father who gives sleep to his beloved children (Ps. 127:2). If a day of Sabbath rest each week provides a foretaste of eternity, then naps are like the little sips from the spoon while the soup simmers. If Sabbath rest is our eternal destination, then in every season of our lives, naps keep pointing us in the direction of our forever home.

1 Seinfeld, Season 8, Episode 18, "The Nap", April 10, 1997.
2 A good summary of several studies on the physical benefits of napping can be found in the article "The Science of Naps", *American Psychological Association,* Vol. 47, No. 7, 2016: https://www.apa.org/monitor/2016/07-08/naps. The article also describes findings that not everyone benefits equally from naps, but I'm skeptical.
3 Galadriel Watson, "Nap time is the new coffee break. Here's how to make the most of it," Washington Post, February 1, 2021, https://www.washingtonpost.com/lifestyle/wellness/nap-pandemic-home-how-sleep/2021/01/29/d2cc6cbe-6015-11eb-9430-e7c77b5b0297_story.html.
4 Jim Janknegt, "A day in the life and a meditation on Wendell Berry's 'Manifesto: The Mad Farmer Liberation Front,'" A Sacramental Life, June 7, 2019, https://www.tamarahillmurphy.com/blogthissacramentallife/56npnyhl6k6xdvloea7zffgaccrc35/2019/6/6.
5 You can see photos of Hersey's performance art and site specific installations here: http://www.triciahersey.com/community-care.html
6 The Nap Ministry and Free Street Theater installed a Nap Revival at Gage Park on the South Side of Chicago for Night Out in the Parks: https://thenapministry.wordpress.com/2018/08/21/rest-a-immersive-performance-and-installation-with-free-street-theater. I will never again read Jesus' invitation in Matthew 11:28 to "come rest" without thinking of Tricia Hersey.
7 The Nap Ministry, "A Meticulous Love Practice," Instagram, May 22, 2022, accessed August 22, 2022, https://www.instagram.com/p/Cd3Lz_VuPkP/
8 The Nap Ministry, "Lay Yo Ass Down," Instagram, June 18, 2022, accessed August 22, 2022, https://www.instagram.com/p/Ce95aumOOrz/
9 I'm forever indebted to Kathleen Norris for her book *Acedia & me* to help me discern the nature of Psalm 91's "noon-day" demon who tempts me to seek counterfeits for real rest.
10 *Rule of Saint Benedict,* "Chapter 48: The Daily Manual Labor," *Monastery of Christ in the Desert,* accessed August 22, 2022, https://christdesert.org/rule-of-st-benedict/chapter-48-the-daily-manual-labor/
11 Philip Kosloski, "Did St. Benedict invent nap time?", *Aleteia,* October 8, 2019, https://aleteia.org/2019/10/08/did-st-benedict-invent-nap-time/
12 Rachel Hall, "Keep it short and before 3pm: what the sleep scientists say about naps," *The Guardian,* August 27, 2021: https://www.theguardian.com/lifeandstyle/2021/aug/27/keep-it-short-and-before-3pm-what-the-sleep-scientists-say-about-naps.
13 Ally Betker, "How Tricia Hersey Wants to Travel into 2021," *Here Magazine,* accessed August 22, 2022, https://www.heremagazine.com/articles/tricia-hersey-nap-ministry-packing-list
14 Archbishop Anthony Bloom, *Beginning to Pray* (Mahwah, NJ: Paulist Press, 1970), p. 90.

COMIC BOOKS

Pow! Fwip! Snikt! and Excelsior!

You ain't done makin' mistakes, bub, not by a long shot.
—Wolverine, *X-Men* Vol. 1 #139

Long before I picked up my first comic book, you could find me running around with my buddy, Will, each of us with a towel safety-pinned around our necks as capes, inspired by the 1966 Batman show with Adam West and Burt Ward. I was always Batman and Will was always Robin, and his dad's T-top Corvette was our Batmobile. You also may have spotted me in our backyard climbing the tall holly tree as Spider-Man.

Matthew Clark, *Batman*, etching

Many years later, on a road trip to Florida, my dad bought me my first comic book. I don't remember the exact issue, but I know it was an *Uncanny X-Men* comic, and it was the summer of 1986. My brother Jeff got a Spider-Man book, and my brother Matt got a Thor book. We traded these books round and round the whole rest of the drive to Florida. I am sure my parents thought the silence and lack of bickering made it the most peaceful drive to Florida we ever had. As I look back over the last thirty-six years of comic book collecting, I can see the glory of God mirrored to me from the pages of the comics I read.

It may feel odd to be discussing God's glory in the context of comic books. Certainly within the mainstream comics culture it is absolutely uncool, and possibly dangerous (from a career standpoint) to be openly Christian. There are some artists who have been open about their Christianity—Doug TenNapel, Sergio Cariello, and Jason Brubaker being some fine examples. And there are some publishers and groups that support Christians in comics (New Creation Comics, the Christian Comic Arts Society, and GG4G—Geeky Guys & Gals 4 God), but most comic book creators tend to be as quiet as possible in public about their beliefs and let their work do the talking. Although gods run rampant in comics (Thor, Hercules, Ares, Gaea, Bast, Ra, etc.), Jesus rarely shows up. Most super heroes are agnostic. Some examples of religious heroes include: Daredevil, Blue Devil, Huntress, and Nightcrawler (Roman Catholic); Captain America, Superman, Human Torch, Rogue, and Cannonball (some sort of Protestant); Shadowcat and the Thing (Jewish); and Ms. Marvel and the Simon Baz Green Lantern (Muslim). I've never seen a good Presbyterian minister in any comics I have read, but there have been some strong Roman Catholic priests (eg. the "Born Again" arc in *Daredevil* and the 1983 limited series of *Cloak & Dagger*), and of course, priests are handy to have around when fighting demons. But rather than looking to comics for explicitly Christian stories and themes, it is better to read them as a way to explore good and evil in a more broad way. Comics are a laboratory where we test the boundaries of our ethics and morality. They allow us to envision a world where light is victorious over darkness, even if it takes a year's worth of issues to get to that point. Comics allow us to process our guilt and shame as we relate to the characters' desperate search for redemption. The truth is, when light is victorious over darkness, when true justice stands firm in the face of injustice, when Captain America knocks out Hitler on the cover of *Captain America #1* (Timely Comics, 1941) we see blurry images of the character of God.

Before I get too far into the discussion of seeing the glory of God in comics, I would like to make an argument for the comic book genre. Why read comic books when you could receive the same benefit through a book or through a well-done movie? The answer is: *you can't.* Comic books offer a distinct experience that can be better than a book or a movie. Scott McCloud states that "Comics offers tremendous resources to all writers and artists: faithfulness, control, a chance to be heard far and wide without fear of compromise . . . it offers range and versatility with all the potential imagery of film and painting plus the intimacy of the written word."[1]

When you read a book your imagination uses the author's description and does much of the interpretation for you. Movies, on the other hand, take all the imagination out of the experience. We know that Wolverine looks like Hugh Jackman and Black Widow looks like Scarlett Johansson. There isn't much space for imagination at all. But comic books combine the mediums: they give words and pictures with just enough info that your Spider-Man and mine look similar, but they still allow us plenty of space to imagine the other aspects of the story. Your imagination fills the spaces between the panels and the gaps left by the text. Comic book art gives us common images with enough space to use our imagination.

One comic book character that especially fires my imagination is Wolverine. Wolverine is a mutant who has a healing factor: his body heals as he takes wounds. As a result of his ability to heal, he was used in an experiment to cover his bones with a fictional metal called *adamantium.* He also has three claws that come out from between the knuckles on each hand. Wolverine drinks too much. Wolverine is a brawler. In the midst of the fight, Wolverine is direct. He always wants to go right at the enemy. (Of course he does: his healing factor makes him nearly immortal.) Wolverine is one of the few X-Men who struggle with the team's ethic of not killing. Wolverine struggles with this ethic because he is trained as a soldier, an assassin, but also because he has an animalistic nature. He can get overwhelmed in the fight and go into a "berserker rage." But Wolverine is written as a complex character. This same beer-drinking, rage-fighting, can't die brawler is known throughout the comics as a character who loves his team. He is committed to the team. He is a father figure to a number of the younger female characters. Wolverine has trained, advised, and cared for characters like Kitty Pride, Psylocke, Jubilee, and many more.

One of the best Wolverine stories of all time is *Old Man Logan*, written by Mark Millar and illustrated by Steve McNiven, is a story that takes place in an alternate future where the heroes lost. The country has been run by the villains for fifty years. Only a few heroes remain, and Wolverine is one of them—except he doesn't go by Wolverine anymore. He has abandoned the superhero life and now lives quietly, going by a nickname, "Logan." He lives a quiet life in the West, married and raising a family. He doesn't fight the villains; in fact, he doesn't fight at all. He watches and suffers injustice at the hands of the Hulk Gang without ever popping a claw.

Benjamin Schipper, *Wolverine,* digital

Wolverine struggles with deep shame by hiding from himself and the rest of the country. The reason that his team, the X-Men, were not available to battle until the end is because Wolverine killed them. He was tricked, of course, but the shame runs deep. As Wolverine is talking with his friend Hawkeye, the archer says, "You murdered the X-Men?"

Wolverine responds, "Stabbed every one of 'em. Right through the heart. But I didn't know it was them, Hawkeye. Mysterio made 'em look and feel and even smell different. I swear to God. I had no idea."

As the weight of the deed sinks in, Hawkeye asks, "What happened then?"

Wolverine says, "Who knows? All I remember was walkin' through the woods and trees, sobbin' and cryin'."

I don't know about you, but I connect to the idea of shame. There are things that I have done and said that can still make me sick to my stomach. And my instinct with shame is to hide it. I don't want to remember it and I don't want anyone to know it. I may not be a nearly immortal superhuman, but I get shame.

As you read *Old Man Logan* and see the injustice of a country run by the villains, you so desperately want Logan to be restored. You desperately want to see the sound of his claws coming out of his hands on the page—"SNIKT." The thing is, Wolverine's claws can't come out until his shame is dealt with.

I love reading comics with Wolverine. He has unbelievable power and has overcome all sorts of challenges. He defeats the bad guys. He brings about justice.

But we see the blurry image of God in comics not when our heroes and antiheroes are their most powerful, but when the weakness of these characters is exposed. Wolverine can't do it all. For all the enemies he defeats, he can't overcome his shame. This is where I live. I don't have unbreakable bones or claws that pop out of my hands. I do have a life filled with resources and opportunities. And still, there are things I just can't beat. This is where Jesus, my need for Jesus, starts to jump off the page of my comic books. Hebrews 12:2 encourages us to look to Jesus, "the founder and perfecter of our faith, who for the joy that was set before him endured the cross, despising the shame, and is seated at the right hand of the throne of God." The cross was a shameful way to die and Jesus overcomes it. Jesus overcomes shame where Wolverine and I cannot. He doesn't just overcame the shame of dying on a cross, but He carried the shame of my sin so that I didn't have to. Reading about Wolverine's struggle—and ultimate failure—to be truly and wholly redeemed drives my heart to seek God's face. Comics show me a broken, blurry picture that aches to be whole. My hope for these characters allows me to practice hope for myself—which can be found only in Christ.

1 Scott McCloud, *Understanding Comics: The Invisible Art* (Northampton, MA, Kitchen Sink Press, Inc., 1993), p. 212.

DANCING

Life Revealed Through Living Shapes

Dancers are sculptors of the air, creating images with shapes and patterns through space. To a dancer, an empty room is a blank canvas waiting to be filled with living, breathing creativity through the artistic medium of the human body.

However, dance is not merely the act of creating shapes and abstract images; these shapes serve as an incarnation of the human condition. The word *incarnate* means to embody in flesh. Dance is not meant to simply show an audience an experience, but it is an *actual embodiment* of our spiritual and emotional selves. Dance puts flesh on what could not be seen before. Contemporary artist Makoto Fujimura says dancers fuse the body and spirit and embody our souls in the public arena.[1]

Dance can embody suffering, injustice, sorrow, or even joy in ways that words prove inadequate for. Our longings, dreams, and prayers can be revealed even to ourselves through the expression of dance. Suddenly what was invisible and only hidden in the human heart becomes visible and named through moving patterns and shapes sculpted through the air.

Scripture says, "So God created man in his own image, in the image of God he created him; male and female he created them" (Gen. 1:27). Being created in the image of God, when we see a clearer version of ourselves, we see more clearly the God who formed us.

One of the shows I've helped co-create with a colleague is based entirely on the Book of Psalms. It's the book of the Bible in which we find the widest range of human experiences, from the lowest point of despair to the highest peak of joy and wonder. In our rehearsal process, even the dancers began to see how they experienced the highs and lows of the psalms in their own lives and familiar scriptures became more tangible and real as they related to one another through the movement. In one piece, I based the choreography on Psalms 40–43, which talk a lot about despair. Through the instrument of their bodies, my dancers and I worked out what a deep depression would look like on a tangible, visceral level. We brainstormed words such as *listlessness, weighted, invisible* and how to actually put flesh on those qualities. Part of the storytelling of that piece was to not only embody the depression but to pull back the curtain on what it might look like in the spiritual realm. As a solo dancer expressed the depression swallowing her up, she was then lifted into the air by eight other dancers. I thought, that's how it would look if we could see a collective community loving and praying us through our darkest hours. Or what if we saw angels doing battle for someone's spirit trapped in despair? For that, I had dancers enter the perimeters of the stage engaging in movement with what looked like an invisible realm.

After our performances, this particular piece, which I titled *The Glass Wall,* received a lot of feedback. The consistent message I received from audience members was "Thank you for telling the story of depression," because what they usually experienced in isolation and hiddenness had now been named and revealed. It was not called out with callousness or condemnation; instead, they saw their suffering being cared for through the story the dancers were incarnating.

The dancers served as vessels of God's glory that incarnated the unseen and connected our stories of isolation with one another. God is glorified in the communal act of sharing one another's stories. When we clothe our stories in flesh, so to speak, we can recognize our place in the narrative of the story God has written us into. The veil is lifted from our eyes, and we can also recognize the God who formed us, sees us, and knows us. It's accepting and living in this reality that transforms us from glory to glory: "And we all, with unveiled faces beholding the glory of the Lord, are being transformed into the same image from one degree of glory to another. For this comes from the Lord who is the Spirit" (2 Cor. 3:18).

The show was entitled *Dialogue of the Heart,* and it became exactly that. Several audience members said they

Tang dynasty, *Female dancer,* tomb pottery

couldn't describe what was happening to them while watching it but they felt something they'd never felt before. One woman who attended was an officer in the police force and was regularly immersed in the darkness of humanity from working in the homicide unit. She said she felt transported from the darkness into the light while watching the show. This is the transformative glory of God at work in creative collaboration through us and the Holy Spirit. His glory moves us from darkness to light.

In this sharing of one another's stories, dance becomes a great act of generosity. Dancers give themselves, mind, body, and spirit, fully over to their audience, to their craft, and to each other. This giving echoes the lavish generosity of God, who gave Himself fully in physical form to show His love through His son, Jesus. Jesus did not come as an idea or an abstract concept, but in a living, moving body.

John 1:1 says the Word became flesh. When Jesus came to this earth as a baby, He defined humanity with His own body. He put flesh on the living God and therefore gave the weight of glory to the human body. He showed us that Love requires physical presence. Love has a physical body. Jesus showed us, through servanthood and the sacrifice of His own flesh, that loving generously requires us to walk closely among each other, willing to be woven into each other's lives in ways that have impact, in ways that change us and sculpt us. Much like the choreographic process of a dance that weaves bodies through time and space, often transcending the practical with generous acts of grace and beauty.

Often the least understood art form, dance is also the most fully human, acting as a deeper language than mere words. I like to imagine that movement could have very well been the first language spoken between God and Adam and Eve. I've always wondered how they communicated before language with words, as we know it, existed. The first communication we see between God and Adam is through breath in Genesis 2:7, where God breathed the breath of life into the man's nostrils and the man became a living person. Even when we are born, our first act of communication is to inhale and the next is to exhale with a cry that signals new life. From birth we are wired to learn and communicate somatically, through the body, which echoes that first somatic experience that began the relationship between God and human. As God breathed life into Adam, I wonder what happened next. Maybe Adam exhaled with a cry of praise.

There are several Hebrew words in Scripture that refer specifically to the use of the body for praise.[2] *Yadah,* which is derived from the Hebrew word for *hand,* indicates the lifting of hands in praise. We find this in Exodus 17 where, for Moses, the raising of his hands meant battle. As long as his hands were raised in prayer, Israel prevailed in war. The story goes that Moses had to have others hold his arms to keep his hands raised, as he became too weak to do it himself through the duration of the battle. We see here that hands raised have power and purpose in prayer and worship. So much so that God instructed Moses to keep them raised in order to continue to be victorious. Maybe there's a battle you're fighting in life where you just need to bring your *Yadah* praise to the situation and let God do the rest. This is the body testifying to the spirit in prayer and worship.

Similar to *Yadah,* we find the word *Todah* which is also derived from the word hand in Hebrew. However, *Todah* carries the essence of giving thanks with our hands in praise.

"I must perform my vows to you, O God; I will render thank offerings (*Todat*) to you" (Ps. 56:12). The word *barach* is another Hebrew word referring to the body in praise and worship. It refers to the physical posture of kneeling as well as a Hebrew common term for blessing. I love the imagery of kneeling in surrender and receiving God's blessing in return.

This is by no means an all-encompassing list of Hebrew words for praise, but it helps us see that the Hebrew language allows for the body to be a part of the language of glorifying God in worship and prayer. There's specificity even to which part of the body is used for different types of praise. Sadly, our Western church culture has a history of intentionally excluding the body from worship and has failed to recognize the power and purpose God intended for the body in bringing our whole selves to glorify Him.

The beginning of Genesis is my favorite part of the Bible. Verse two of the entire Bible says, "The earth was without form and void, and darkness was over the face of the deep. And the Spirit of God was hovering over the face of the waters." The word *hovering* in Hebrew is *rachaph* which means to tremble or flutter like a mother bird hovering over her nest. We see the first act of creation in the very next verse when God says, "Let there be light" (Gen. 1:3).

Creation begins with movement, with the Spirit of God hovering.

I wonder if we can recognize God hovering in our darkness, stirring up the waters, ready to birth new creation where maybe we can see only chaos and a formless void. As I create through dance and fill empty spaces with living sculptures of movement, I am echoing that first creative act of bringing shape and order where there is emptiness. This is what art can do. It helps us make sense of the senseless and gives shape to empty places in our lives. It reveals a God who has been hovering over us the whole time, waiting to create new life within us. Our own creative acts of faith glorify God every time as they testify to His creativity dwelling within us.

1 Makoto Fujimura, *Refractions: A Journey of Faith, Art, and Culture* (Colorado Springs: Nav Press, 2009).

2 "Hebrew & Greek Words for Praise," *Worship Basic 101,* https://sites.google.com/site/worshipbasic101/about-praise--worship/hebrews--greek-words-for-praise.

TRAFFIC

Minivans and Monasteries

Growing up in Canada's Yukon Territory, the busiest roadway I'd ever driven was Two Mile Hill. It's the stretch of highway that most people use to get to and from work, and the most likely place a Yukoner would mention when referring to traffic. The word came up just like it did anywhere else, but in a town that small it was safe to assume that if someone was late, they probably just didn't leave the house on time. "I hit a moose on the way here" was a more geographically appropriate excuse. My hometown still has no real traffic to speak of, and I can say this with full confidence since I've spent the last ten years living in Austin, Texas—one of the twenty-five worst congested cities in the nation.[1]

Sitting in painfully slow traffic is now a part of my daily life. I spend about an hour out of every weekday on the interstate alongside 18-wheelers and frustrated commuters, baking in the Texas heat in shiny metal boxes.[2] We're close enough and driving slowly enough to have conversations, but we don't usually look at each other. We save our interactions for moments of extreme idiocy, such as merging too soon, exiting too late, or driving the speed limit. Calling bad traffic "congestion" has always seemed to suggest that there's some impending cure for this malady. I'm no city planner and I'm sure there are potential remedies to this issue, but my hunch is that traffic jams are here for the foreseeable future.

One day, I hope to spend a lot less time in my car. But for now, I'm going to suggest something kind of crazy: I think traffic is making me a better person. And I think, if you let it, it could do the same for you. I realize this might be a hard sell. I'm like a parent extolling the virtues of broccoli to a two-year-old at dinner time. "Try it! You'll like it. It's a tree you can eat!" You're the wary toddler eyeing the green lumps on her plate, arms crossed, mouth firmly shut—you're unconvinced. Let me see if I can put some metaphorical cheese on this unsavory assertion.

A lot of people drive big trucks in Texas. When I first moved here, I assumed this was so they could haul hay around or avoid getting stuck in the mud. But after finally summoning the courage to drive on the interstate, I witnessed one big reason a truck can come in handy: when cars are nearly at a standstill and idling, bumper-to-bumper, Texas truck drivers can (and do) pull what a Texan once hilariously described to me as a "Texit." No exit for another mile? No problem! Make your own exit wherever you please, by driving down into the ditch, across a field, and up onto the frontage road running alongside the highway, escaping the monotony in store for the rest of us.

I drive a minivan that bottoms out in potholes, so no "Texits" for me. And since I can't opt-out of the tedious, mind-numbing waiting, and since this is an unavoidable part of millions of peoples' lives, it has to be an area of life that God can work through. His work in this case is just as unexciting as we'd expect. We won't miraculously enjoy being crammed into hot cars, blissfully coasting around with grateful smiles. It will still be frustrating, boring, and feel like a waste of time. Precisely because it is all of these things, we can be formed and changed by it. If we let it, this "wasted" time could make the rest of our life outside of the car better and our hearts more whole.

In my case, traffic has become an unexpected means of sanctification. Sanctification can blandly make its way into our lives through our daily routines and the repeated motions we make. We turn the key, check the mirror, signal to turn, and (if you're me) cuss a little at the person behind you who's driving too closely. Yes, sometimes I swear at strangers from the safety of my car. In fact, part of the reason I'm convinced that God can use traffic to change me is because this daily ritual has exposed something ugly in me that needs my attention: my uncontrolled anger.

It's not like my life before traffic didn't involve anger. I just thought I had a handle on it, that I could manage it respectably, and that it wouldn't bubble over and embarrass me. Most of the time, and for most of my life, I've managed to keep a lid on it. But it's hard to ignore your vices when they are provoked daily by the monotony, and necessity of traveling slowly in a confined space. This became more evident to me a few years back, thanks to my young kids.

For a while, driving was the time I used to catch up on current events on public radio. That all changed when the kids pulled their pacifiers out and started asking questions, reflecting on what was being fed to them over the speakers. Suddenly they wanted to know why there was a war, who died, and who the president was going to be. "Why does there have to be a president anyway?" one of them once cried out, bursting into tears. They were starting to pay more attention, so it was inevitable that they'd notice the obvious: Mommy gets mad in the car.

One day, as I was pulling out of the neighborhood with my kids in tow, I grumbled loudly about someone who cut me off. I chose one of the least colorful words I knew to chastise the other driver; I was practiced in exercising enough restraint to save the real zingers for drives absent of little ears. Even so, an astonished little voice rang out from the backseat, "Mom, you just called someone made in God's image a moron!" Yes, I recognized that line. It came straight from my own parenting playbook—now turned around by my child to teach me.

I felt gross. I realized that my outburst in front of the kids wasn't a slip-up. I had been practicing this behavior in my car for years under the false assumption that I could save acting on my worst impulses for times when I was alone. And worse than that, my behavior revealed my mistaken belief that my nasty, unforgiving comments about people didn't matter or that they got sucked into some kind of cosmic holding area for my contempt. Instead, the truth broke through to me: the angry words I spoke were indeed landing somewhere. They were circling back to settle, like a foul cloak, on my shoulders.

I'd love to say that this moment of realization produced an immediate change. In reality, I'm still a cranky driver. To modern city-dwellers like me who greatly value efficiency and productivity, time is a precious commodity. Spending so much of it in the car feels like a colossal waste. I think this is a large part of why bad traffic infuriates and brings out the worst in so many of us.

For now, driving is a significant part of how my light is spent,[3] and I've begun to let go of the notion that I can somehow redeem this "lost" time; I've started to treat my car like my own moveable hermitage—a modern, solitary cell. When I know I'll be alone in the car, I choose to keep it quiet—no radio, podcasts, or music. Without any distractions, I am more aware of the emotions I've been avoiding, the worries I'm constantly combatting, and my real need for the presence of God.

This forced confinement has now become a time of confession and examen for me, of exposing the messy state of my soul to myself and to an already all-knowing God. With the A/C blowing in my face, I tell God how I've messed up. I cry over the ways I've hurt my friends, my family, random strangers, and admit the ways in which I've been hurt. It's an unconventional way to practice prayer, but I feel that God honors this odd, new ritual of mine. I believe that through times like these, He's slowly healing me, revealing the roots of my anger, and providing forgiveness and comfort through His presence.

No, it's not beautiful. It's not the serene cloister I'd rather spend these prayerful moments in, but it's the space I have. I've begun to count on this time of slowing down and choosing silence, accepting where I am, and letting God speak into that cramped, strangely intimate place. And so, most days, you'll find me in my snack-littered minivan, inching along the interstate with the radio off, resisting the urge to mentally "Texit," talking aloud to invisible ears, and for the most part, staying in my lane.

1 "United States of America traffic," Tomtom, accessed August 8, 2022, https://www.tomtom.com/en_gb/traffic-index/united-states-of-america-country-traffic/.

2 The Police, "Sychronicity II," from *Syncronicity,* A&M Records, 2003, https://www.youtube.com/watch?v=XLEyIE_TMU8.

3 John Milton, "Sonnet 19: When I consider how my light is spent," Poetry Foundation, accessed July 1, 2022, https://www.poetryfoundation.org/poems/44750/sonnet-19-when-i-consider-how-my-light-is-spent.

CHRONIC PAIN

These Broken Bones

As I knelt down and touched my hand to the water of Henry David Thoreau's famous Walden Pond, I pondered his legacy and the words he penned in the quaint cabin across the water:

"I went into the woods because I wanted to live deliberately . . . I wanted to live deep and suck out all the marrow of life."[1]

But instead of "sucking out all the marrow of life," it felt like *life* was sucking all the marrow out of *me.*

As I stood up from the pond's edge, my head pounded and fuzzy stars flashed across my eyes. I began blacking out with every few steps. Pain pierced me from my head to my feet, and I wavered in and out of dizziness as the pond spun around. Waves of nausea came and went like the water lapping at my feet.

Stumbling around Walden, I thought cynically about Thoreau and his fellow transcendentalists. Spirituality, they promised, was best accessed in nature, beyond our corporeal bodies. The concept of transcending the physical is very romantic. But what about those of us imprisoned by sick bodies, unable to transcend the physical? I would have loved to walk around Walden immersed in a sensational, spiritual experience. But instead all I could think about was mustering up the energy to put one foot in front of another without promptly keeling over.

In eighth grade, I was diagnosed with a few different conditions, all of which are common and not life-threatening. But even so, every day for me is a different battle. I certainly spend a portion of life feeling normal, but most days are laced with bodily pain, exhaustion, blackouts, and nausea. These symptoms have followed me through the most important days of my life. I ended my honeymoon with a $6,000 hospital visit. I saw the Colosseum through dizzy eyes. I graduated high school aching unbearably all over my body.

Somehow, I know that bodily pain is a part of lived redemption. My freshman year of college a close friend quoted Psalm 51:8 to me: "Let me hear joy and gladness; let the bones that you have broken rejoice." Over and over again I have read and memorized the mantra of Psalm 61:4, where the writer praises God that he is "safe beneath the shelter of your wings" (NLT). The Christian life is no stranger to pain, both physical and emotional. But how can broken bones rejoice? How can joy and pain coexist without some kind of deafening dissonance?

Most of my experience with sickness is feeling my body slowly fade. Laughing hurts. Sadness overwhelms me. I have spent many gatherings and celebrations in a quiet room listening to fellowship while I nurse a swollen and shaky body. I battle to live normally and inevitably lose. It is because of this that I believe my illness is particularly mundane. I take eight or nine pills at night and hope I don't regurgitate them. I have alarms on my phone reminding me to drink enough water. I pray that I will feel well enough to do "that thing" that we've been planning for months; I pray I won't ruin it for everyone else. There is a day-in, day-out boredom to the routine of treatment. If I become lazy and pass on my medicine, eat the wrong thing, or stay up too late, I may suffer from days or weeks of relapse. I spent the first three weeks of my marriage in a strict "don't leave the house unless necessary" attempt to heal from the stress of the wedding. It is from these situations that I have learned: most of chronic illness is not dramatic hospital visits, it's just missing things. Forced boredom. Silence.

Despite how lonely a chronic illness feels, my loved ones have coped in delightful ways. My husband has learned sweet mantras and rituals for my bad moments. Every time I sloppily say, "I don't feel good," he gently responds, "Well, you look good." Sweetly I'll hear him say, "Just a dizzy girl in a dizzy world," as I lean on him to conquer a flight of stairs. In NYC, a friend accompanied me up eight flights of stairs in between debate competitions, and teased me gently when I ran to the bathroom to throw up. When our flight was canceled and the whole team spent the night in the airport, I was one of two students allowed to spend the night in a hotel, because, and I quote, "You don't look so good." When my husband watches me stand up quickly, "on a mission" as I always am, he quickly rushes to my side, knowing I will soon start to fall over. When blood flow to my brain is inhibited, I can pass out, experience migraines, or (rarely) undergo seizure-like symptoms and lose control of my extremities. But, sometimes, the poor blood flow simply makes me "loopy," as my friends say, and sends me into a state of silliness, slurred speech, and complete lack of inhibition. Loopy Sarah is fun at weddings but has also been known to spill root beer all over people at Applebee's. Loopy Sarah bonds with strangers, urges people to pursue their dreams, and, when asked what she wants on her burger, says simply, "Not mushrooms. Please not mushrooms." I have not even slightly begun to understand this ridiculous mood my brain puts me in, but at least there are some fun things about the illness.

Still, I look back on most of my life and just remember exhaustion. Mitski's song "Washing Machine Heart" relates the feeling of your heart being put through a washing machine, tossed and turned, soaked and dried, wearing it out and stretching it thin. This is the burden of chronic illness.

It is inherently lonely. To have an invisible yet debilitating illness following you through life requires fierce advocacy of your reality. I live in a world that others cannot see. Because of that, even my closest friends and family have questioned whether I'm being honest about my symptoms. My illness is detectable via MRI and blood tests and vital numbers, but my doctors still rely on me to communicate precisely and thoroughly about the experience of living in this body. Without that communication, treatment is impossible. Most of the time, people cannot look at you and tell that you are sick. You must advocate for and trust yourself, or you will battle feelings of insanity. Because of this, chronic illness is also an invitation to know your body intimately. I have learned its intricacies and signals, and now we have a complex language. I have learned to feel things that I cannot put into words and communicate back. It is an invitation to deep intuition.

Solitude is the second sacred invitation of chronic illness. I've waited alone in hospital waiting rooms, sat for hours alone in a claustrophobic MRI tube, and curled up silently in my room as everyone is making memories downstairs. These moments of solitude have afforded me plenty of time to contemplate. I have come to believe—whether by inspiration or necessity—that solitude is a holy communion between you, your body, and the Holy Spirit. Three inseparable entities. I have grown to love this solitude and guard it as sacred.

Albrecht Dürer, *The Doubting Thomas*, from *The Small Passion* (detail), woodcut

Finally, chronic illness is an invitation to recognize the God-given dignity of your body. I have heard the famous quote: "You don't have a soul. You are a soul; you have a body." Though this is often incorrectly attributed to C.S. Lewis, it comes from a Walter M. Miller novel.[2] I have had this quote indelicately, yet kindheartedly, thrown at me by people saying "You will transcend your body! Your body is the least important thing about you!" I do not find this compelling. When Jesus resurrected, He did not "transcend" His body. He realized it. He resurrected it. He redeemed it. His scars remain as a sign of His violent victory over death. He invited his apostles to touch and feel Him. When they reached out their hands, they did not find a ghostly mirage.

They found flesh and bones. I am a body and a soul, and both of those are sick in this world. And one day, I am promised, both will be healed.

Learning the spirituality of my body, learning to communicate with it and sense its sadness, joy, relief, and fear has taught me much about the human condition. The solitude and loneliness of chronic illness has given me a greater capacity for the profundity of the body. Day by day, I gain a more personal understanding of what the psalmist means when he says "Let these bones you have broken rejoice." We may weep and mourn over these broken bones—yes! So, too, does our Savior. We may cry out in the dead of night for someone to take away our pain, and we may feel our souls fading into non-existence as another day starts and ends with misery. Still, He understands.

Every Moment Holy's "Liturgy for Those Enduring Lasting Pain" cries out for "grace to endure what I cannot on my own." Can I be content with Christ to just hold me in the pain, to "meet me in the secret place of my torment" and to "tend to my distress"?[3] Years of illness have refined me until I can finally answer yes. But this is not without exhaustion and protest. I have spent years never entrusting this pain to God, too cynical to breach the subject. When I have prayed, my prayers have become tirades against a God who has permitted my suffering. Sometimes I wonder how many times Jesus has uttered "Forgive her Father, she knows not what she does" on my behalf. I worship a savior whose body, too, was broken. Together we will stand in eternity with perfected forms and praise unlimited.

A few years into my illness I still battled with fainting spells. One such incident came on Thanksgiving break, as my family made breakfast. Usually, I can calmly sit down before the darkness overwhelms me. But at that moment, I could not. With my limbs violently shaking, and no control over my movement, I realized that I would soon fall. I felt my face hit the ground and I heard my family rush to me, but I could not speak to them or even turn around. Looking back, I want to tell this scared child that her body is not her enemy. She feels out of control, but there is a Savior holding that broken body. He knows her broken body is trying its best. Jesus loves this body and mourns the pain that plagues it. I want to tell her that the day she so anxiously awaits is not the day when she will leave her body, but rather the day when her body will be realized, resurrected, and redeemed, made perfect and sent onward on its mission as an agent of eternal praise and glory.

I will likely not heal in this life. But for now, with eyes fixed ahead, I take refuge in the shelter of His wings, pulling together my broken bones for another day of rejoicing.

1 Henry David Thoreau, *Walden* (London: Macmillan Collector's Library, 2016, orig. publ. 1854), p. 98.
2 Walter M. Miller, Jr., *A Canticle for Leibowitz* (New York: HarperCollins, 1959), p. 293.
3 Douglas Kaine McKelvey, "Liturgy for Those Enduring Lasting Pain," from *Every Moment Holy, Vol. 2: Death, Grief, and Hope* (Nashville, TN: Rabbit Room, 2021), p. 83.

MOVIES
Celluloid Sanctification

When we are moved by the magic of movies, we welcome the emotions welling up in our chests; we grip our seats with white knuckles during a thrilling scene; our stomachs churn over a character's dilemma; we cry even as we smile uncontrollably. We embrace movies that embrace us into their worlds. We journey with the characters and lose ourselves in their tales. A major reason we enjoy movie-watching is that it allows us to escape into a "secondary world,"[1] whether magical lands of elves and dragons or business offices of suits and ties. But is movie-watching more than a shallow amusement that diverts us away from the things that matter?

Movie-watching can be surprisingly God-glorifying. According to Scripture, God has used secular storytelling to teach wisdom and foster faith, as the case for Daniel (Dan. 1:4, 17). Robert K. Johnston writes, "We seldom notice God's sacramental presence in the ordinary experiences of life, including our moviegoing. We fail to hear God speak. For this reason, we rarely respond theologically, whether critically or experientially."[2] Spaces where God shows up can be outside the church walls on a Sunday morning and even in darkened theaters on a Friday night. If we want to engage God where He appears we must be mindful—we must notice Him.

Mindfulness does not require us to be so serious that we cannot enjoy movie-watching. Rather, mindfulness requires an integrative mindset: God's sovereignty can not only invade secular storytelling but can even empower storytelling for His good purposes. When we integrate theology and art, we are able to experience God's fingerprints in movies. We're truly entertained when we are enriched by the spiritual substance woven in the art. There are at least four ways movie-watching glorifies God.

CULTIVATING COSMOS

We try to make sense of life, seeking meaning in an array of experiences from triumphs to trials. Kelly James Clark writes, "Narrative seeks the unity of a life amidst the diversity of life-events."[3] We search for the story in our lives, trying to understand seasons of life as purposeful chapters.

Story harmonizes events into a meaningful whole, whether glorious triumphs, treacherous trials, or downtrodden tragedies. Clark writes, "The impulse to tell stories is rooted in our desire to understand ourselves and others . . . to make sense out of the apparently disparate events in our lives."[4] Story tells us life is going somewhere and we're not trapped in a mundane ticking of time without reason or purpose. Story inherently relates to God's creativity.

Genesis introduces God as Creator. Genesis 1:2 shows us the canvas the Creator worked on was an earth "without form," that was "void," where "darkness was over the face of the deep." The earth was shapeless and disordered. It was also destitute and lifeless. Upon this chaotic canvas, God's Spirit came.

Then, God commenced a dramatic performance of creativity, a step-by-step fashioning of cosmos out of chaos. God's nature as Creator is to create. His will is not for chaos, but for order and wholeness. God created everything to be *good*, declaring, "It was good." A good reality is fraught with beauty, dignity, and flourishing. This is the meaning of cosmos.

Good stories cultivate cosmos by serving as mirrors and maps for finding our narratives out of apparently disparate experiences. We discover that successes are meaningful parts of our story and struggles have a purpose. We realize that relationships, like other characters, are crucial to our development but can also be challenges to our goals. We learn that we must grow in character to move forward in our journeys.

The Lord of the Rings helps us find hope amid hostility. *News of the World* shows us how to embrace

John Hendrix, *Barad-Doodle*, ink

a new love by relinquishing guilt. In *Up,* we see a way to navigate through loss to seize the freedom for a new adventure. *Cast Away* inspires us to survive despite temptations to hopelessness and loneliness. *Wonder* encourages us to love those who are different from us and who face discrimination. *Hidden Figures* reminds us that people can rise above discrimination through intelligence and perseverance. *Shawshank Redemption* shows us the value of preserving human dignity in a demeaning, dehumanizing environment.

Movie-watching that cultivates cosmos in our lives glorifies God as Creator. When movie-watching helps us pursue cosmos, it glorifies God by aligning with His creativity.

ICONS FOR ILLUMINATING TRUTHS

There is no cultural domain that God's grace cannot touch. God "makes the sun rise on the evil and on the good, and sends rain on the just and on the unjust" (Matt. 5:45). In fact, "every good gift and every perfect gift" comes from God (James 1:17). So, John Calvin instructs, "As truth is most precious, so all men confess it to be so. And yet, since God alone is the source of all good, you must not doubt, that whatever truth you anywhere meet with, proceeds from Him, unless you would be doubly grateful to Him."[5] Truth wherever it is found comes from God. According to Abraham Kuyper on *progressive common grace,* God works through humans, Christian and non-Christian, to disseminate measures of his grace and truth.[6] This includes scientists, engineers, educators, artists, and moviemakers. God can and will exhibit His truths through good stories in movies as His gracious act to mass audiences.

Movies do not display truths in informational ways, but portray them with luster and palpability in story, using metaphors, emotions, and human experiences. Truths are uncovered in a character's arc through discovery. Truths in movies are not told but illuminated.

Icons are historically part of the Church's practice of faith. A term derived from Scripture (Matt. 22:20, Col. 1:15), icons are artistic creations that illuminate Scripture. Icons serve as windows to God's truths and wonders. They are aesthetic instruments for enlightening minds about God and enriching hearts to a deeper faith.

Good movies serve as icons by illuminating truths. Robert K. Johnston writes, "We might almost say that we are within the film as icon, within a series of images that are not metaphoric of some other, unseen images, but are rather a series of images in which the unseeable is shown."[7] Movies can direct us to a beyond—to universals and philosophies about God, the universe, and being human. Johnston writes, "A story is the embodiment or mediation of the 'more,' that is, that which lies beyond the perception of the reader, the horizon or atmosphere that frames our conscious critical day-to-day existence."[8] Movies can facilitate contemplation of truths.

Movies by nature are truth-seeking, grasping for what is true. By God's grace, they can be wisdom-building. Through movies' aesthetical impact, we not only learn life lessons and universal truths, but we experience them in a felt way, as movies stir our emotions and imaginations.

Saving Private Ryan illuminates how doing the "decent thing" serves as an answer to malice and chaos. *Inside Out* teaches us not to ignore sadness, but to include it, in a healthy way, with joy. *The Martian* shows that a way through an insurmountable ordeal is to perseveringly solve one problem at a time. *Doctor Strange in the Multiverse of Madness* shows that a life on mission for a greater good does not idolize personal happiness. *Just Mercy* shows that giving unmerited grace fosters justice and equality. God is glorified when movies illuminate truths.

Ned Bustard and John Hendrix, *It's All True,* linocut and ink

DEEP QUESTIONS DEEPEN FAITH

Our world is marred by original sin. Although beautiful in original design, reality is also broken under the fall. In many aspects, the world is hurting and life is painful. Not all movies present beautiful solutions, but some help us understand brokenness.

Movies glorify God by causing us to wrestle with deep, dark questions that are important for deepening faith. Movies can draw an audience to see brokenness with greater honesty. In that honesty, God is glorified because evil and suffering are not ignored or superficialized. Ephesians 5:13–14 reads, "But when anything is exposed by the light, it becomes visible, for anything that becomes visible is light." Craig Detweiler writes, "Prophetic voices have always arisen from unlikely places . . . today's most creative filmmakers, desperate to understand why things are so broken, echo the heart and mind of the Creator God. Their haunting questions to audiences are actually God's recurring questions to us."[9] Movies can be honest voices about the ugly aspects of reality.

By wrestling with ugliness, movies charge us to see evil for what it is, provide insight on complex problems, and respect suffering. Sometimes a most dignifying act toward those suffering is to make their suffering seen. Then indirectly, we're challenged to consider redemptive responses to brokenness. These dark questions deepen our faith by refining our grasp of the need for redemption and maturing our beliefs on how the gospel applies to brokenness.

Parasite exposes the dehumanization of an economically disparate society. *Silence* troubles us and causes us to examine our faith in the face of vicious persecution. *The Tragedy of Macbeth* depicts the calamity of pride. *Me Before You* questions whether assisted suicide can be just for the suffering who choose it. *La La Land* considers the disappointments of chasing dreams amidst the complexities of love and obstacles. Some movies are not about happy resolutions, but deal with matters of a broken reality. In honestly dealing with the deep, dark questions, movie-watching can glorify God.

REDEMPTION THROUGH SACRIFICE

Lastly, redemption through sacrifice in movies glorifies God. Many movies depict self-sacrifice as the necessary way to save others. Self-sacrifice is a super-human kind of deed, because it defies the basic instinct of self-preservation. Surrendering one's own well-being for the good of another is the bravest and most gracious act of all.

The sacrificial character is an age-old archetype—the "messiah archetype." It is pervasive in classic myths and contemporary films. Self-sacrifice is a fundamental trait of heroes. Christopher Vogler writes, "A Hero is someone who is willing to sacrifice his own needs on behalf of others, like a shepherd who will sacrifice to protect and serve his flock."[10] Vogler's definition of a hero echoes Jesus' self-identification: "I am the good shepherd. The good shepherd lays down his life for the sheep" (John 10:11). The sacrificial character echoes the gospel principle of substitutionary atonement.

Ned Bustard, *Potter,* linocut

Self-sacrifice to save others conveys grace—someone freely paying a personal price for the redemption of others. It nurtures the belief that grace is a necessary bridge for salvation.

Films hallowing the sacrificial character include (beware of spoilers) *Braveheart,* the *Harry Potter* series, *Avengers: End Game, Terminator 2, Edge of Tomorrow, Star Wars: Rogue One, Star Trek 2: Wrath of Khan, The Dark Knight Rises, Big Hero 6, The Iron Giant,* and many more. It is as if God drips notions of the gospel across stories to orient people toward Jesus! Movie-watching that involves experiencing the gospel principle of sacrifice for the redemption of others glorifies God.

In these four ways, we can celebrate and honor God in movie-watching, an entertaining activity that can minister to us while God is glorified. So, enjoy watching a movie and be truly entertained!

1 James W. Sire, *How to Read Slowly: Reading for Comprehension* (Colorado Springs, CO: Waterbrook Press, 1989), pp. 92–93. Sire used this term from J.R.R. Tolkien.
2 Robert K. Johnston, *Reel Spirituality: Theology and Film in Dialogue,* 2nd ed. (Grand Rapids, MI: Baker Academic, 2006), p. 173.
3 Kelly James Clark, "Story-shaped Lives in Big Fish," in *Faith, Film and Philosophy: Big Ideas on the Big Screen,* ed. R. Douglas Geivett and James S. Spiegel (Downers Grove, IL: InterVarsity Press, 2007), p. 42.
4 Clark, "Story-shaped Lives," p. 41.
5 John Calvin, *Letters of John Calvin,* Vol. 2,, trans. Jules Bonnet (Philadelphia: Presbyterian Board of Publication, 2018), p. 192.
6 Abraham Kuyper, *Wisdom and Wonder: Common Grace in Science and Art,* ed. Jordan J. Ballor and Stephen J. Grabill, trans. Nelson D. Kloosterman, (Grand Rapids, MI: Christian Library, 2011), p. 40.
7 Robert K. Johnston, *Reframing Theology and Film: A New Focus for an Emerging Discipline* (Grand Rapids, MI: Baker Academic, 2007), p. 297.
8 Johnston, *Reframing Theology and Film,* p. 311.
9 Craig Detweiler, *Into the Dark : Seeing the Sacred in the Top Films of the 21st Century* (Grand Rapids: Baker Academic, MI, 2008), p. 256.
10 Christopher Vogler, *The Writer's Journey: Mythic Structure for Writers,* 3rd ed. (Studio City, CA: Michael Wiese Productions, 2007), p. 29.

WRITING
Grace, Justice, Humility, and Recognition

My writing life has been mostly spent in the company of ordinary people, teaching and learning about writing. I spent the first decade of my professional life in elementary school classrooms, surrounded by third grade girls printing their breathless exuberance on paper and third grade boys whose stories were all gore and football. Now I work with college students, coaxing writing out of both traditional undergraduates, fresh from high school, and adult learners, who are often returning to school after lifetimes of work and ministry and sometimes pain and struggle. My students have taught me much about writing and the glorifying of God through writing. I think specifically of the lessons they have taught me about grace, justice, humility, and recognition.

WRITING AND GRACE

I think I learned the most about writing while teaching third grade in a wonderful independent school in Philadelphia. Rather than using report cards listing letter grades or generic "Exceeds Expectations," teachers were required to write narratives on each of our students twice a year. While there was some boilerplate verbiage about texts read, skills mastered, and concepts introduced, the rest of the narrative was a customized story about each child. A former editor was on staff at the school, and she read all our narratives and offered gracious and personalized feedback. I learned how to cram a half-year's worth of learning into a concise, yet vivid, document.

Because the school was located next to universities and hospitals and law firms, many of the students' parents were highly educated, ready to parse our writing and analyze our comments. However, I found that they were just like other ordinary parents. They wanted grace. How many of us parents reverently and nervously approach our children's report cards, hoping for grace? Will my daughter's teacher see beyond her reading comprehension and math skills to that one special thing I love about her? Does my child's teacher understand that, despite the fights with classmates or the rambunctious behavior during morning meetings, my son is trying his hardest?

In writing those narratives, I could offer assessments and evaluations, or I could offer grace. Gracious narratives led to gracious conversations with parents who were thrilled that I saw what they saw in their children. In the context of grace, parents could trust me with those hard conversations about real struggles with learning, challenges with social skills, and difficulties with third grade life. As I wrote those narratives, and then talked about them with their subjects' parents, I had the opportunity to see those children through the eyes of the people who loved them the most. And those conversations reminded me that those parents, in grace, had entrusted their children to a young, flawed teacher who was still learning, just like their children. It was such an opportunity to learn to write with grace and then to share with and receive it from others!

WRITING AND JUSTICE

> Learn to do good;
> seek justice,
> correct oppression;
> bring justice to the fatherless,
> plead the widow's cause. (Isaiah 1:17)

Last year, my family spent Thanksgiving in Alabama. We visited Birmingham, a hub of the civil rights movement and the site of the 16th Street Baptist Church bombing and the Children's March. Propelled by my sons' passion for football, we drove to Tuscaloosa and marveled at the University of Alabama football stadium. We ate soul food every day. Finally, we traveled to Montgomery and spent an afternoon at The Legacy Museum: From Enslavement to Mass Incarceration. If you can make your way to Alabama, visit this powerful place. Through its interactive narrative, you experience this country's history of racial inequality. One corner of the museum demonstrates the discrimination surrounding voting rights. Visitors can attempt to pass a sample "literacy test" like the ones African Americans in the Deep South were required to complete in order to vote just sixty years ago. The questions on the test range from the technical to the ludicrous. Here are a few examples:

- What do a Writ of Certiorari, Writ of Error Coram Nobis, and Subpoena Duces Tecum mean?
- How may the county seat be changed under the constitution of your state?
- How many seeds are in a watermelon?
- How many bubbles are in a bar of soap?
- Divide a vertical line in two equal parts by bisecting it with a curved horizontal line that is only straight at its spot bisection of the vertical.

The test's intention to obliterate the right to vote is clear. It is a powerful example of how every element of life was positioned to exact injustice, and how writing, specifically, was leveraged to enforce oppression.

In my work, I get to meet with individual students to develop their writing. Many of my students are African American, primarily middle-aged or older women. A number have grown up in communities and schools devastated by the long-term effects of poverty and racism. When I meet with them, they often share stories of heartbreak surrounding their experiences with the hardships of life. They often must share those stories before we can get to writing.

In my foolish pride, I have questioned the efficacy and efficiency of these writing sessions. One evening, after a litany of selfish complaints, my husband, whose long career in legal and racial justice is my north star, encouraged me to consider these sessions as "reparations." These brave students, in pursuing higher education, are doing the hard work of reaping for themselves justice for the challenges, both systemic and personal, they've faced. They are, as in the words of Isaiah, seeking justice and correcting oppression. In working with them on writing, I get to play a minor part in this process of reparations. It's a privilege I don't deserve.

WRITING AND HUMILITY

Writing is an act of humility. Those of us who try to write anything beyond a quick text or post or email will find ourselves faced with the infuriating disconnect between what we imagine and what lands on paper or on the screen. As one of my favorite authors, Ann Patchett, puts it: "The journey from the head to the hand is perilous and lined with bodies . . . Only a few of us are going to be willing to break our own hearts by trading in the living beauty of imagination for the stark disappointment of words."[1]

This is what makes students like the ones I describe so brave and so humble. They are willing to engage in a process that challenges and frustrates, that so often does not capture their thoughts and ideas in the way they desire. They humbly seek out feedback. They enroll in courses during which all their thoughts and ideas may only be assessed by writing. They choose writing to represent them. That humility is at the center of the writer.

If writing is an act of humility, then writing classrooms and communities call for "humble listening."[2] Those of us who work with writers must respond with love for our neighbor, an openness to learn rather than simply a dispensing of judgment, a "gesture of hospitality" that makes space for another's views amidst our own.[3] I work with a team of student writing tutors who do this so well. I've watched them sit down with their peers, listen, and draw out ideas with thoughtful questions. They give honor to the vulnerability with which their classmates share their writing. They don't measure a classmate by a piece of writing but rather view that writing as part of a continuum of growth and learning.[4] For those students whose past experiences with writing have been marked by condemnation, shame, or anxiety, these experiences with "humble listening" can be empowering and transformative. They feel respected, understood, and strengthened to continue in the task of writing.

WRITING AND RECOGNITION

> And I tell you, you are Peter, and on this rock I will build my church, and the gates of hell shall not prevail against it. (Matthew 16:18)

> Truly, truly, I say to you, when you were young, you used to dress yourself and walk wherever you wanted, but when you are old, you will stretch out your hands, and another will dress you and carry you where you do not want to go. (John 21:18)

At the beginning of their earthly relationship, Jesus renames Peter Cephas, which means "rock." Towards the end, Jesus forewarns Peter of his death by which God will be glorified. He provides Peter with a template for his life, one of strength and suffering. Within this frame, this glorious and impetuous man will live a life that will bring extraordinary glory to God. Upon Peter will the church be built. Everything in Peter's life will come to this.

Over the last year, I have had the lovely experience of writing profiles for a college magazine. As I ask questions that coax people into talking about their lives, as I prompt them for stories and memories, I can often connect a thread of God's work through their stories. While a life is long and varied, within it I can often find a single purpose for which God has used this "one wild and precious life," to borrow the celebrated Mary Oliver phase. My hope is that as each person reads their profile, they feel seen and understood, that they recognize themselves. For each person, I hope that their profile reinforces for them who they are and how God has been working in them and through them, often in very remarkable and consistent ways.

It is often in the most unselfconscious people, those who have truly embraced dying to themselves so that others might live, that this true self, created for a single but complex purpose, shines most brightly. Over the last year, I've worked with an adult student who came to this country as a refugee. He's a member of a persecuted ethnic group that was expelled from Myanmar by its government. He now pastors a large church made up of refugees and their families. We connect virtually and discuss grammar and sentence structure. I try to translate academic jargon into everyday English, which he then translates into his own language. He works so hard and is uniformly cheerful in the face of due dates and citations and comma usage. What I've noticed is that his heart of a refugee and his heart for refugees spills into every assignment. All his writing overflows with the needs of refugees. He looks for articles and cites firsthand experiences. I think his eagerness to learn is fueled by love for his countryfolk who have made America their home and by a desire to serve them better. The thesis of his writing and his life is care for the sojourner, love of the foreigner.

That's the beauty of writing. Given the freedom to do so, our best writing will circle who we are and what we care about. In a time and culture that celebrates endless choices, I find this reassuring. In his wonderful memoir, *The Pastor,* Eugene Peterson recounts a conversation with his son. Peterson's son declares that "novelists only write one book. They find their voice, their book, and write it over and over . . . You only preach one sermon."[5] This author of many books and *The Message* preached only one sermon. Perhaps we all have one sermon and, when given the opportunity and support to do so, discover it and preach it to God's glory, with our writing and with our lives.

1 Ann Patchett, *This is the Story of a Happy Marriage* (New York: HarperCollins, 2013), p. 25.
2 Richard H. Gibson and James E. Beitler III, *Charitable Writing: Cultivating Virtue Through Our Words* (Downers Grove, IL: InterVarsity Press, 2020), p. 49.
3 Gibson and Beitler, *Charitable Writing,* p. 58.
4 Stephen M. North, "Training Tutors to Talk About Writing," *College Composition and Communication* 33, no. 4 (Dec. 1982): 434-441, https://www.jstor.org/stable/357958.
5 Eugene H. Peterson, *The Pastor: A Memoir* (New York: HarperOne, 2011), p. 297.

LOVEMAKING

I Am My Beloved's and My Beloved is Mine

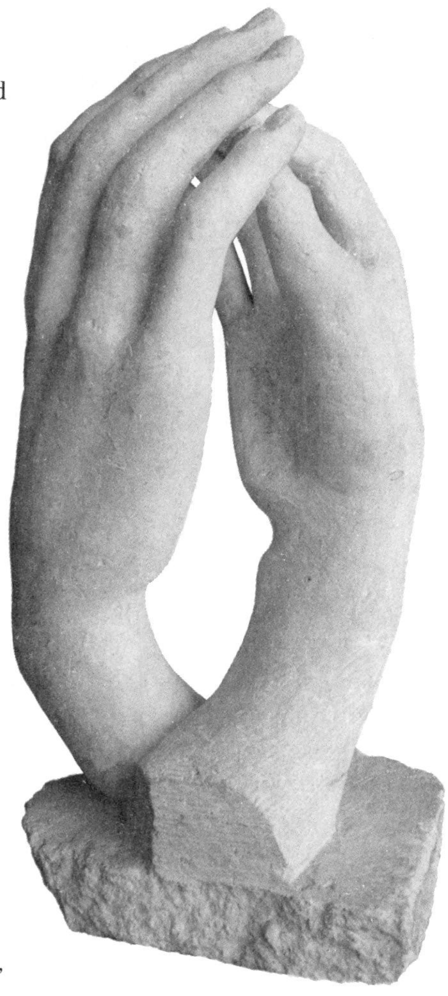
Auguste Rodin, *The Cathedral*, stone

One of my favorite pieces of art by Auguste Rodin consists of two intertwined right hands almost touching. It has been reproduced many times, and in various materials. I've read that it was originally entitled *The Ark of the Covenant,* although it is now commonly known as *The Cathedral.*[1] And from certain angles, it bears a strong resemblance to a pointed gothic window or an arch in a medieval cathedral. But I almost prefer the original title because the sculpture seems to me to be one of the most beautiful visual representations in Western art of marriage's covenant renewal ceremony: *lovemaking.*[2]

In contrast, there is an amazing sculpture by Gian Lorenzo Bernini in the Galleria Borghese called *The Rape of Proserpina.* I was dumbstruck when I first saw it. It is a magnificent work of art and also the exact opposite of what lovemaking to the glory of God should look like. The god of the Underworld smiles, appearing to find gratification in the young girl's fruitless attempts to resist his taking advantage of her. The art is breathtaking, but the message is evil, because pleasure must never be derived

Gian Lorenzo Bernini, *The Rape of Proserpina* (detail), stone

from "something that causes your spouse discomfort, embarrassment, humiliation, pain, or harm."[3] Instead, lovemaking is a calling for those who are married—which they are to joyfully carry out—that will both do good for them and help fulfill the cultural mandate. For the husband, it is an act of self-sacrificial service to and care for his wife; for the wife, it is a mysterious embodiment of the relationship between Christ and the Church, given for the good of her husband and the good of the world.

As our society flounders, gasping for air while we are sucked down again and again in the swirling wake of the Sexual Revolution, it might be impossible to conceive of any way in which we could glorify God while "doing it." Yet this is not a new dilemma. The Bible itself is replete with documentation of sexual excess and abuse,[4] and certainly the Roman world in which the Church first began was dishonoring to God in its use and abuse of human sexuality. Roman religion utilized sex as part of worship, pornography was found everywhere, prostitution was legal throughout the empire, and homosexual activity was common. But compared to our current time where homosexuality is celebrated with parades, prostitution is glamorized in our films, pornography is on our cellphones, and "my body my choice" is a national creed, it is hard to say which society is more obsessed with defying God through the perverting of sex.

Everybody in the world is bodied and therefore should be using their bodies in a way that is glorifying to God.[5] The apostle Paul tells us that we "were bought with a price" (1 Cor. 7:23) and that everyone should each "lead the life that the Lord has assigned to him, and to which God has called him" (1 Cor. 7:17). For me, this has included the callings of son, student, husband, father, artist, and church elder. Some of those callings are for a season, some will be for my entire life, and some callings I will never have—mother and CPA being two safe bets. For three decades one of my callings has been to be a husband. In that calling I am instructed to carry out the marriage sacrament, not depriving my wife (1 Cor. 7:5), but faithfully and regularly giving her her conjugal rights (1 Cor. 7:3).

God's word insists on limiting sexual activity to the marriage bed (Eph. 5:3). Therefore, not everyone is called to glorify God through lovemaking—only husbands and wives (Heb. 13:4).[6] Our bodies are not our own[7] but were purchased by God and must be used to bring Him glory (1 Cor. 6:19–20). Those called to lovemaking do so as a good work, an essential duty that is a joyful and sweet thing, that "goes down smoothly" like the best wine (Song 7:9). Yet even when work is enjoyable, it is still work. "Love doesn't just sit there like a stone, it has to be made, like bread, remade all the time, made new."[8] The making and remaking is woven into us from the dawn of time. Before sin entered the world, lovemaking was part of our parents' job description in the Garden. In Genesis 1:26–28 the cultural mandate was given to Adam and Eve, giving them dominion over all animals (Gen. 1:26), the task of tending the garden (Gen. 2:15), and lovemaking.[9] And though we have been banishedfrom the Garden of Eden, we still glorify God through fulfilling the cultural mandate, and marriage is

Ned Bustard, *Winelily*, linocut

"the garden where we both still grow, Where making love is always making more."[10]

This goodness of lovemaking "comes neither from ecstasy (how good the sex is) nor frequency (how often you have it) but mainly from intimacy, which occurs as love, trust, security, and respect deepen through the longevity of a monogamous, self-giving, covenant relationship."[11] It is within the hothouse of a Christ-centered Christian marriage that the uniting act of two becoming one is ideally carried out. And, as with all other aspects of life after the fall, lovemaking is work that is not simple or easy, even for followers of Christ who set apart their bodies for the glory of God. For example, my wife and I were both virgins when we were married but we still brought mental, emotional, and spiritual baggage into the marriage bed that resulted in many awkward years of trying to make lovemaking a joy.

Thankfully, we had the safe place of the marriage covenant in which to do the work. "God's design is that sex would only ever take place in the context of a committed, life-long relationship between a man and a woman in marriage. Sex is protected and purified by this commitment to tender, faithful, self-sacrificing, other-serving love."[12] Yet to conceive of intercourse as self-sacrificial and other-serving in this day

Julius Schnorr von Carolsfeld, *Song of Solomon*, engraving

is akin to defending a flat earth theory—bizarre, silly, out of touch, and likely harmful. But when the Bible connects lovemaking with the death of Christ on the cross, there really is little room to think of it in any other way. The marriage bed is a place for giving and receiving care, receiving and giving honor under the banner of love, and thinking of your spouse more than yourself. A marriage is a place of mutual submission (Eph. 5:21) and care, one for the other, with the husband expected to lead the way in loving his wife "as Christ loved the church and gave himself up for her" (Eph. 5:25). This self-sacrifice should be evident in every area of a marriage relationship, but not least of which when lovemaking. Therefore, when Ephesians 5 is our model, we should expect to find lovemaking that is

> Intimate, affectionate, gentle, sacrificial, personal, and pleasurable. Just as God deals with us gently, so we should be gentle with our partners. Just as God in Christ sacrifices His life for His people, so we should put the pleasure of our partner before our own pleasure in intercourse.[13]

To glorify God through lovemaking is not to give up on pleasure but to put it in its proper place, as a good gift from God to be used in the way He intended, and for His glory. Paradoxically, just as it is true that those who lose their lives for the sake of Christ end up finding their lives (Matt. 16:25), so also those who give their lives over to their spouses find even greater delight. "Christ's love is a spousal kind of love—the love of total self-giving," writes Christopher West. "Spousal love is the love of total self-donation . . . It is 'precisely that love in which the human person becomes a gift and—through this gift—fulfills the very meaning of his being and essence.'"[14] Lovemaking is often equated with passion, and think of the Passion Week of Christ. When did He consider His needs before His bride's? When did He rush to satisfy Himself instead of caring for the Chosen? Never. West, again, points out that

> the Christian revolution transforms sexual union from something that is *worshiped* into something that *is* worship. When lived sacramentally and liturgically, spouses are not seeking ultimate satisfaction in their union. Rather, they find in their union a sign, a foreshadowing, of ultimate satisfaction. And in that sign, through the sign, they offer praise and worship *to God* with a living hope in the consummation of the Marriage of the Lamb. It is union with God—participation in the eternal bliss of the divine exchange—that alone satisfies the heart's thirst.[15]

A bride and groom have the privilege to foreshadow the Consummation of all things at the end of Time. And this good work begins right now. Hear the bride express her desire for her husband:

> As an apple tree among the trees of the forest, so is my beloved among the young men. With great delight I sat in his shadow, and his fruit was sweet to my taste. He brought me to the banqueting house, and his banner over me was love. Sustain me with raisins; refresh me with apples, for I am sick with love. His left hand is under my head, and his right hand embraces me![16] (Song of Solomon 2:3–6)

Hear the groom replies, praising her:

> Behold, you are beautiful, my love, behold, you are beautiful! Your eyes are doves . . . and your mouth is lovely . . . Your two breasts are like two fawns, twins of a gazelle, that graze among the lilies. Until the day breathes and the shadows flee, I will go away to the mountain of myrrh and the hill of frankincense. You are altogether beautiful, my love . . . you have captivated my heart with one glance of your eyes . . . How much better is your love than wine. (Song of Solomon 4:1–10)

As with the husband in the Song of Songs, so too this was my song on my wedding night over three decades ago—or it would have been, if I weren't so nervously trying to undo the buttons and lace adorning my bride. Has there ever been a husband who delighted more in the wife of his youth than I did? (Prov. 5:18–19) But that was then. Now, I lie in bed with a middle-aged woman who is fighting breast cancer and melanoma. The surgeon's knife and a battery of drugs have altered the curves of her hourglass figure in ways which cause her great sadness. In this new season what song should I sing? When my wife looks in the mirror with despair, do I add to her lament?

No, I sing: "How beautiful and pleasant you are, O loved one, with all your delights!" (Song 7:6) and she responds, "It goes down smoothly for my beloved, gliding over lips and teeth. I am my beloved's, and his desire is for me" (Song 7:9–10). This calling of lovemaking—this good work—has not changed because the lines of my wife's silhouette have been altered. Long before the dawn of time, the Lord planned good works for me to do, and, graciously, one of them has been to joyfully carry out my calling upon our marriage bed. This is a good thing for me, for my wife, and for the kingdom of God. It is an act of self-sacrificial service and care by me for my wife, and a mysterious embodiment of the Church by her for me and for the good of the world.

In Rodin's sculpture of the two hands we see a fittingness that characterizes the marriage sacrament, a cherishing of the beloved, and an intimacy that cannot be described in words. It is a visual reminder that marriage is a place where the four loves—affection, friendship, eros, and charity—all meet together, and kiss. "God made sex to be intimate, physically and emotionally, for both partners,"[17] both needing the intimacy provided through lovemaking. The two hands point towards the gentle caresses, the loving foreplay of two lovers naked and without shame exploring each other, and towards the blessed climax, where physical and mental and relational tensions are released in a great crashing wave.

Ned Bustard, *The Marriage Bed,* linocut

Those two hands—the lovemaking—are also, in a way, a set of scaffolding. They are building something together that transcends individual expression and is a collective making of something new. There is a holy worship of each other in the marriage bed, where *The Ark of the Covenant* is fitting, but perhaps it *is* better to call lovemaking *The Cathedral.* In the wonderful poem, "Scaffolding," the Irish poet Seamus Heaney speaks of building the scaffolding with the goal that, in the end, it is taken down, "Showing off walls of sure and solid stone."[18] But the goal in lovemaking (as, ideally, it was in the great cathedrals of old) is not to make the windows and archways. They are simply letting light in; they are creating the required negative space needed for their calling. Through lovemaking we are building that joyful, mysterious thing *between* the walls, between the hands. We are making those pillars of solid light in which we can glory in the rapturous ecstasy of the goodness of God.

1 Originally modeled in 1908 (to learn more, see: "The Cathedral," Musée Rodin, accessed August 31, 2022, (https://www.musee-rodin.fr/en/musee/collections/oeuvres/cathedral). My first encounter with the work was probably seeing the bronze version, cast in 1925, that is now in the collection of the Philadelphia Museum of Art.

2 Tim Keller writes, "The Bible is full of covenant renewal ceremonies. When God enters into a personal relationship with someone, he is not so unrealistic as to think that mere emotion can serve as the basis for it. He knows that human emotions come and go and that there needs to be something binding to provide consistency and endurance. So God requires a binding, public, legal covenant as the infrastructure for intimacy . . . The ultimate covenant renewal ceremony is the Lord's Supper. The sacrament of the Lord's Supper renews the covenant made at baptism; through the breaking of bread and the pouring out of wine it reenacts the selfless sacrifice of Jesus to us . . . In the same way, marriage is a covenant, one that creates a place of security for vulnerability. But though covenant is necessary for sex, sex is also necessary for covenant. The covenant will grow stale unless we continually revisit and reenact it. Sex is a covenant renewal ceremony for marriage, the physical reenactment of the inseparable oneness in all other areas—economic, legal, personal, psychological—created by the marriage covenant. Sex renews and revitalizes the marriage covenant."covenant" ("The Gospel and Sex," Redeemer City to City, accessed August 31, 2022, (http://static.squarespace.com/static/53189f41e-4b0ee73efed7b5a/t/53405ed7e4b02233d743c913/1396727511326/The_Gospel_and_Sex.pdf).

3 Sheila Wray Gregoire, Rebecca Gregoire Lindenbach, and Joanna Sawatsky, *The Great Sex Rescue: The Lies You've Been Taught and How to Recover What God Intended* (Grand Rapids, MI: Baker Books, 2021), p. 198.

4 For example, polygamy (I Kings 11:3), adultery (2 Sam. 11:2–4), homosexuality (Gen. 19:5), rape (2 Sam. 13:2–16), domestic violence (Judges 19:20–29), and incest (Gen. 19:30–38), just to name a few.

5 Nancy Pearcy has a great book called *Love Thy Body: Answering Hard Questions about Life and Sexuality* which is extremely helpful and insightful.

6 Also Exodus 20:14, obviously.

7 It is common to hear people appealing to their needs and rights, but, as Wesley Hill has observed, "strictly speaking, we have no 'inalienable rights.' God reserves all rights for himself. And this extends even to the realm of our sexuality—what we humans do with our bodies" (*Washed and Waiting: Reflections on Faithfulness and Homosexuality* [Grand Rapids, MI: Zondervan, 2010], p. 86).

8 Ursula K. Le Guin, *The Lathe of Heaven* (New York: Scribner, 1971), p. 159.

9 Genesis 1:28 says, "Be fruitful and multiply"—that is, engage in the lovemaking and parenting required to populate the planet..

10 Malcom Guite, *The Singing Bowl* (London, UK: Canterbury Press), 39.

11 "The Problem with Sexual Compatibility," The Gospel Coalition, July 18, 2013, accessed February 8, 2017, https://www.thegospelcoalition.org/article/the-problem-with-sexual-compatibility.

12 Paul David Tripp, *Sex in a Broken World: How Christ Redeems What Sin Distorts* (Wheaton, IL: Crossway Books, 2018), p. 128.

13 Chester then continues to extrapolate the implications of an Ephesians 5 approach to sex, concluding that "masochistic sex, sadomasochistic sex, aggressive sex talk and sex involving some form of domination or enacted domination, even when these involve mutual consent, *must* be regarded as bad sex. Because they don't model Christ's sacrificial love for His people." Tim Chester, *Gospel-Centered Marriage* (Epsom, UK: Good Book Company, 2011), p. 82

14 Christopher West. *Heaven's Song: Sexual Love as it was Meant to Be* (West Chester, PA: Ascension Press), 32–33.

15 West, *Heaven's Song*, p.130.

16 At the time of the initial composition of the Song of Songs, apples and raisins were considered aphrodisiacs.

17 *The Great Sex Rescue*, p. 37

18 Seamus Heaney, *100 Poems*, (London: Faber & Faber, 2018), p. 13.

GRANDPARENTING
A Blessed Crown

We are all familiar with the Christmas song that begins, "Over the river and through the woods to grandmother's house we go." Our family traditions often create memories of everyone gathering at the grandparents' house for feasts with extended family. However, the beautiful images of this idyllic family scene often fail to capture most people's experience. It can't be a surprise that something as beautiful as grandparenting would be disrupted by relationship struggles at all the different family levels. The trinity of child, parent, and grandparent presents opportunities for conflict between each pair in the group. So how do we grandparent to the glory of God?

GRANDPARENTS' LOVE

I often hear people talk about how we can take the grandchildren for a limited time and then we get to send them home. It can be tiring to care for young children as we age. But I prefer to think that we send our grandchildren home enriched with the blessings of affirmation, loving communication, and joyful experiences.

Grandparents play a special role in the lives of their grandchildren that is unlike the connection between any other family members. I remember the special love I had with my grandparents and I rejoice in the way I am able to love and be loved by my grandchildren. I have had little grandsons grab my hand as soon as they arrive at my house and drag me away from the adults to a quiet place where we can read books, play with cars and trucks, or sit and watch TV together. One grandson quoted the dialogue from the first five minutes of a Disney film from memory while perched on my back. There are times when a grandson will burst into tears when told it is time to go home. Young grandchildren often share a deeply loving mutual affection with grandparents.

As those children grow up, the relationship changes, and they offer the grandparent a completely different experience. My grandchildren range in age from their thirties to under six. The love between grandparent and grandchild continues, but the conversations move to a deeper level. There are fewer cozy moments reading books and playing with toys and more opportunities to revisit fond memories, share adventures in the kitchen, and talk about important issues. Adult grandchildren have their own lives, but it is such a joy when they make time to come over. We eat food, share what is going on in our lives, and say "I love you" repeatedly.

It should not be a surprise that adult grandchildren make choices that are not what the grandparents would wish for them. The grandparent is not obligated to approve of everything that the young adult does. But the grandparent is obligated to love that grandchild where he or she is. What I have found is that if the grandparents love the grandchild and emulate how God loves us (slow to anger, compassionate, and merciful), the grandchild will respond with the same love. As we care for each other, we may have fruitful conversations. The intent of such conversations is not to simply change the grandchild. Rather, the intent is to share experiences, wisdom, and lessons learned, and to give the grandchild access to new information. Godly words, often drawn from Scripture, allow the grandchild to think new thoughts and begin to evaluate his or her actions. As Proverbs 16:23 says: "The heart of the wise makes his speech judicious and adds persuasiveness to his lips. Gracious words are like a honeycomb, sweetness to the soul and health to the body."

It is not our job to "fix" the grandchild. Our job is to care about the grandchild in word and deed when we are together and to pray for our grandchildren regularly. The Spirit of God is the one who changes hearts and minds. To really love grandchildren is to call upon the Spirit of God to touch their hearts and work in them for their good and God's glory.

LET'S HAVE A DO-OVER

For some grandparents, a new grandchild presents an opportunity for a do-over. Parents are inevitably flawed. When we parent, we bring into our role the impact our parents had on us. Sometimes we want to parent just like our parents. For others, the objective is to parent in a completely different way than we were parented. We must beware of parenting in a way that simply reacts against how we were parented.

Christian counselor Diana Di Pasquale has observed that it is not helpful to parent using the flip side of the same coin. She says using the flip side is "a technique we use to prevent us from repeating a detrimental behavior done to us by determining we will behave the opposite. This is unwise thinking. What we need is a new coin altogether."[1]

During our parenting years, we normally have the stressors of a relatively new marital relationship, relationships with in-laws, financial limitations, multiple demands on our time, possible relocation to a new house/city/state, and the struggle to figure out the best parenting methodology. Our view of parenting is often limited to copying our parents or avoiding copying our parents. But there is a better way.

It often takes us a long time to recognize that we are to parent as God parents us. If we spend time thinking about how God parents us, we come to recognize a number of ways He parents better than anyone else. God catches us every time we do something wrong, but He doesn't impose strict penalties on each individual sin. Rather, He is gracious and merciful, slow to anger and compassionate. God often teaches us, whether through Scripture, the words of wise advisors, or circumstances, how to be a better child of God. He never disciplines out of anger (or we would be destroyed) but He does allow us to experience the consequences of our actions. He blesses us when we are faithful and calls for us to be in constant communication with Him. He provides, protects, encourages, and helps. He calls us His children and His heirs, and promises to be with us forever.

I am comfortable saying that we all fail to live up to that example. That is why grandparents look forward to a do-over. With age, we hope, comes wisdom. We normally have fewer stressors, although health problems can begin to more strongly impact us. Grandparents are not normally the primary disciplinarians, which allows us to be more thoughtful as we attempt to emulate God's parenting example. Our children may object, "But Mom/Dad, that is not how you treated me when I was their age!" We can only respond by agreeing and apologizing for the ways we failed to parent like our holy and gracious God.

Grandparents face a number of challenges that may require wisdom. Parents have the primary responsibility for their children, and if grandparents are not on the same page with the parents, there can be conflict. This conflict can come from the grandparents overstepping boundaries, behaving badly, or repeating unhealthy patterns. Or it can come from parents disciplining too harshly or not at all. Parents may feel the need to defend their territory, correct grandparent interaction with their children, or establish new boundaries. In most cases, as would be expected with imperfect people, both parties, parents and grandparents, contribute to the conflict. That is why wisdom and emulating how God parents us is so important.

The most important question a grandparent must ask is, what is my responsibility? We do have a responsibility to report physical, sexual, or significant emotional abuse. But in the absence of that, we are not the parents, and we are not responsible for fixing what we see as the errors our children are making in parenting their children. We are responsible for loving our children and building a loving relationship with our grandchildren.

THE LOST GENERATION

In today's world, for an unusually large number of grandparents, access to their grandchildren is denied or severely limited. This is something I have experienced. I am not talking about seeing grandchildren infrequently because the grandparents live far away. Rather, I am talking about grandchildren who are intentionally withheld from grandparents. Assuming no abuse by the grandparents has taken place, the withholding of grandchildren is a source of sorrow, both to the grandparents and often, to the grandchildren as well.

This can occur due to divorce, not wanting grandparents to have an undue influence, fear by the custodial parent that secrets will be revealed, or antagonism of a parent against the grandparents. It would be nice if there was a simple solution to this problem, but normally there is not. The paths of forgiveness, reconciliation, peacemaking, and honest communication can offer hope. If improved communication and relational repair can be accomplished, all parties are truly blessed. But when these options do not produce fruit, there is another approach available. Even in the absence of an in-person relationship, prayer offers hope. It may be that we will never meet our grandchild this side of heaven, but we can pray for their welfare and pray for their souls. The God who is our loving heavenly Father knows how to care for us. He tells us the prayer of a righteous person has great power.

AN UNEXPECTED ARRIVAL

I became a grandfather at age thirty-six and a great-grandfather at age sixty. Needless to say, the arrival of a grandchild without the prior establishment of a stable two-parent home is a challenge. Parents and grandparents often find themselves pulled in two directions. The unmarried child having a baby has acted unwisely, but the new baby is a blessing from God. We all react to unexpected grandchildren in different ways. I remember the general confusion about how I should feel and act. The unexpected surprise can create a lot of noise and conflict that may distract from what is really important.

What is not important is the embarrassment some grandparents experience, as though they thought they raised perfect children. What is important is living out the gospel before our children and grandchildren. Living the gospel involves emulating the God who Jonah criticized, saying, "I knew that you are a gracious God and merciful, slow to anger and abounding in steadfast love, and relenting from disaster" (Jonah 4:2). The challenge is in figuring out how to live out grace, mercy, and steadfast love as we interact with our child and grandchild.

We face a difficult balancing act as we deal with an unexpected pregnancy. We want to help and to celebrate the birth of this new baby. At the same time, we do not want to make the situation so normal and so easy that the child having the baby doesn't see any of the consequences of their action. There is no magic formula. If we recognize that we have been too indulgent with our child, we may want to emphasize allowing the child to feel the consequences more. If we have been too harsh or if the child recognizes she is responsible but made a mistake, it could be that we mitigate some of the consequences.

In the midst of all this confusion, the one stable place we can stand is in asking how God parents us when we fail to keep His commandments. He deals with each of us individually, and He always works for our good. His example is the model for our response.

SURROGATE/ADOPTIVE GRANDPARENTS

We have been blessed to have dear friends who are about the age of our children. Their children have been a joy as we watched them grow up and flourish. While they have grandparents, distance and health issues sometimes prevented those grandparents from attending events where the grandchildren were performing or being honored. We loved attending these events and were able to be there when the grandparents could not.

There are a number of reasons why surrogate grandparents are a valuable resource for children (of any age). Some children do not have access to grandparents. The grandparents may be dead, live far away, or may not be interested in playing a significant role in the grandchildren's lives. Sometimes the grandparents are living a lifestyle that is in sharp disagreement with the parents' values.

Regardless of the cause, the absence of biological grandparents provides an opportunity for loving older people, with a natural connection to a family, to build a relationship as surrogate grandparents. The surrogates do not replace existing grandparents. Rather, they express love for those children by attending grandchildren's events and providing love, wisdom (we hope), and encouragement that children need. In my experience, the surrogate grandparent relationship is similarly rewarding to the biological grandparenting relationship.

Old nurse holding a child, 4th century B.C., terracottas

Another category of grandparenting comes from the marriage of your child to someone who already has children. My parents had to address that when I married my wife, who had two children. My mother made the most of the opportunity: my oldest daughter still has treasures my mother made for her. Believers who become adoptive grandparents already know what it is to be the adopted children of God. So this new relationship should feel somewhat familiar. The situation is similar to surrogate grandparenting as there may be existing grandparents. This is an opportunity for the grandparents to love the stepchild or adopted child in a way similar to surrogate grandparents.

CONCLUSION

Grandparenting is a challenge whether the grandchildren are biological, surrogate, or adoptive. Yet there are legions of adults who credit their grandparents for their successes. For many, the memories of grandparents who cared, nurtured, and loved them are among their greatest treasures.

Grandparents are able to imitate their Heavenly Father by demonstrating sacrificial love, undeserved love, and affirming love to grandchildren. Our constant theme with grandchildren is to love. We are to love wisely, generously, and fully. As Ephesians 5:1–2 says, "Therefore be imitators of God, as beloved children. And walk in love, as Christ loved us and gave himself up for us, a fragrant offering and sacrifice to God."

Loving grandchildren in any of the various categories is a blessing that comes from the Lord. It is one of the greatest joys we can experience. We hope that our grandchildren may actually hear and sing, "Over the river and through the woods to grandmother's house we go" and feel the warm embrace of loving memories of grandparents who loved them well. As the Scriptures say, "Grandchildren are the crown of the aged, and the glory of children is their fathers" (Prov. 17:6).

1 *Speaking Code page #?*

PAINTING
The Face of God

C.S. Lewis famously said there are no mortals, "no ordinary people."[1] In other words, we live and work and marry and mistreat and bless *immortals* every day of our lives. As a painter who studies human faces and figures all the time, and especially having had the privilege of collaborating with poet Malcolm Guite and composer J.A.C. Redford on the *Ordinary Saints* project,[2] I have been utterly overcome at times by the reality that there are no two faces alike. Even so-called identical twins are not identical at all—they're easily distinguishable if you pay close attention. And that kind of caring attention must be paid if we are to glorify God as we look, as we paint, as we attempt to respond adequately to the beauty and complexity and mystery of the human person.

First, from Exodus 33:20: "You cannot see my face, for no one may see me and live" (NIV); from Psalm 27:8: "Seek my face." It this contradictory? I would like to suggest that we are being told that *illicit* looking on God's face is forbidden (more about that later) but that when we are invited to adore and draw close to God in intimacy and trust, there is nothing more beautiful, nothing more joyous than gazing upon God's holy face. And now that God has made His dwelling place among humans, with the incarnation, we are not only given permission, we are lovingly invited to the very table of God, to feast on and rejoice eternally in God's presence—to become, as Jesus says in John 15:15, God's friends.

Why dwell on this question of facing God, human faces, and Lewis's quote above?

Because at the heart of our faith is the face of Christ. There is no other face more beautiful, and yet the prophet Isaiah speaks of the Messiah as "one from whom men hide their faces" (53:3). He writes, "He hath . . . no beauty that we should look upon him" (53:2 KJV). This apparent contradiction is in truth a lesson in the making: it is our distorted vision that makes His face unattractive, makes His kingdom seem unreal or worse, a failure against worldly kingdoms. Yet as the Apostle Paul says, in 2 Corinthians 3:18, "And we all, who with unveiled faces contemplate the Lord's glory, are being transformed into his image" (NIV)—restored to that image in which we were originally created.

But is there an illicit gazing upon God? Yes—just as there is a corrupt way of looking at our fellow humans. It is the look of one attempting to seize control, to master another, to use or abuse or objectify another person. Only the vulnerable gaze of self-giving love is genuine. Only openness and curiosity about the other person yields the joy and beauty we hunger for in God, in one another. In our collaboration, Malcolm Guite writes:

The ordinary saints, the ones we know,
Our too-familiar family and friends,
When shall we see them? Who can truly show
Whilst still rough-hewn, the God who shapes our ends?
Who will unveil the presence, glimpse the gold
That is and always was our common ground,
Stretch out a finger, feel, along the fold
To find the flaw, to touch and search that wound
From which the light we never noticed fell
Into our lives?

It is through our very fragility and woundedness that we sometimes are enabled to draw closer to God in submission and obedience and love. Experiencing our dependent condition and realizing that we are but dust helps to clarify the difference between that distorted, colonizing gaze—wants to control or possess—and the look of love. The "gold" that Malcolm refers to, the "light we never noticed," is indeed the image of God that is glimpsed in a dim or scratched mirror, but that we will one day see face to face.

But how are we better able to move closer to that heavenly vision, the beatific vision in which we glimpse that gold of the other's infinite worth? By surrendering our tendency to seek dominance and reduce others to our pawns, our objects. There are no mere mortals—and it is fundamentally impossible to reduce a person to property. Enslavement can only affect a person's body, and though humans are able to subject one another to terrible tortures and abuses, the soul—that image of God—cannot be taken away, cannot be reduced to an object to be used or owned. A person can only ever be loved to be known. You may enslave me, but by doing so you will utterly miss who I am and will have only a small fraction of me under your control.

As a painter I must gaze deeply into another's face to see the minute particulars, the micro-expressions that animate that particular person's visage. I have sometimes been completely frustrated in that process because an almost imperceptible shift of color or brush-mark or tonality will irrevocably change the sense of who is communicated through a face. The face is the meeting place of persons—but it can also become a hiding place, a mask. Penetrating that mask is essential if a portrait is to be made. As my friend, the painter George Wingate, once said to me, "Every portrait is also a self-portrait," by which he meant that we inevitably paint a unique interpretation of the person we are portraying. And that is because in essence we are painting a *relationship.*

And it is relationship for which the entire cosmos exists. The language of marriage is used throughout the Old Testament to describe the relationship between God and God's chosen people, His "bride." And Jesus refers to Himself over and over as the Bridegroom. Finally, the entirety of Scripture is summarized in the last chapter of Revelation when heaven comes to earth, the Bride is adorned for her Beloved, and the cosmic consummation takes place. This is a mystery too deep for words. And yet I believe we are called to contemplate that mystery every time we worship or partake of the Eucharist, the Lord's Supper—that table to which we have been invited.

. . .

Bruce Herman, *Malcolm* (detail)

Bruce Herman, *The Artist's Father* (detail)

In making a painting of a human face there is a risk and a sacrifice. The risk is that it is something one can only do with all oneself: intellect, imagination, will, heart, memory, and soul. You cannot make the portrait half-heartedly or it arrives stillborn, a mere effigy. The sacrifice is that if you are to make the portrait "live" it requires a humility and surrender to the process that is unparalleled. In all the other kinds of painting I practice, I try to similarly give myself away in the process. But in making a painting of another person, someone I love, I feel much more vulnerable. And that vulnerability is the means by which the other person's unique qualities can find their way into the painting. In a very real sense this is not something that I can control or command at will. Often, I must repaint a portrait over and over in order for this element to appear, and sometimes I stand back amazed having achieved that life-like quality quite unconsciously.

I'll end with a story about a particular portrait in the *Ordinary Saints* project. In fact, it was the very first painting in that series and is quite literally the "father" of the entire project. In early August of 2009, I was outdoors working on a house-repair project when my wife, Meg, brought me the phone saying, "It's your brother Marty and he sounds quite upset!" I took the phone and my brother told me he'd found my father dead in his bedroom, the victim of an apparent massive heart attack. Over the ensuring months, as I had to be the executor of my father's estate, I realized the only way I could work through my grief was to paint him. And I remembered that about four or five months earlier, the last time I'd visited my parents, I'd taken a lot of photos of them both. I went back to those images and out of about a hundred, I found only one that truly seemed to capture my dad's unique personality.

When I finished the painting, I stood back and burst into tears—not tears of grief (though of course I was still grieving), but tears of joy. I had done it. I had painted the person, not the effigy. It not only looked like Dad, it *felt* like him. I showed it to Meg (who is my most honest and direct critic) and she said, "That's Dad!" Since then, many people have commented how they feel that somehow they know him, feel close to him, even feel loved by him, when they gaze on the painting. It was this painting of my father that Malcolm Guite saw at a CIVA conference about seven years ago; he then approached me about allowing him to write a sonnet in response to the painting. That sonnet required that he come and visit the painting in its "natural habitat," and so the next time he was in the United States he visited for an entire weekend, staying at our house and camping out in my studio.

By that time, I'd painted my mother, my wife, my son, my daughter, and one of our grandkids—and intended to keep going in a series of portraits of all the people I love. Malcolm ended up taking notes on all these and other paintings as I completed them—and the result was a body of ekphrastic poetry (poems written to describe and respond to works of visual art, with John Keats's *Ode on a Grecian Urn* perhaps being the most famous in our tradition) that later was combined with amazing music written for our collaboration by J.A.C. Redford—tender, tough, penetrating music and poetry that honors the people I love more than I could ever adequately express. It has been the joy of a lifetime, and the most fulfilling experience as an artist I've ever had.

Here is the poem that Malcolm wrote about the portrait of my father:

Here is your father, looking out at us
From this dark room where shadows furl and fold,
Patiently present to whoever comes,
Still on his battered sofa, at his ease.
He looks out from the darkness of the world,
The copper blotch and mottle of old time
Whose tarnishes and patina reveal

Strange beauty in the saints we love and leave,
Whose leaving leaves us burnished as we grieve.
He meets us here, at home in his own skin,
Which holds more colours than the eye can trace,
More substance, more humanity and grace
Than paint on wood can possibly contain,
All in the clarity of his kind face.

Soli Deo Gloria

1 C.S. Lewis, "The Weight of Glory," from *The Weight of Glory and Other Addresses* (New York: HarperCollins, 1949), p. 46.
2 To learn more about the *Ordinary Saints* collaboration, visit https://ordinary-saints.com/.

PRETZELS

Preachers Don't Know Nuthin'

4 YEARS OLD (1981)

Ten p.m. on a Friday night at the Frederick Fair in Maryland and I'm lying on a homemade bed of boxes and lawn chairs under one of the counters, wrapped in a sleeping bag, fighting to stay awake. All around our massive tent I can hear the nighttime sounds of the fair, where my family gathers for ten days every year to run a large concession stand.

My grandfather shouts out to the passing crowds, "Get your ham and cheese sandwiches!" The guy in the small tent beside ours, selling his wares, "Now, step right over here, sir. You won't find prices like these anywhere else . . ." The tractors in the tractor pull grind their way along the grandstand. The distant laughing screams of people sound out from the rides I'm too scared to even watch.

"You okay?" my mom asks, squatting down and checking on me. She tucks the sleeping bag in around me. She wears a white apron to which clings small bits of ham and Swiss cheese. "We're going to start cleaning up soon. Then we'll head back to the motel."

I nod, my eyes heavy. Surrounded by my family and my parents' friends, the noises of the fair pressing up against the tent, I fall asleep.

8 YEARS OLD (1985)

Inside the fairground gates, I run ahead of my mom, duck down the secret passageway between a row of campers, and sneak into the back of my grandfather's tent. The smell of funnel cake and caramel apples and popcorn chase me, friendly ghosts.

"Hey!" I shout, and it seems like everyone erupts with joyful shouts, as if they haven't seen me in years.

My dad is already there, running ham and cheese over a big slicer (one year, when I am older, my aunt nearly cuts her finger off on the spinning blade). I hug my dad and slide down the narrow aisles strewn with extension cords and empty cardboard boxes.

"Hey, grandpa!" I say, and my grandpa looks at me, pretends not to recognize me.

"Who's this?" he asks in a gruff voice, his jowls growling, his eyes glittering.

"Grandpa!" I complain. "It's me!"

"Oh, yes, you," he says with a smile. He looks around, trying to be sneaky, then he holds out his hand. I play along, reaching. My grandfather hands me a ten-dollar bill, an extravagant gift to an eight-year-old in 1985.

There is a large spinning wheel. It costs one dollar to play. If you win, you get a bag of Snickers. I win a lot—suspiciously so. The carnival worker must be stopping the wheel on the winner's spot with his foot. I walk back to my grandfather's tent, loaded down with bags and bags of candy bars. I dole them out to my cousins like newly-minted million-dollar bills.

Country music blares from the old speakers. I crawl under one of the tables, pile up three or four broken down cardboard boxes, and spread a sleeping bag there, in the dark corner. I crawl inside, tasting its warmth, my belly full of treats. I can hear my family working around me, shouting out orders, laughing with their customers.

The cool autumn air has turned chilly—it blows in under the table, and I give in to sleep, dreaming of tilt-a-whirls and cotton candy and the day when I'll be old enough to work in that tent for Grandpa.

14 YEARS OLD (1991)

It is the first year of the fair after Grandpa died, and we keep finding things that remind us of him: the old tables he built by hand; the note written in permanent marker on the outside of the meat case in his scrawled handwriting; the wide broom he'd used for at least twenty years, practically worn down to the nub. My mom sighs a lot while she works. My dad finds another relic of Grandpa's and clears his throat loudly, walks away.

I am old enough to handroll soft pretzels for the duration of a twelve-hour shift, and I spend my days at the fair cutting off narrow strips of dough, rolling them out, twisting them in the air, and then placing the pretzels on a tray and in the oven. The children stop and watch. Hundreds and hundreds of pretzels a day. Over and over again. I roll until my shoulders ache and my wrists are sore.

I remember Grandpa that year with nearly every pretzel I roll. How can someone be gone and also present? Away but also home?

I take a break at the end of the day. A cool autumn breeze blows through and the tent inhales, exhales. The sides billow out and then pull in. It is not the same place without his weathered grin, but it is also not less than it was before—it is somehow more.

21 YEARS OLD (1998)

There is a new couple who run the kettle corn stand across the way from our tent, and we get to know them. She is lively and smiling with bright, flashing eyes. He is gruff and quiet and pushes his hand truck through the crowd with a certain kind of simmering at the world around him. I am not sure how to talk to him.

A year passes, then two, and we become friends with the kettle corn couple. Jim and Suzy. They meet my wife, Maile, get to know our kids when we come together for that one week every year. They remark on how much they've grown.

One year while I'm rolling pretzels Jim slides over and we start talking. He tells me about his daughter, how she was murdered by her husband, how it darkened his life. I ask him a few questions. He answers quietly. When he walks away, I realize I didn't know him until that moment.

35 YEARS OLD (2012)

If my grandfather was still alive, he would wear black shoes like that, and an old black belt like that one, and probably even sport those grayish, navy-blue trousers.

"Hey," I shout to the man outside the tent. "You need a drink?" I keep rolling soft pretzels.

He smiles, and I don't see many teeth in there. He walks slowly toward our tent, as if each foot weighs about fifty pounds. The wrinkles around his eyes are deep, eroded streams feeding the Grand Canyon.

"I remember your grandpa," he says with that toothless grin. "He was a firecracker."

I laugh and roll another pretzel.

"Where's your old man?" he asks me, smiling.

"My dad? He's a preacher. He's at home today, at church, but he'll be here tomorrow."

The old man's eyes glaze over and I can tell he's somewhere else, somewhere besides these fairgrounds.

"You go to church?" I ask.

"Nah. Well, I did when I was a kid, every Sunday. My parents made me go. Then I joined the Army and spent eighteen months in Korea."

He has forgotten I am there.

"When I got back from the Army I went back to church, and I gave the pastor money, you know, to fix some ceilings and stuff. Then we walked outside and I put my hand on his shoulder like this—" he puts his hand on my shoulder and squeezes my collarbone—"and I told him, 'You don't know nothin'. I just saw my friends get blown apart. Who took care of me over in Korea? Not the church. Not God. It was my buddies. We took care of each other.' That's what I told him."

He kept talking. Fourteen years he's been around The Great Frederick Fair and I've never spoken to him for more than two minutes. Now he can't stop.

"You know what? I kept going to church. Then my old man died. The pastor stood up there at his funeral and he kept talking about how great my dad was, how he was in heaven this and heaven that. But I knew different. I knew he stole stuff—if he was here he'd steal these pies when you weren't looking! My old man did stuff. And that preacher just stood up there and talked nonsense. I walked up to the front of the church and said, 'If my dad didn't go to hell, then I don't want any part of this.'"

He looked back at me. I handed him a bottle of Coke. He looked at it like I was handing him a foreign language.

"The cops came and kicked me out. I never went back to church after that," he said. "Them preachers don't know nothin'."

42 YEARS OLD (2019)

By now I've been coming to the fair for over four decades. Grandma and Grandpa are gone. I run the stand with my parents, my wife, my own children, nieces and nephews, my sisters and their families. I look around at all the young employees and realize I'm one of the older ones now.

And I'm still rolling pretzels. Slice the dough, stretch it out, flip it around, lay it on the tray, bake it for five minutes. Over and over again, thousands of times in a week.

But it was never about the pretzels. Was it? It was about Jim and Suzy and Chuck and Jackie and John who thought preachers didn't know nothin'. It was about these weeks spent together over forty years and getting to know people by increments.

Poppy? Where is our youngest daughter, Poppy?

I roll out the last dough of the night, put the last tray of pretzels in the oven, and wash my hands before making the rounds. It's my responsibility now to collect the money from the registers, put down the tent flaps at the end of the day, make sure the ovens are turned off. Our friends and employees laugh and joke with each other as they clean—it is always a relief when another day is done.

Most nights, my dad isn't at the fair anymore. He makes a few trips down every week, bringing supplies and giving our employees a ride back and forth. My mom still makes sandwiches, just like my grandma used to, standing at one of the large tables my grandpa built, methodically adding ham and cheese to the soft rolls.

I check at the table in the back, the one covered with crayons and paper, but Poppy's not there. I ask my sister if she's seen her. She shakes her head. I go behind the trailer, back where we've arranged some metal shelves to create a private room of sorts, and there she is, asleep on a lawn chair, a blanket up to her chin, a cool September breeze pressing the canvas tent in and out. I bend in close and push her hair out of her eyes, tuck the blanket in around her.

Another autumn.

MENTAL ILLNESS

Blessings on Your Head

No smartphone. No backpack. No sharp objects like pens. No shoelaces. They all went into a box and into a locker. The first time I walked into a city-run psych ward I felt like I was stepping into a movie set filled with terror and confusion, green linoleum floors, and fluorescent lights. As I tried to talk to and pray with a congregant's teenage daughter her eyes were vacant. She stared at the ceiling, at the window, or nowhere in particular. I wondered how much she understood.

Finally, she spoke, "Do you hear what they are saying?"

"Who?" I asked, dumbfounded because the other patients were quiet in the row of beds.

"The angels over there, they're talking to me." Then she drifted back into a vacant stupor, likely caused by the drugs more than her illness.

This was my introduction to schizophrenia up close. I didn't get it. It felt alien.

My pastoral counseling preparation had, frankly, not prepared me for what I had to do to be helpful. I could pray and listen, but those seemed like insufficient offerings to an ordinary saint who was living in an alternate reality. How could I relate to her suffering?

. . .

Our generation is steeped in pop psychology, prescribed medication, and armchair diagnosis. Elementary school children talk about ADHD or anxiety or depression as if they learned the DSM right after their ABCs. Today 21% of Americans are diagnosed with a mental disorder, mostly anxiety or depression, including 5.6% with a severe mental illness.[1]

Yet Christians in some quarters deny the existence of mental disorders saying they are an excuse for sinful and faithless actions. Admittedly, whenever someone hides behind a label so that they do not have to deal with their own problems, they avoid the hard work of change. At the same time, whenever someone denies underlying mental health issues, they hamstring their ability to seek the wisdom that the Christian community offers.

What if sin and suffering are not mutually exclusive?[2] Knowing how to parse the difference is more complicated when it comes to mental illness. We can see most physical ailments and offer compassion to the elderly, infirm, and sick. Mental illness is inside other people's heads. The only symptoms we know about are the ones that they tell us or the behaviors we observe. Since we are inaccurate about our own internal reality, how can we hope to understand other people? Is she lazy or depressed? Is he just a jerk or does he have borderline personality disorder?

Christians around us suffer with serious mental disorders like anxiety[3], depression, traumatic stress, age-onset dementia, autism, hoarding, insomnia, medication-induced personality changes, and a host of other conditions, all of which impact people's lives in ways that defy simplistic categories of sin. They cannot be overcome with a weekend retreat, a trip to the pastor's office, or a Christian self-help book. Long-term care, support, compassion, and patience are necessary to love our saints who suffer.

Two even more severe mental illnesses are in a whole different league, however. Schizophrenia and bipolar disorder are less common (but technically not rare) diseases that require medication in nearly all cases in order to function, and sometimes those medications do not alleviate severe symptoms.[4] They help us see our humanity when our minds are malfunctioning. If we can't think clearly, what is our relationship to God based on?

The picture we have about severe mental illness more likely comes from Hollywood than a psychiatry textbook.[5] So how should we as thoughtful, caring Christians react when we are approached by a family member or congregant who suffers from a diagnosed severe mental illness? If we offer cheap pious advice that amounts to "pray more and you'll get better," shun the sick, retreat in fear, or ignore the biological nature of mental health problems, we will add pain on top of acute suffering.

Instead, we could learn much from those who faithfully struggle with things many of us cannot fathom and yet still see the saint under the diagnosis. Kathryn Greene-McCreight, a priest with bipolar disorder, reminds us that internal despair with hope in the resurrection is a deep form of faith.[6]

. . .

The first step Christians can take is to simply understand enough about these severe disorders to recognize people who potentially suffer from them. Essentially 1% of the worldwide population suffers from schizophrenia. Symptoms collectively present a nightmarish experience for patients as they descend into the illness.[7] Some are hard to distinguish, such as decreased motivation (laziness? depression? faithlessness?), while others are red flags (hallucinations or not sleeping for days on end). People from every walk of life may exhibit a thought disorder. These brain diseases are so complex that no single cause is known despite advances in DNA analysis.[8]

Since most people suffering with these illnesses cannot tell that they have symptoms (called anosognosia)[9], evidence comes out in their interaction with others. Elyn Saks describes her side of a conversation with her professor as she was sinking into psychosis:

> "The memo materials have been infiltrated," I said, looking at my shoes. "Jumping around. I used to be good at the broad jump. Because I'm tall. I fall. Is anyone else in this room? It's a matter of point. There's a plan. People put things in and then say it's my fault. I used to be God but I got demoted. Are you God?"[10]

Another nearly 1% are diagnosed with the affective[11] disorders Bipolar 1 and 2. Bipolar signs are symptoms of mania alternating with long-lasting depression, although the scale of either pole can vary, leading to different types of bipolar diagnosis.[12] As mania begins, the ride up can feel exciting before the roller coaster drops. "The world was filled with pleasure and promises; I felt great. Not just great, I felt really great. I felt I could do anything, that no task was too difficult."[13]

Both illnesses can wreak havoc on a person's life—ending careers, destroying relationships, causing damage and potential self-harm, driving people into illegal drugs as a form of self-medication and frequently pushing them onto streets or into prisons.[14]

Several biblical accounts show the intense stigma surrounding mental illness. When David acted insane so that he could escape Achish, Achish responded, "Do I lack madmen, that you have brought this fellow to behave as a madman in my presence? Shall this fellow come into my house?" (1 Sam. 21:15). These and other ancient writings show us that for millennia, people with mental illness have been outcasts who also brought shame upon their family. They are often declared unproductive, unpredictable, and seen as a heavy burden. The stigma can be worse than the suffering.[15]

So, who's to blame? Like the disciples with the man born blind (John 9:2), we imply that ailments are God's judgment for something. Someone has to be the cause of mental illness, and severe mental illness was often blamed on mothers (of course! Mom's always at fault). Relatively recent understanding of these as specific brain diseases has not eliminated our culture's assumption of blame on families or even the patient. However, Todd Stryd of CCEF compassionately reminds us, "Schizophrenia is an affliction. Your loved ones didn't do this to themselves. You couldn't have stopped it from happening."[16]

Christians have an ability to undo shame by pointing to our Savior who took all of our infirmities of the flesh into Himself, promising a new heavens and earth where all things will be made new (Rev. 21:5). Our acts of faith, shown as moving toward those who suffer with mental illness, reflect the heart of Jesus.

If I claim that I am saved by God's grace alone through faith alone, then I need to extend that same level of grace toward other members of God's household. My mentally ill brothers and sisters are not objects of fear and scorn. They are my family, united in Jesus with me. I will sing praises with them forever. How can I doubt their faith simply because I do not understand how their minds work?

Our binary method of classifying people into normal/abnormal ignores the truth that our orientation to God determines our true reference.[17] As previous Christians have taught us, our humanity and our relationship with Jesus is rich and full and beautiful even in the midst of (and in spite of, or even because of?) any illness we face. Todd Stryd explains, "Just as schizophrenia cannot erase your loved one's humanity, schizophrenia cannot keep your loved one from exercising the fruit of the Spirit—faith, hope, and love. Schizophrenia nuances moral responsibility and faith, but does not extinguish it. It cannot diminish the value, dignity, or relevance of a person."[18]

We do not have to merely pity ordinary saints who suffer this way, we can learn from them. For example, many great artists, poets, writers, and performers suffered from symptoms of manic depression. Their bursts of creativity, genius, and insight may have been enhanced by their mental illness, despite the destructive force it took on their personal lives.[19]

Charles Spurgeon and the hymn writer William Cowper exhibited patterns of "melancholia" that could have been in this category.[20] Where would we be without some of Spurgeon's brilliant insights or Cowper's *Olney Hymns*, insights gleaned from their inner turmoil? Cowper graphically paints his severe depression: "A thick fog envelopes every thing, and at the same time it freezes intensely . . . Nature revives again, but a soul once slain, lives no more."[21] Amazingly, through the love of friends like John Newton and others, he frequently survived to the other side of his "thick fog." Few hymn lyrics are as poignantly hopeful as William Cowper's, which acknowledge the genuine struggle that nearly all of us face in seasons of darkness and pain. Cowper's hymn "God Moves in Mysterious Ways" encourages all of us: "You fearful saints, fresh courage take; / The clouds you so much dread / Are big with mercy and shall break / In blessings on your head."

Kathryn Greene-McCreight courageously writes of her battle with bipolar disorder and describes how her steady application of spiritual disciplines holds her to reality, even when it is merely a tiny thread of sanity. Despite her "broken brain" that cries out to end her own life, she hangs on to the daily office, memorized Scripture, and the hope of the resurrection. Any saint that holds on to hope while suffering a severe mental illness is a witness to God's preserving love for His children.

> The soul is not the seat of sickness in the mentally ill. The brain is broken: its synapses and neurons and receptors. At least for the time being. But the soul, as the self in relation to God, continues healthy in anyone as long as that

person is in Christ, relating to and acknowledging God. The soul that to Jesus hath fled for repose, I will not, I will not desert to its foes.[22]

God's glory is manifested even more in saints whose souls rest in Him despite their broken brains. If only I had known that I could have given comfort and hope to that teenage girl suffering from schizophrenia. I could have seen her without fear and seen Jesus more clearly through her fractured interior experience. Maybe I could have heard the real angels rejoicing over her life.

1 "Mental Health," National Institute of Mental Health, updated January 2022, https://www.nimh.nih.gov/health/statistics/mental-illness.

2 Matthew S. Stanford, *Grace for the Afflicted: A Clinical and Biblical Perspective on Mental Illness,* 2nd ed. (Downers Grove, IL: InterVarsity Press, 2017), pp. 53–54: "Although I believe this is a legitimate concern, we need to be careful to separate sin from illness. It is not a sin to be ill, even mentally ill."

3 See Charles Marsh's memoir *Evangelical Anxiety* (New York: HarperCollins, 2022). He describes his life-long crippling anxiety within the confines of his evangelical background and academic religious career.

4 Daphne Merkin, "Can You Cure Mental Illness? Two Centuries of Trying Says No," *The Atlantic,* July 10, 2022, https://www.theatlantic.com/books/archive/2022/07/-desperate-remedies-book-review-mental-illness-cure/670480/?utm_source=feed. "[Andrew Scull's book *Desperate Remedies*] is an effort to provide a sight line through the often turbulent currents of the field, touching on its strengths and (mostly) its shortfalls, from the start of the psychiatric endeavor to the present moment. His hope, I would suggest, is to provide readers with a way of thinking about people with mental illness as part of us rather than as alien or weird presences, best drugged into compliance or shuttled off to an institution. Understanding the long, sordid history of how these diseases of the mind have been treated is a necessary first step toward bringing people with even the most debilitating disorders into the fold and finding the solutions that might aid in their healing or, at the least, alleviate their suffering."

5 Multiple personalities, serial killers, raging lunatics, or end-of-the-world prophets sell tickets or streaming subscriptions. None of those are accurate portrayals of people with schizophrenia. They are no more dangerous than the rest of the population and tend to experience more violence *against* them than they cause, and what violence they do cause is, usually by accident. The violent antagonist of a psychological thriller more likely has one of the more extremely rare disorders, such as sociopathic disorder or a fictional illness invented by the screenwriters.

6 Kathryn Greene-McCreight, *Darkness is My Only Companion: A Christian Response to Mental Illness* (Grand Rapids, MI: Brazos Press, 2015), loc. 2520–2523, Kindle: "This is an exceedingly important lesson: despair can live with Christian faith. Indeed, having despair while knowing in your heart that God has conquered even that is a great form of faith tried by fire. And the counterpart to despair is hope ... Christian hope looks to the future, to God's promise of the resurrection."

7 Schizophrenia symptoms that are not normal experiences: delusions, hallucinations, disorganized thinking, and disorganized behavior. These are the most obvious symptoms that we can see. Negative symptoms are also present: flat expression, decreased motivation, reduced speech and social interaction, and inability to feel pleasure. Not everyone experiences all of these symptoms, and they can vary in degree. See Stanford, *Grace for the Afflicted;* and also E. Fuller Torrey and Michael Knable, *Surviving Manic Depression: A Manual on Bipolar Disorder for Patients, Families, and Providers* (New York: Basic Books, 2002); Michael Emlet, *Descriptions and Prescriptions: A Biblical Perspective on Psychiatric Diagnoses and Medications* (Greensboro, NC: New Growth Press, 2017); and Lynn DeLisi, *100 Questions and Answers About Schizophrenia: Painful Minds,* 3rd ed. (Burlington, MA: Jones & Bartlett Learning, 2017).

8 Stanford, *Grace for the Afflicted,* p. 52: "The vast complexity of the brain makes it possible for a disorder to result from an imbalance in a single neurotransmitter or a combination of several."

9 Xavier Amador, *I Am Not Sick, I Don't Need Help!: How to Help Someone With Mental Illness Accept*

Treatment (New York: Vida Press, 2012), p. 11, Kindle: "When once again a bottle of medication is found in the trash or stuffed under a mattress, when we are told to mind our own business––that we are the only one who has a problem, when yet another doctor's appointment is missed, we all come one step closer to throwing our hands up in despair. Sometimes, whether or not we walk away, our loved ones do. They disappear for hours, days, weeks and even years. My brother Henry was in the habit of disappearing for days and even hitch-hiking cross-country."

10 Elyn R. Saks, *The Center Cannot Hold: My Journey Through Madness*, (New York: Hachette Books, 2007) loc. 2015, Kindle.

11 Affective diseases are not the person, but they do alter someone's personality. E. Fuller Torrey and Michael B. Knable, *Surviving Manic Depression: A Manual on Bipolar Disorder for Patients, Families, and Providers* (New York: Basic Books, 2002), p. 21..

12 Bipolar disorder is diagnosed by the severity of the mania (grandiosity, decreased need for sleep, pressured speech, racing thoughts, distractibility, agitation, uncontrollable urges) and the depression stage lasting two weeks or longer (depressed mood lasting all day, lack of interest, unplanned change in body weight, insomnia or hypersomnia, agitation, fatigue, worthlessness, diminished thinking ability, pondering death). See Torrey and Knable, *Surviving Manic Depression*, loc 275. A subset of patients has schizoaffective disorder which is a combination of schizophrenia (thought disorder) and bipolar (affective disorder).

13 Kay Jamison, in Torrey and Knable, *Surviving Manic Depression*, p. 21.

14 I'm writing mostly from an individual perspective in this essay, but the social impact of our national approach toward treating mental illness exacerbates the problem. Treating severe mental illness is extremely expensive (schizophrenia is the second-most costly illness behind cancer), and long-lasting. Families are ill-equipped and unable to handle the most severe cases. Most states closed mental health institutions in the 1960s–1970s because of their terrible reputation of abuse and questionable results. Rather than reforming their system, the majority of patients are given psychosis medication and released to independent living. Given the nature of the disease, that resulted in patients forgetting their medication and living on the streets.

15 Greene-McCreight, *Darkness is My Only Companion*, loc. 977–981, Kindle: "The worst thing about mental illness, besides the pain, is this very stigma. The pointing. The staring. The laughing. Stigma draws its energy from fear of the unknown, fear of the other who is not like us. Stigma creates fear both of and in those of us who live with mental illnesses. It directs the fear of those who are healthy towards those who are ill."

16 Todd Stryd, *Schizophrenia: A Compassionate Approach* (Greensboro, NC: New Growth Press, 2018), p. 3.

17 Michael Emlet, *Descriptions and Prescriptions: A Biblical Perspective on Psychiatric Diagnoses and Medications* (Greensboro, NC: New Growth Press, 2017), Kindle: "At the end of the day, 'normal/abnormal' is not the only (or best) binary to categorize people because it doesn't, in and of itself, reference the reality that we are image bearers who stand before the living God as responsive and responsible people (Genesis 1:26–27; Romans 1; Colossians 3:10). A person without a diagnosed mental disorder (('normal' according to the DSM) may in fact be living a life oriented away from God (and thus 'abnormal' as it relates to God's design for humanity). A person with a diagnosed mental disorder ('abnormal' according to the DSM) may in fact be living a life oriented toward God ('normal' as it relates to God's design for humanity)."

18 Stryd, *Schizophrenia: A Compassionate Approach*, p. 8

19 For example, Emily Dickinson's self-reflective musing:

> "And Something's odd—within—
> That person that I was—
> And this One—do not feel the same—
> Could it be Madness—this?"

quoted in Kay Redfield Jamison, *Touched With Fire: Manic-depressive Illness and the Artistic Temperament* (New York: Free Press, 1996), loc. 898, Kindle.

20 Bipolar-like disorders also include unipolar cycles of severe depressive disorder.

21 William Cowper, in Jamison, *Touched With Fire*, loc. 363, Kindle.

22 Greene-McCreight, *Darkness Is My Only Companion*, loc. 1617–1620, Kindle.

PORN

Hope for Ordinary Pornographers Who are Ordinary Saints

"Wait . . . what? How can an essay on pornographers (those who use and collect pornography) be included in a book about ordinary saints living their lives to the glory of God?" Maybe we would find it more acceptable to title this essay, "Ordinary Saints Caught in Extraordinary Sins." These sins could be any number of addictive, self-soothing behaviors like drugs or alcohol abuse, cutting, lying (including pesky little fibs), stealing (oops, cashier mistakes in our favor!), grumbling, sexual addictions, gambling, excessive buying, overeating, under-eating, and so on. But how can a sin like grumbling or lying be anything like viewing pornography? For the purposes of this essay, let us agree that while all these addictive behaviors ensnare followers of Christ, few are as secretive and shame-producing as pornography.

LEVELING SIN'S PLAYING FIELD

Before discussing pornography, we must level sin's playing field for believers caught in sin (be it grumbling or pornography), lest we devalue Christ's sacrifice for us. Leveling the playing field allows porn users to see their sin as every other person sees theirs. We *all* are in need of Jesus' redemptive blood and God's forgiveness. A level playing field gives hope both to the porn user and grumbler at the foot of the cross.

Read the word of the Lord:

> For I do not want you to be unaware, brothers, that our fathers were all under the cloud, and all passed through the sea, and all were baptized into Moses in the cloud and in the sea, and all ate the same spiritual food, and all drank the same spiritual drink. For they drank from the spiritual Rock that followed them, and the Rock was Christ. Nevertheless, with most of them God was not pleased, for they were overthrown in the wilderness. (1 Corinthians 10:1–5)

According to Paul, *his* ancestors (the nation of Israel, into which we have been grafted) are *our* spiritual lineage. What things or activities did our spiritual ancestors do that we also do? They were under the same cloud, passed through the same sea, were baptized into the same Moses, ate the same spiritual food, and drank from the same spiritual rock. While most of their activities do not necessarily correspond to ours, Paul makes an interesting observation in verse 4. Paul says Jesus is the spiritual rock from which we and our ancestors drank. His living waters equally satisfy all who drink from Him (be they porn users or grumblers) thereby establishing a level playing field for all. Let's see how the specific sins and consequences of our ancestors speak to us today. Read the word of the Lord:

> Now these things occurred as examples to keep us from setting our hearts on evil things as they did. Do not be idolaters, as some of them were; as it is written: "The people sat down to eat and drink and got up to indulge in revelry." We should not commit sexual immorality, as some of them did—and in one day twenty-three thousand of them died. We should not test Christ, as some of them did—and were killed by snakes. And do not grumble, as some of them did—and were killed by the destroying angel. (1 Corinthians 10:6–10 NIV)

Talk about the consequences of sin: bodies scattered in the wilderness, twenty-three thousand dead in one day, death by snake attacks, and an angel gone wild! Whether we follow in the specific sins of our ancestors listed in the passage above, or fall headlong into another sin of our own choosing (like pornography), we must recognize from where sin originates. If not, we will rank one sin above another. Christians often find solace in ranking sins from Not-So-Bad at one end to Really-Really-Bad at the other. For example, we often will find ourselves thinking that idolatry, sexual immorality, and testing the Lord are far worse sins than grumbling. This hierarchical organizing of sins causes us to believe our sins aren't as bad as the sins of others. The key to leveling sin's playing field is in Paul's strict warning to believers against "setting our hearts on evil things." People caught in pornography feel inhuman, causing them to believe their sin is too big for God to fix. But Paul says all sin starts in the human heart, placing all sinners on the same level ground. For proof, Paul says that the sin of grumbling unleashed a destroying angel upon our ancestors. Porn viewers (and grumblers!) need to embrace their humanity as they deal with the shame of their sin. Jesus' redemptive work shines because He died for the sins that come forth from our hearts.

Dear Ordinary Saint who views pornography, your sin originated in your heart. And your heart is exactly where Jesus wants to begin your healing, for God is greater than your heart (1 John 3:19–21). With this level playing field, let's look at how this helps you (as well as grumblers) live to the glory God. Read the word of the Lord:

> Therefore let anyone who thinks that he stands take heed lest he fall. No temptation has overtaken you that is not common to man. God is faithful, and he will not let you be tempted beyond your ability, but with the temptation he will also provide the way of escape, that you may be able to endure it. (1 Corinthians 10:12–13)

Any sin can make us fall. We must all be careful, even if we believe we are standing firm. The porn viewer and grumbler both stand on the same level playing field. They both rest on the faithfulness of God, who knows our ever-wandering heart. Our faithful Lord promises that He will be measured in His discipline and will not give us more than we can bear. In fact, God provides a way out. Yet we must remember that bearing up and finding a way out is very different for the porn user than it is for the grumbler. There is no ranking of our sins—sin's playing field is level—but it is unkind and unwise to equate how the porn user and the grumbler struggle in their sin. Pornography is tied to brain chemistry and can be as addictive as heroin. Grumbling is not.

SIN IS AN IDENTITY ISSUE

I explain in my book *Speaking CODE: Unraveling Past Bonds to Redeem Broken Conversations* that we all have things in our past that form our identity. These are often responsible for the sadness in our lives and lead us to make sinful choices—including the heart decision to view pornography. The addictive nature of pornography almost always becomes an idol that users must worship in secret as they publicly live life. This wrecks the user's important relationships and makes communication with them soul-crushing; their ritualism becomes all-consuming. How can ordinary saints live life to the glory of God, while active in their sin?

When sin moves us away from Jesus, sin also moves us away from ourselves. We replace our true identity, which is hidden in Christ, with a false identity, which is hidden in our idolatry. Pornographers, trapped in sin, identify themselves by that sin, making it hard to live life to God's glory. But this is a lie. Christians trapped in sin do not belong to that sin. Ensnared or not, ordinary saints who view pornography belong to Jesus because Jesus owns their heart. Instead of sin's false identity, the accurate self-identification for a porn user is, "I am a child of God who is at war with pornography, which makes my life feel like a raging storm over which I have no control." This new identification becomes a starting point to live for God's glory.

PORNOGRAPHY AND . . . JONAH?

Here is where we meet Jonah, a prophet of God who was told to go to Nineveh and preach against its evil. Read the word of the Lord:

> Now the word of the LORD came to Jonah the son of Amittai, saying, "Arise, go to Nineveh, that great city, and call out against it, for their evil has come up before me." But Jonah rose to flee to Tarshish from the presence of the LORD. He went down to Joppa and found a ship going to Tarshish. So he paid the fare and went down into it, to go with them to Tarshish, away from the presence of the LORD. (Jonah 1:1–3)

God's voice is the first voice we hear in this book. He tells Jonah to go where He sends him to go and do what He tells him to do. Sounds pretty God-like, especially since Jonah is His prophet. Yet Jonah disobeyed God and boarded a ship headed to Tarshish, fleeing from God's presence. Many times, porn users confess that they hear an inner voice of warning, but the addiction overpowers it. Sadly, like Jonah, they often flee from God's presence (as they ignore that voice) and indulge themselves in whatever "Tarshish" offers. As we learned in 1 Corinthians 10:6, sin's playing field is level— human decisions to sin begin in the heart.

Sometimes we may offer Scripture passages to porn viewers, thinking this will help them overcome their sin. But often our brothers or sisters who are using porn believe they are fighting a losing battle and Bible verses aren't enough. There may be times when the pornographer experiences success in response to our help, yet sadly, that success turns to failure when the porn user succumbs to the idol's allure.

In Jonah 4, the prophet accuses God of being gracious, compassionate, slow to anger, and abounding in love. These attributes angered Jonah because he did not want to preach repentance to Israel's enemies. He knew God would relent of the coming disaster that would befall Nineveh if, in fact, they repented. Jonah likely self-identified as a Nationalist, and his anger idol led him to conceive a plan to thwart God's purpose. Jonah's sin originated in his heart, helping him devise his plan.

Much like Jonah, a pornographer's heart creates idols based on desires that oppose God's commands regarding lust and inappropriate sexual experiences. Their hearts tell them they cannot find satisfaction in life without giving in to their sinful desires. Both Jonah's and the porn user's hearts feel aggrieved that God does not seem to understand their wants and needs. As they pursue their idols of choice, they justify their sinful behavior. The porn user sees disruptions in his life that need to be soothed. Whatever the motivations that cause their self-identification, porn users and Jonah embrace their idols and flee from God's presence.

Unfortunately, idols are relentless and insatiable. For Jonah, there was no satisfaction in Nineveh's repentance, nor in the plant God created for his comfort. Jonah's heart was full of anger, anger which led to his behavior. Likewise for the porn user, the stimulation from images viewed today will not provide satisfaction tomorrow. In his heart, the pornographer despairs that he will ever live life to God's glory.

Both Jonah and the porn user believe that because they worship their idols in secret, only they are affected by their disobedience. But is that true? While the idol worship may be secretive, the practical outworking of the sin is not. Nearly everyone in Jonah's life was affected by his rebellion. Likewise, nearly everyone in the pornographer's life is impacted by his sinful behavior. Let's briefly compare the porn user and Jonah's behavior and how it affected the people in their lives.

THE STORM

God pursues ordinary saints to help them live life to His glory. Jonah 1 identifies the players who were directly affected by Jonah's secret sin: the mariners, the captain, and Jonah. All played a role and were significantly impacted by Jonah's decision to flee from God's presence.

A violent storm arose and terrified all those on the ship. The mariners prayed earnestly to their gods. Then they threw their valuable cargo overboard, incurring great loss. But as the storm was raging, Jonah went into the inner part of the ship and fell asleep. The captain went below deck and sought him out. He ordered Jonah to call out to his god for mercy. Still nothing stopped the fierce storm.

Antonius Wierix, *Jonah Cast on Shore by the Fish*, engraving

The mariners drew lots, and the lot fell to Jonah. He confessed he was responsible for the calamity and suggested they throw him overboard. After rowing against the storm, they finally called on the Lord, asked for mercy, and did the unspeakable: they picked up Jonah and hurled him into the sea. The storm stopped and the men offered sacrifices to the Lord and made vows.

Jonah, meanwhile, was sinking. But in his mercy God sent a fish that swallowed him whole. Interestingly, while in the fish's belly Jonah confessed that "those who pay regard to vain idols forsake their hope of steadfast love" (Jonah 2:8). Sometimes, when saints are feeling completely trapped, they confess what is true. In this case, Jonah confessed to paying regard to his vain idol. In moments of clarity, pornography users will sometimes acknowledge that their addiction is also a "vain idol."

Life quickly breaks apart for the pornographer, just as Jonah's ship threatened to burst into pieces. Idolizing pornography catapults the user into the harsh consequences of the natural world, where they may lose jobs, relationships, possessions, and hope for the future.

THE MARINERS

There are many similarities between the account in Jonah and the life of a pornographer. The path that leads us away from ourselves and God is never traveled alone. The mariners on board the ship are similar to the people in a pornographer's life. Spouses, parents, children, family members, friends, coworkers, church leaders, casual acquaintances, and even strangers can get caught up in the pornographer's raging storm. Intentionally or not, porn users pull everyone into their ritualistic idol worship, just as the captain and the mariners were unknowingly pulled into Jonah's sin. We wonder if pornographers, like Jonah, realize how their addiction affects those around them.

Jonah and the mariners are thrown together in a relationship. They looked to Jonah to help them find a way to survive. But Jonah had caused the chaos, and he seemed unconcerned that the mariners would die if God wreaked vengeance on the ship. Similarly, porn users can show little regard for the mariners in their lives. Loved ones are left in the dark about the user's porn addiction. Friends and family often pour their own resources into the pornographer's recovery. Counseling appointments and expensive medications deplete financial resources, as pornography viewers are likely to suffer from mental and physical issues. This causes a financial strain on everyone. Money disappears from bank accounts. Work wages are lost due to missed days. Sometimes porn users even lose their jobs because they used work computers to gratify their addiction idol. It appears from the text that Jonah entertained suicidal thoughts, just as many pornographers consider suicide as an escape from the hopelessness of their addiction.

As they tried to save his life, the mariners showed more regard for Jonah than he did for them. Often, loved ones demonstrate care for the porn user that seems to be one-sided. Loved ones forgive beyond rationality, while the pornographer promises a change that rarely happens.

THE CAPTAIN

In assessing the critical situation for his crew and ship, the captain found Jonah below deck, fast asleep. We can almost hear his indignation as the captain calls out to Jonah, "What do you mean, you sleeper? Arise, call out to your god! Perhaps the god will give a thought to us, that we may not perish" (Jonah 1:6).

The captain calls on Jonah to pray! We sinners should not miss the significance of prayer. Prayer affects our hearts and connects us to God, who loves us and helps us in our weakness. The power in prayer is that prayer speaks directly to the sin we conceive in our hearts before the behavior gets established.

Captains play a critical role in the porn user's life, often to their own peril. Captains are typically the ones in charge and are responsible for making impossible decisions. They can be parents, grandparents, relatives, friends, church leaders, siblings, and especially spouses. Captains feel trapped when porn users drag them into the results of their sinful behavior. As with Jonah, captains hopelessly try to arouse the pornographer from his deep sleep as they question his choices. Captains may even ask the porn user for solutions to remedy the chaos he created, just as the captain asked Jonah to help fight against the raging storm.

FINDING HOPE

How can ordinary saints caught up in pornography live life to the glory of God while actively struggling in their addiction? We see in the account of Jonah that, regardless of the prophet's sin, nothing interferes with God's glory. This suggests that pornographers can find rest in God's sovereignty as well.

Porn viewers can find hope because Jesus leveled sin's playing field at the cross. The heart that causes your sin and my sin are equal before God. Let that encourage you, even though you believe that pornography degrades you. God's love pursues us right to the cross. God's pursuing love proves His connectedness to us. Allow these truths to aid you as you glorify God in your everyday life. People trapped in pornography can live out the first and second greatest commandments, and thereby glorify God in their lives. Because God both initiates love and then pursues us in love, pornography users can respond to God with love that includes their heart, soul, and mind. This love motivates sinners to hope in God with a renewed understanding that their addiction does not have the final word in their lives—God's initiating love does. God loves each one of His dear children with specificity.

God's initiating love equips a pornographer to love himself. This prepares him to love his neighbor, because one cannot love his neighbor if one does not love himself. Surprisingly, believers caught in extraordinary sin understand love for God, others, and themselves in a way few of us can ever appreciate, for he who has been forgiven much, loves much (Luke 7:47).

Pornographers (like other saints) suffer from repeating the same sin over and over. How can one live life to the glory of God if the pattern of failure continues? Jonah chapters 2–4 shed light on this. In the belly of the fish, Jonah called out to God in his distress and God forgave him. But the account is not over. And Jonah repeats his sins in chapters 3 and 4 until the fullness of Jonah's disobedience is revealed.

Viewing pornography can cause you to enter into a shame cycle. Rather than spiraling downward, remember: God has not abandoned you. Your realization of your fall shows that He has not finished speaking into your life. Setbacks often reveal the fullness of our idol worship. In speaking of repeated sin, Paul reminds us that God's grace is sufficient for the pornographer (and all of us), because God's power is made perfect in weakness, and for Christ's sake, when we are weak, then we are strong (2 Cor. 12:10). Remember, prayer is the primary strategy for ordinary saints living life to the glory of God.

The book of Jonah shows that salvation belongs to God. As porn users read this essay, may they find a level playing field knowing God is after their heart. Finally, pornographer, in the humiliation of your sin, may God lift up your head to Him, the King of Glory as expressed in the word of the Lord:

> Lift up your heads, O gates!
> And be lifted up, O ancient doors,
> that the King of glory may come in.
> Who is this King of glory?
> The Lord, strong and mighty,
> the Lord, mighty in battle!
> Lift up your heads, O gates!
> And lift them up, O ancient doors,
> that the King of glory may come in.
> Who is this King of glory?
> The Lord of hosts,
> he is the King of glory! *Selah.* (Psalm 24:7–10)

Sandra Bowden

COLLECTING
A Visual Heritage of Glory

I just returned from a trip to England visiting towns northeast of London, where my mother's relatives lived in the sixteenth and seventeenth century, and searching for churches where they had worshiped before they emigrated to the New World. Some of the churches were in small villages and others had to be ferreted out by driving miles down narrow hedged roads and past fields of spring hay and intense yellow rapeseed to spot a bell tower through a cluster of trees. Most appeared quite plain from the exterior, but walk inside these thousand-year-old structures and another world appeared.

Sandra Bowden, *Sanctus*, collagraph

Inevitably, in every sanctuary we found somewhere among all the art and liturgical embellishments a sign that read, "To the Glory of God." Stone-carved baptismal fonts, painted organ pipes, stained-glass windows, painted and polychromed altarpieces, elaborately carved pews, sculpted angels, intricately designed wood screens, hand embroidered altar coverings . . . you get the idea. These congregations created meaningful objects of beauty to enhance their worship and, in doing so, left a visual record that faith was alive and well in their time.

Art is so often thought of as an add-on, even as frivolous, of less importance than the supposedly more essential elements in the life of the church. The historic church understood and perceived it as so important that even the smallest worship space required art. It was necessary to communicate the faith visually, to find ways to help the viewers understand the Bible more deeply, and also to inspire and bring the parishioner closer to God.

As both a Christian artist and collector, this is so reassuring. To know that my roots are securely planted in the soil and tradition of creating art that brings glory to God gives me great joy, reminding me every day of my purpose and that it is worth dedicating my life and ministry to this work.

GLORY

What does it mean to bring glory to God through the visual arts? First, God's glory is revealed and made visible through the visual arts. The Bible itself reveals what is God's glory. In the Old Testament God's glory is almost exclusively revealed in physical form as found in these passages: "The cloud covered the tent of meeting and the glory of the LORD filled the tabernacle" (Ex. 40:34) Moses said, "Please show me your glory" (Ex. 33:18); "The heavens declare the glory of God" (Ps. 19:1); "And thou shalt make holy garments for Aaron thy brother for glory and for beauty" (Ex 28:2, 28:40 KJV). In each of these passages God's glory was seen.

In the New Testament, Jesus is the physical presence of God's glory. The main purpose of the Bible is to reveal God's glory. Yes, it is also to unveil His plan for salvation, but the overarching purpose of God's word is to reveal His glory. Jesus is the ultimate manifestation of God's glory. John 1:14 evidences this: "The Word was made flesh and dwelt among us, and we beheld his glory" (KJV). Hebrews 1:3 further demonstrates this point: "He is the radiance of the glory of God and the exact imprint of his nature." Jesus was seen.

Edward Knippers, *Christ Risen*, linocut

Second, glory is reflected, showing its source. In Paul's first letter to the Corinthians, he extols, "So, whether you eat or drink, or whatever you do [whether you are creating or collecting art], do all to the glory of God" (10:31). Here again, the glory of God refers to honoring God with one's life. For artists, honoring God means, in part, honoring Him with the art we create. If glory is manifested, seen, and artists are making visible an invisible reality, then this is a strong mandate to see our work as a reflection of the one we worship. When we work, we are giving glory to God.

From early in my career as an artist I have strived to reflect my faith in the things I created. This quest has taken me in many directions, but in reflection, I realize that each series I created was a conversation with the past. First I explored geology, inspired by Psalm 85:11: "Truth springs up from the earth" (NLT). Then I studied Hebrew and integrated it into the layers of my collages and collagraphs. In the late 1990s, my focus turned to art history and how the many crosses and altarpieces were crafted to reflect God's glory. My latest work has been creating a series of gilded encaustic panels, each covered with 22-carat gold. The name of the show is *Reflecting the Glory*. I have come to realize that my life's work is to reflect the glory of the one I worship.

COLLECTION

It is not that unusual for an artist to also be a collector. There have been many before me, such as Rembrandt, Leonard Baskin, Robert Rauschenberg, Jeff Koons, and Damian Hirst, as well as my contemporary, Edward Knippers. I have been called to be an artist but also a collector of art that reflects God's glory, how He works among His people, and the story of the Bible. The pieces in Bowden Collections show that at various points in history faith was alive and well. We need the insights, the understandings, and the illumination that comes from this art.

I believe it is important to collect and preserve those objects of beauty and meaning for another generation. True collectors know that what they have bought is not truly theirs. In reality the collector is one link in a chain of collectors that goes back to the artist's studio. We own a wonderful "corpus" from around 1420. It is not in perfect condition as the arms are missing; nevertheless, for nearly six hundred years there have been individuals who believed that this fragile sculpture was worth protecting. Furthermore, through wars, catastrophes, and personal tragedies, there have been individuals who have had enough faith to know that there would be collectors yet to come who would see the intrisic worth of this crucifix. I am privileged to be in that lineage.

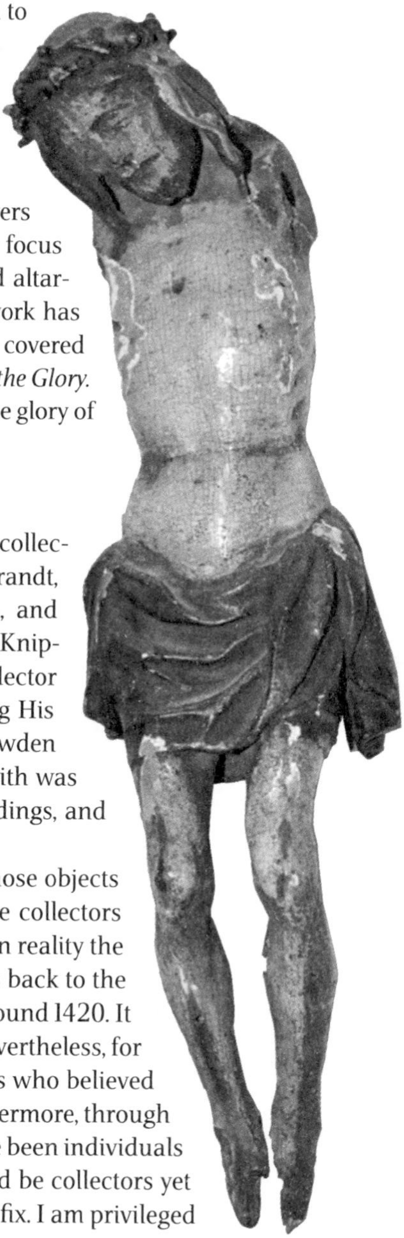

Corpus, wood and polychrome, c 1430

Many have asked me how I got started collecting religious art. The first important piece in our collection came when I was having an exhibition of my collagraph prints that contained Hebrew text at a gallery in Connecticut. The owner of the gallery was Jewish. While at her home I noticed Georges Rouault's etching from the Miserere Series, *He Was Obedient Until Death, Even Death on the Cross.* I asked her how she came to own that piece. She explained that her father was the manager of Brentano's gallery in New York City and that he had given it to her. She also told me that she was dying of cancer and her children intended to destroy it. She asked if I would be willing to purchase this important print. Of course, the answer was yes. That was the beginning of a very fulfilling and exciting journey as collector. Never did I imagine the rich experiences and sheer joy that would result from this first acquisition.

Others ask, why do you collect religious art? First, this topic is of the utmost importance to me personally. Second, I believe that the art I have chosen will have greater value for coming generations because it has a focus. I also know that art opens us to the transcendent in ways that words cannot do. We own a large thorn wrapped silver chalice, called *Can You Drink This Cup I Am About to Drink?* by John Kiefer, that takes the viewer by surprise. Yet as we contemplate its meaning, we realize that it brings into focus the sacrifice of our Lord in arresting ways. Can you imagine being offered this cup on Good Friday? The artist has made visible an intangible reality of our faith with more power and potency than just words.

It is a wonderful time to be collecting work with biblical or Christian themes because the art market in general is not interested in religious work. It is not exactly politically correct, unless the work is outsider art, a Rembrandt or Dürer, or some other very famous name that becomes an investment opportunity. I found a little gem in a crammed bookstore in Wisbaden, Germany, where everyone told me I'd find no religious art. It is a gouache, *Christ Placed in the Tomb* by Barent Fabritius, who was a student of Rembrandt. Now is the time to gather and preserve some of these past treasures—many of which are in jeopardy. I could recount many stories of pieces that I literally rescued.

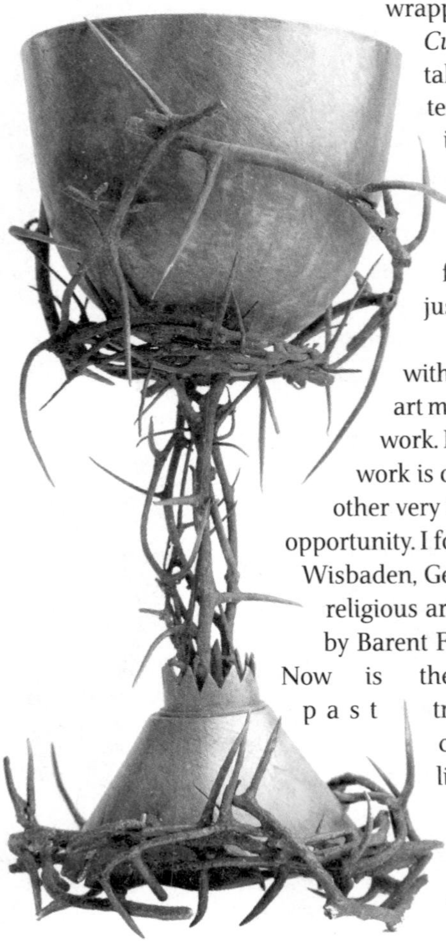

Fr. John David Kiefer, *Can You Drink this Cup I Am about to Drink?*, silver and other metals

Barent Fabritius, *Burial of Christ*, gouache

Over the last thirty years I have been collecting significant works of art, and I have placed them in safe environments in order to preserve them for future generations. I came to believe that I needed to do more than collect: I should curate exhibitions from the art that I had gathered, offering them to museums, colleges, churches, and seminaries for public display . . . This is how Bowden Collections was formed. The first exhibition was eighteen pieces from Georges Rouault's Miserere Series, and today there are nearly twenty shows that are traveling throughout the United States. My hope is that God's people will come to know their rich visual heritage and gain a deeper and richer understanding of His presence among us.

Bowden Collections does not only contain antique works. Private collectors, churches, and universities need to be creating collections of the art by some of our best contemporary artsts. There is a large body of work being created, right now, by a wide variety of artists of faith whose work offers rich insights into the world and the faith experience. I believe it is time for the Christian community to rise to the task of gathering those works of art that are reminders of how faith is envisioned in our time.

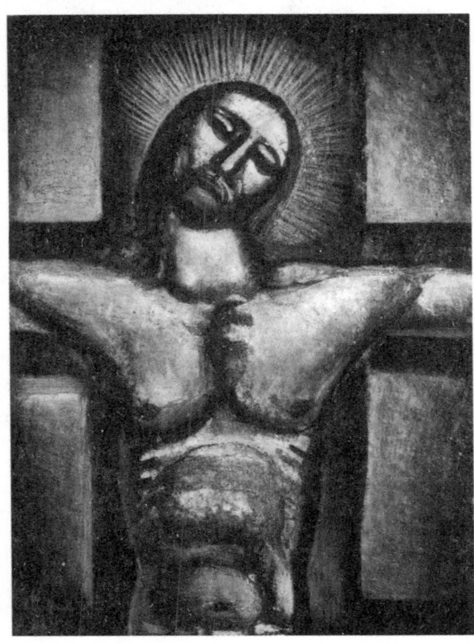

Georges Rouault *Miserere Series Plates 30* (top) and *57* (bottom), aquatint

CHALLENGE

We have a great challenge in front of us if we are to be serious about preserving our visual heritage which has brought glory to God. It is going to require the dedication and imagination of many private collectors, the commitment of corporations and institutions to seriously gather and preserve the art that will continue to inspire generations of the faithful.

It is my challenge to you as an individual to consider how you can participate in this movement to engage the visual arts in the life of the community of faith. How can we all insure that our visual faith traditions can be preserved for the good of all? How can we continue using the visual in ways that bring glory to the Lord?

It is my question to each of us and to the church at large: with the world so hostile to Christianity, how can we count on others to be interested in art of religious content and intent if we are not willing to lead the way in using our resources to preserve our rich visual heritage? How can we expect those who do not hold our faith to support the contemporary artist of faith if we are not willing to take up that challenge and responsibility?

It takes a vision, an understanding of its importance, a determination, a sense of urgency, and yes, some money. I invite you to join me on this journey of preserving our visual treasures that inspire and offer a glimpse of God's glory.

WORK
. . .is it Really Good?

My first year of college had ended and I found myself gainfully employed that summer working for an electric utility company. I was working to afford my "full time" job: grinding through four years of college. I worked a night shift at multiple buildings as part of "project crew," a euphemism for "janitor will travel," at the lowest rung possible, mopping floors and cleaning toilets for my fellow employee "customers".

They were a colorful cross section of humanity at one location in particular; line crew, truckers, and mechanics who were a pretty rough group; office staff, who would hide small items to ensure I was cleaning properly; and dispatchers and control personnel who, in select cases, managed to juggle work and sordid relationships while on the premises. For a relatively empty building, it was a busy place at night. My project crew coworkers were also hard at work themselves. However, apart from a saintly older cleaning woman, when they weren't high or intoxicated, most were working hard at finding ways to avoid work and amuse themselves.

My work was far from glamorous or mentally challenging, but partway into my tour of duty I noticed the sorry state of the floors at one of my assigned locations. For reasons that were not apparent to me at the time, I decided that I would turn these tired and dull pathways and rooms into polished mirrors. By summer's end the day staff was unexpectedly abuzz with talk of this surprising transformation. Unfortunately, my less motivated coworkers were not as pleased. I had unknowingly created a dichotomy between my work and theirs. They had preferred their work life of avoiding work, and their anger was palpable. Had they been given the opportunity, I likely would have physically experienced their displeasure.

Over the years I've hardly thought of that early period in my Christian life because it didn't seem relevant to life in the present. But now that I'm looking at more of my life in the rearview mirror than ahead, I have developed a very different perspective, even an appreciation for this experience, and that is the value and calling of work. First though, I need to connect a few dots essential to my point.

When we work, we demonstrate our God-given creativity as image bearers and stewards of His creation as we were created and instructed to do in the beginning

(Gen. 1:27–31).[1] The fact is that for the vast majority of people, work will occupy more of our waking hours than any other part of our lives. The fall has not changed that created order, it has only added brokenness and hardship in our flourishing, multiplying, and subduing (Gen. 3:1–29).[2]

Secondly, although there are some exceptions, I would offer that considering the previous point, there is no such thing as secular or sacred work, only life occupations that fulfill the stewardship mandate (Gen. 1:1–3:23).[3]

Third, I would assert that the value of our work is not measured by the type of work we do (society's reasonable measurement) but by our loving obedience to God and our love of humanity as a form of worship. Further, Scripture makes the essential distinction that our life (including our work) is either in worship of Him (through Christ) or ourselves (Matt. 22:37).[4]

Fourth, I want to focus on one particular strand of the goodness of work and that shows how our sanctification as Christ followers is substantively intertwined with our primary occupation. Stated differently, if we picture work as a multistranded rope which uses our bodies for the good of others and ourselves in accomplishing God's creation mandate, it now includes a sanctifying element. If I am to worship God in all I do, and to love my neighbor, then I cannot take over half my life and segregate work simply as an unrelated activity. No, it is essential that we see work as, among many things, a sanctifying crucible that allows us to participate in the sufferings of Christ and to be transformed into His image. With this perspective we can then truly evaluate success (kingdom and not earthly), the exercise of our abilities, and growth in the understanding of who we are.[5]

How do you describe your work? More than likely you talk about *what* you do, which is certainly a reasonable response. You may also discuss your disposition, dare I say feelings, about that work as well. If we are willing to wade into these thoughts further, we will find that they often reveal our heart's observations about our occupation, exposing the affections of our hearts in ways we readily overlook when simply relegating work as an activity. My response to daily interactions at work reveals any obvious or hidden expectations I may hold in my heart. For example, I may protect my reputation, harbor grudges, disdain subordinates or peers, envy those in authority, or feel entitled through self-justification. I may actively promote discord or gossip and revel in the downfall of others. Maybe I'm exasperated with my place in life or with the work community I engage daily. Maybe I have a brewing anger or resentment towards people. I might carry a sense of self-righteousness and elevated personal values and may render judgment on others. Am I grasping, boasting, entitled, or arrogant? We may likewise suffer injustice or hardship, and be on the receiving end of someone else's judgment or self-righteousness. We may also revel in our work, what we do, with its joys, challenges, rewards, and countless other aspects. The list is practically endless, but all these examples give us a chance by God's grace through the Holy Spirit to critically examine our motives and expectations as they collide with the work environment around us to the end we are shaped and transformed in Christ.

My early life's work was to attend college. I still remember envisioning the glory of academic success I would surely claim. What I didn't envision was the hardship and trials those years would yield, nor the ignominious conclusion resulting in barely graduating. If my dreams of academic grandeur weren't sufficiently shattered, my escape to a paying occupation early in my career didn't fare much better. For the most part, if I were to measure the success of nearly a decade of my life by normal standards, it was anything but. I could not tell at the time that my ambitions were a form of boasting in myself, and yet God in His mercy revealed my heart through some of those same frustrations and difficulties. Hardship caused dependence. Dashed expectations brought lamenting inquiry. Confidence in my abilities yielded hopelessness but moved me to a place of an expectant hope in His purposes. Failure was really success but not in the way I understood, and all of this was the result of my occupation as a student and employee, not through my home, family life, or church.

The forty years since have only served to illustrate even more how my occupation has served as an essential sanctifying environment where God works in and through me in ways I never appreciated earlier. At the right time, broken as I was, God gave me a different heart towards the purpose of my work. The organization I would eventually have the privilege of leading also became a place of service for me to work on behalf of those who worked for me. It enabled me to enter the lives of a unique work community in ways I never imagined, and allowed me at times to visit those who were hospitalized or dying, lament with those who were grieving, encourage those who were sick, and listen to those suffering with family struggles and divorce or overwhelmed by their own work. All the while, I was presented with the stark contrast between my expectations and feelings about my work and the people I worked with and the kingdom work God was daily calling me to. In retrospect, it is easy to see that my heart's boasting in my opening illustration was incompatible with the servanthood I was to demonstrate in and through my work.

So how do I evaluate my early summer job experience as a janitor now if I consider my observations and feelings present at that time? Certainly, it played a role in subduing the boasting of my heart and helped me understand, in an uncomfortable context, the goodness of work despite the circumstances. I was given the opportunity to express diligence in the midst of temptation, to serve others (however at first unappreciative), to suffer a level of disdain and condescension, and to witness the brokenness and messiness of the lives of those who pursued the hopelessness of self-fulfillment. I was young in life and my faith and ill-equipped to understand my work other than considering it simply as a job. But God has demonstrated not only the tangible value of work as a necessary part of our kingdom stewardship, but also its goodness as a tool in our sanctification. Through it He reveals the rocky soil of our hearts exposed in our thoughts and feelings about what we do and those we do it with.

1 God commanded living creatures, including mankind to "be fruitful and multiply" but He uniquely appointed humanity to subdue the earth (mission directive) and have dominion (created order) over all creatures—whether in the sea, air, or land—reflecting a delegated authority. In verse 29 it is further understood that the plant world was subordinated to act as the food source for everything that has the breath of life. The preeminence of mankind over the earth is also portrayed in Gen 2:19–20 where Adam is uniquely tasked by God to name all the land animals and birds He had created as an exercise of mankind's dominion.

2 The account of the fall identifies a curse, brokenness, and frustration but maintains the mandate to be fruitful and multiply as well as subdue the earth. The physical world is now cursed, and in a sense, in rebellion to mankind. Pain, although not absent, is greatly multiplied in fulfilling the procreation mandate and pain, futility and frustration are now present in working to live. This is all in direct contrast to an unfallen mandate to work and partake of the fruit of the garden.

3 It is important to understand that the account of creation, mankind, and the fall was first delivered to the Israelites through Moses. The hearers, like you and I, were given a story to explain events of immense comprehensive significance and complexity and yet provide a structured understanding of mankind's purpose and fall. Consider in particular several key words God issues as an open-ended command which we take for granted—fruitful, multiply, and subdue. Fruitful is markedly different from multiply, although the "fruit of the womb" is an acknowledgment of both fruitfulness and multiplying. Fruitful implies abundance and advancement in part through control and harnessing creation. The Jews witnessed a form of this in Egypt and understood this in the lives of the patriarchs. Multiply necessitates expanding demands on what it means to be fruitful—think families, communities, tribes, nations. Lastly, subdue embodies in part, domination through exertion. This stands to reason, it would take effort to bring the world into order before the fall (Adam was to work the garden!), and as we know all too well, after the fall in world that has been cursed.

Rule it, be fruitful in it, multiply in it, cover the earth. Imagine a society not made of fallen but sinless beings of unbroken intellect, logic, and understanding in loving and perfect relationship to God.

4 Christ testified to the summation of all the Scriptures in our love of God and man but with the crucial distinction that our fallen love is incapable of this apart from the imputed righteousness of Christ on our behalf.

5 For additional reading consider some of the following resources:

Work Matters: Connecting Sunday Worship to Monday Work, by Tom Nelson (Crossway)

Every Good Endeavor: Connecting Your Work to God's Work, by Timothy Keller and Katherine Leary Alsdorf (Penguin)

Working in the Presence of God: Spiritual Practices for Everyday Work, by Sharron Vandewarker & Denise Daniels (Hendricks)

WINE
A Liquid Odyssey

One of the earliest photos I have of myself is slowly yellowing and beginning to show signs of wear and tear. These days, it barely leaves the memorabilia box it's been stored in for years. I'm not sure why I keep it out of sight, especially because when I do see it, I can't help but laugh and think of how that moment has foreshadowed who I have become. The image documents my first birthday in 1977. In it, I'm standing on my maternal grandparents' kitchen table wearing a three-piece suit (yes, a three-piece suit—I mean, how else would you show up to your first birthday party?). Standing with a smile on my face, I'm holding an empty magnum of Prosecco to my mouth as if I'm getting ready to take the final sip. No other faces are in the photo, but on a closer look, you can see a number of elbows and arms as family members surround me during this momentous event. Torsos are turned towards me, and I'd like to think that all eyes were on me as I mimed the act of consumption. I assume I was being prompted to act as if I was taking a sip, but for the sake of personal lore and legend, I'd like to think at the wise age of one, I was following social cues and contributing to that convivial moment. I'd also like to believe that at such a young age I embraced the Italian proverb *"A tavola . . . non si diventa mai vecchi,"* or "At the table . . . one never grows old," and in some way, shape, or form, began making it my life philosophy.[1]

Throughout elementary and middle school, while most kids were playing outside, I was in the alimentary trenches. I would spend my afternoons at my grandparents' house watching my grandmother in the kitchen and my grandfather in the yard. Most kids in the neighborhood were riding their bikes or playing baseball in their yards; I, on the other hand, was busy helping my grandparents cook or tend the garden. This was totally normal in my world—I mean surely when all the other kids finished their outdoor activities, they returned to their homes to help their families in some similar fashion. My parents emigrated to the United States in the mid-1960s. For a brief time, both sets of grandparents lived in close proximity to me and my family. My extended family was also close to us as they were in the neighboring towns not more than ten minutes away via car. My mom's family remained in the United States, while my father's stayed for several years before opting to return to Sicily in the early 1980s. Family gatherings were frequent and not resigned to major/personal holidays. They were large and loud events that lasted for hours and included several movements of food and wine. Everything was homemade and usually came from my grandfather's or uncle's gardens. Even the wine was homemade. No, neither my grandfather nor uncle had a vineyard, but they did have their own wine presses. Every year, in the early fall, we would make the trip to the Farmer's Market in Hartford, Connecticut, to get grapes to press, ferment, and bottle. As a young kid I was included in every aspect of the wine-making process. I vividly remember the animated debates concerning wine-making between my grandfather and uncle, the frenetic pace of pressing day, and constantly bobbing and weaving to try and avoid the dozens of fly ribbons hanging from the basement ceiling to keep the flies away from the grapes, must, or juice.

Wine was part of who I was. I had no intention of perusing a career in wine or wine making, but being raised in a family that spent a lot of time around a table sharing meals and stories, wine was always around me. As kids, we were given a small amount of wine mixed with soda water or Sprite at meals. We were taught to be responsible with its consumption. It was a beverage void of any ceremony and without any social or cultural currency attached to it. It was a product my grandfather and uncle made. It was consumed with a meal, and not meant to quench thirst. A derivative of wine, vermouth, was always offered to friends and family when they stopped by for a visit, or mixed with soda water before a meal to sharpen the appetite. Another derivative, grappa, was usually served after meals to settle the stomach and help with digestion. If one had a sweet tooth, a Passito or a small glass of Marsala was offered as a substitute. For my family, there was a purpose to the consumption of wine in its many manifestations—to heighten the pleasure of a meal and time well spent with family and friends. This discoloring photo speaks to that story in my life, a narrative that is always in tune with family, the act of preparing and cooking meals, and spending hours at table.

As I got older, my relationship with wine and my understanding of it evolved. During my undergraduate years I spent a semester abroad, in London, England. Growing up as a first-generation Italian-American, we visited relatives in Sicily during the summers. Since we were visiting family, we remained on the island. My semester in London afforded me the chance, during our breaks, to visit mainland Italy on several occasions. It was also the first time I realized that I didn't actually speak Italian, but had been taught a dialect from southeastern Sicily. In fact, on my first trip to Milan, I encountered a waiter who told me I spoke like an old farmhand (but that's another story for another essay).

It was in London that I began to explore the larger world of wine, and by "larger world," I mean wine that wasn't made by a family member. Having grown up in my grandmother's kitchen, I was usually tasked with cooking meals for my roommates and friends. We would all chip in some money, and try different bottles of wine. Armed with Philip Seldon's *The Complete Idiot's Guide to Wine,* I first began spending time in the grocery store aisles.[2] This was a relatively safe space to begin my liquid explorations. Back home, wine came in one size bottle and had no label. It was table wine. It was always red. And it always tasted the same. There was no hierarchy or snobbery attached to its consumption. Not only was it consumed as part of a meal, but most often than not, it was also used in the cooking process. The more time I spent in the wine aisles, the more I realized that I was far from home and that wine was a rather liminal and ephemeral substance. Bottles appeared to be volatile and judgements were cast with each glare from those who were in the know and sensed I was a rookie consumer.

At first, I had Seldon's book with me. No, not in my hand as I traversed down the grocery aisles, but in my backpack. In the event I was overwhelmed, I could always dart to a different aisle and get my vinifera bearings. Not wanting to sound like a novice, I tried to get some vocabulary down and make it a point to communicate that I was serious in my searches by dropping some informed lingo here-and-there. Yes, I was an undergraduate on a budget, but knowing my way around a kitchen came in handy as the daily routine to find a bottle or two became more and more interesting. As you can imagine, I stayed in my wheelhouse—Italian wine. I had a general sense of the country's geography and cuisine, and it seemed to give me an air of legitimacy with regard to wine/food pairings by sticking to Italy's alimentary traditions and habits. Later, as I built confidence, I took notes on a particular country or region, and left the book at home. Eventually, I left the predictable aisles of the grocery store and began visiting the bottle shops that were close to our flat. Wine became more of a necessary compliment to meals. I became more intentional with what I was searching for with each and every meal. Every outing became an adventure. Depending on what we were making, the search changed, and I explored new geographies via bottles and tastings. I stayed mostly within the culinary cultures of Italy, France, and Spain; but eventually I explored other countries. In doing so, a new world of flavors and pairings were open to me and my explorations became filled with wonder and wonderful interactions and conversations.

Hieronymus Wierix, *Christ in the Wine Press* (detail), engraving

A lot has changed since then, and continues to change as I make my way through this beautiful world with my family and friends. While capturing these concluding thoughts, I find myself looking at my wine cabinet, which has its own history and will no doubt provide

Georg Pencz, *Wedding at Cana* from his *Life of Christ* series, etching

some more stories to color my odyssey. But that photo of my first birthday reminds me of a new(ish) tradition that began back in grad school while completing my thesis on the Italian Renaissance table as an agent of cultural change. I keep a bottle of prosecco in the fridge. There is no real reason for having a bottle on hand, other than I need to find reasons to pop the cork and share it with others. Good or bad times, victories or defeats, the bottle is there, chilled and ready to go. People tend to fixate on the Bible's admonitions on how to celebrate. The miracle at Cana in the Gospel of John is filled with important reminders about how and why we should celebrate (John 2:1–12). In it, Jesus' divinity is on full display and His love for us is front and center. Imagine the sounds at the wedding feast. The sights and smells. The joy and merriment. While Jesus converts the water to wine in solitude, before and after the miracle, He is with people and enjoys being in their company. He has a tough conversation with His mother, gives authoritative instructions to servants, and enjoys the company of the satisfied guests after they sampled the transformed water. I am to follow His example; I am to do as He does and go where He leads. Along the way, as life happens, I'm not to get distracted but must remain focused and keep my sights on Him. With every step of the journey, I'm to include others, just as He has. Regardless of where I'm headed, the one thing I know for certain is that the only time I've ever worn a three-piece suit was back in 1977.

1 Maria L. Buseghin and Maria G.M. Lungarotti, eds., *Buon vino, favola lunga: Vite e vino nei proverbi delle regioni italiane* (Perugia: Electa Editori Umbri, 1992), p. 287.

2 Philip Seldon, *The Complete Idiot's Guide to Wine* (London: Dorling Kindersley Limited, 1996).

COMMUNITY

The Inevitably Messy Art of Making Scones

With scones, the moment of regret usually comes just after you add the buttermilk and begin to mix. Inevitably, the flour is not only on the work surface, but has found its way into the crevices on your stove and defiantly settled in the grout between your floor tiles. On a good day you remembered to remove your wedding rings and the thick layer of sticky dough has bonded only with your fingers. Later, when the surfaces have been scrubbed clean, the tea poured, and the fresh cream and jam heaped in bowls, you'll emphatically declare that it was worth it. But in the moment when you know the mess is going to get worse before it gets better, you'll find yourself wondering why this ever seemed like a good idea.

In our house, during the COVID-19 lockdown, scones became something of a cornerstone. I remember one night, right at the beginning, when the mood was pretty dark. School was closed, exams had just been canceled, and the reality of isolation was beginning to hit home. My daughters were lying at opposite ends of the sofa, and I was desperately trying to figure out what to say to bring some perspective. Then I got a text telling me to open my front door. On the mat, wrapped in brown paper with a tag that said, "Something for your supper," was a giant freshly-baked scone. I'd like to say we took time to set the table beautifully and put out some napkins and pretty plates. We didn't. We ripped that paper off like savages and dived into the cranberry and raisin spiced goodness, dripping butter and crumbs on a floor that no one but us would walk on for months. Almost instantly the atmosphere in the house changed.

As weeks passed and the daily notches on our fence post accumulated (my husband really did keep track of lockdown that way), making scones became our own way of caring for the people we missed. Over and over, I poured the buttermilk, mixed the flour, and tipped the whole mess onto the surface to cut. We experimented with rhubarb and ginger, lemon curd and coconut, and white chocolate and raspberry. We put together packages in clear gift bags with colorful ribbons and dropped them on doorsteps. Those five-minute conversations from the end of the driveway felt almost holy. Even as an introvert with a tendency towards being socially awkward, those little moments of connection made me long for community in a way I never had before.

Introvert as I am, I was not surprised that I struggled without community. Over the past few years, I've become increasingly convinced that the biblical call to love one another is not only central to the biblical story, but is essential to our growth, our understanding of God's character, our holiness, and even our joy. To some degree the pandemic confirmed in practice what I had long suspected in theory. I was not, however, prepared for the extent to which I struggled. Without the friends who were regularly part of my life, I was a little shocked by how quickly I became disheartened. More than that, I discovered that some of the spiritual disciplines I gave myself credit for proved, in part, to be due to the encouragement of the people I was no longer spending time with. As I sifted flour and shaped dough, I began to re-evaluate my approach to community. Slowly, as I pictured myself rushing with delight into things my more reluctant self so often avoided in the past, my post-Covid life began to take on an ethereal glow.

If lockdown reminded me that I am wired for fellowship, the return to ordinary life has taught me a less romantic lesson. Despite my rekindled enthusiasm, it quickly became clear that while the reality of actual, everyday community occasionally felt like those stolen, distanced conversations in the sunshine, it more often felt like the moment when regret settles like flour in the hard-to-reach places. There is no doubt that the call to love one another runs through the whole of Scripture. Yet, as I wrestle with my post-Covid ideals and the juxtaposed reality that comes when broken people like myself try to share their lives, I've noticed again that the biblical writers never sugar coat the truth. They make no secret of the fact that actual, physical community is as challenging as it is essential. Writing to the church in Ephesus, where differences in background, social status, and culture were creating fault lines that threatened to rip the church apart, Paul exhorts them to make every effort to keep the unity of the Spirit they have been given (Eph. 4:3 NIV). They were to stop at nothing, pouring themselves out to protect the supernatural oneness that is a gift of the Holy Spirit and can be either treasured or squandered by the way they choose to love.

Similarly, Peter tells believers who have been scattered into new communities to "love one another earnestly from a pure heart" (1 Pet. 1:22), using everything at their disposal to fight for the kind of relationships that are a direct response to the truth and reality of the gospel. Later in his letter Peter encourages them to "keep loving one another earnestly, since love covers a multitude of sins" (1 Pet. 4:8), and to "show hospitality to one another without grumbling" (1 Pet. 4:9).

This is not the kind of community I began to idealize in the heady days when we stood on our doorsteps on Thursday nights, clapping and banging pots and pans in honor of our healthcare workers and waving to our neighbors before going back to our movie. No one had to tell me not to grumble when hospitality meant putting my feet up on the sofa with my family and a cup of tea. On a wet Thursday afternoon in January, when my house is less than clean and I'm heading to the supermarket to grab something for an unexpected guest, it's a different story. If we are to love each other *earnestly,* then this is a love that requires effort. If Peter felt it necessary to point out that love covers a multitude of sins, he was anticipating that there would be sins in need of covering. He knew that there would be forgiveness to be offered and accepted, and bridges to be rebuilt.

While the type of community that grew up during the COVID-19 pandemic was a lifeline in that season, the danger for me was that it fit me like a glove. It was a kind of hit-and-run love that cost me little and allowed me to romanticize fellowship. It ran on my schedule and kept people at a distance. I may have poured myself into making scones, but I was long gone before anyone took a bite. I think now, more than ever before, we feel we have a right to control our own time, the space around us, and the people we allow into our circle. When we buy into the idea that community is simply for our benefit, and not the other way around, we miss the very things that make it so intrinsic to who we are.

I'm as convinced as ever that some freshly baked scones can be a great way of loving people, but I'm also convinced that they are best eaten together. I've had some of my best conversations while trying to ensure there isn't flour or cream on my chin. But I'm also realizing that the mixing and the sticky fingers and the cleaning up are the hard work that make the feast possible.

In Ephesians 4, Paul explains that our dogged determination to love one another well is the hard work that enables us to stand firm in a world that is trying to blow us in every direction. As each of us brings what we have to the table and offers it up for the good of the church, we grow, together, into maturity in Christ. The problem is that it's difficult to do that from a distance. If you are going to give what you have and add it to the mix you've got to get your hands dirty. Loving from a distance isn't an option; this is up-close, physically present, sacrificial, messy love.

It's interesting that Jesus commands His disciples to love one another just as He has loved them. Emotions tend not to respond well to command. In fact, if you want me to love something or someone, demanding that I do it is just about the worst thing you could do. Love, in the sense that Jesus commanded it, is so much more than the temperamental feelings-based affection we so often settle for. This is love that is based in the will. It's an active decision to keep turning up. To persevere when it would be easier to throw in the towel. To seek someone else's good when you'd rather seek your own. Usually it's inconvenient, often it's counter-intuitive, sometimes it's downright painful, but it's always for God's glory and our good.

There's a by-product of love that we often overlook, but it's one Jesus was clear about when He said, "By this all people will know that you are my disciples, if you have love for one another" (John 13:35). This is visible love that exists in the public realm. In a world that has become increasingly isolated, polarized, and self-focused, the kind of love that turns a diverse group of individuals into enduring, Christ-centered, loving communities is a living demonstration of the heart of God.

With scones, the moment when you realize it was worth it comes quickly, and that satisfaction is enough motivation to get out the scales and start again. With the hard work of community, it's usually not that fast. When you've experienced the inconvenience, the tension, and the costly grace—it can undoubtedly be hard to keep going. If it wasn't for a husband who is tenaciously and unshakably committed to our local community, I suspect I'd have given up many times. Instead, I'm learning to glorify God by showing up and getting my hands dirty, reminding myself that those holy moments around the table grow out of the work that has been put in beforehand. There are glimpses now of something beautiful: friendships and relationships that have enriched my life and helped me understand God better; the kind of laughter that leaves your muscles sore; the particular companionship found only in shared heartache. But, even in the moments when I'm wondering why this ever seemed like a good idea, I'm trying to live in the light of the knowledge that the day is coming when I will look back and emphatically declare that it was worth it.

HEIDI'S FAMILY SCONE RECIPE

INGREDIENTS:

4½ cups (1 lb. 4 oz.) soda bread flour
2 Tbsp caster sugar
½ cup (4 oz.) butter, softened
2 eggs
1½–2 cups (¾–1 pint) buttermilk
Optional: white chocolate chips and frozen raspberries

DIRECTIONS:

Mix sugar and flour, then rub in butter. Add whisked eggs and ½ pint buttermilk. Mix gently with spoon. If adding white chocolate and raspberries, mix them with a little flour to coat and add them to the mixture, stirring gently to combine. Tip mixture onto well-floured surface, flour top of dough, and press out until around 1–1½ inches thick. Cut into large squares and shape gently into rounds with floured hands. Add more buttermilk as needed—until there are no dry bits. Place on floured baking sheet *(I sometimes use a cupcake tray to keep the shape)* and bake at 400 degrees for around nine minutes or until golden. Serve with jam and whipped cream!

BRIEFCASES

The Unexamined Bag is Not Worth Carrying

The son of a friend told his father that for graduation he wanted a leather briefcase like mine, an eccentric request for a young man about to enter the black Cordura corridors of the American workplace. My friend, the dad, had no idea even where to find such a briefcase. The local luggage store certainly had none. Was there a store in town, he asked me, or would he need to go online?

I cleared my throat. "What does he want, exactly?"

"A leather briefcase," he said. "Like yours."

"Um . . . which one?"

He shrugged. "The leather one."

That did not narrow it down. The reason I have never forgotten this exchange is because it left me feeling exposed. As of today, I have twelve briefcases. To be more precise, I have five leather document cases, an attaché case, five portfolios, and two satchels, one in leather and one in waxed canvas. And believe it or not, mine is a tightly edited collection. It no longer includes, for example, the case that inspired my friend's son, which, on cross examination, turned out to be a custom bag from a well-known San Francisco craftsman who uses a process of his own devising to hand-color the leather. In the quest for perfection, I have bought and sold at least a dozen other bags of various designs, almost always with reluctance. The few exceptions, such as the hideously overhyped Saddleback or the picture-perfect Italian reporter bag with a too-fragile lining, only prove the general rule.

The first point to clarify is this: I am not a *collector* but rather a *user* of briefcases. Yes, I can hear how that sounds, but you will have to take my word for it. This accumulation of bags is simply the result of uncertainty. I have a notion of the perfect briefcase, but I have not managed to find it. Which is why I have to keep looking, and also why I must hold onto every briefcase that might be the one, that might turn out to represent that elusive goal: *as good as it gets.* The problem of the one and the many, of unity in diversity and diversity in unity, is connected in some way to this predicament, and perhaps later I will try to elaborate. For now, accept that my goal is to *use,* not collect.

Furthermore, I do actually use my briefcases. I lug things around in them. I show up at places—coffee shops, church, other people's homes—with a briefcase in hand (or at least back in the car, within easy reach). If you encounter me in the wild and need to point me out to a companion, to distinguish me from the crowd, you can just say, "The guy with the briefcase." That's who I am.

My cases divide neatly into three categories, which I will now (if you'll forgive me) unpack. For me, *briefcase* is an umbrella term for any bag intended to carry what we might call "writing tools," whether pens and paper or laptops and chargers, excluding bags like camera cases, totes, or backpacks, which might serve similar purposes but aren't quite the same. Among briefcases, I will further distinguish between *satchels,* which are made for shoulder carry: *document cases,* made to carry by hand; and *portfolios,* meant to be tucked under the arm. It's true that a satchel probably has a handle, and many document cases have the option of a shoulder strap, and portfolios might even have some kind of vestigial grip, so let's hold these distinctions lightly (apologies again). Still, I think my terms correspond more or less to the intended use of the bags, and if nothing else at least give you a sense of my own mental taxonomy.

My two satchels are concessions to modernity, the bags in my collection most likely to draw no attention in public. One is a brown pebble-grain leather zip-around with soft handles and a shoulder strap, and the other is a capacious, reporter-style, green canvas bag, bristling with pockets, that includes a ridiculously flimsy and under-cushioned laptop sleeve. I couldn't care less, because I frown on the inclusion of built-in laptop sleeves and any bag that features one isn't likely to please me for long.

I won't bore you with a tedious history of the development of the leather document case, a topic I have not bothered to research. Suffice to say, they resemble those craft paper accordion files with a flap cover and elastic closure that people used to stash bills, receipts, and miscellaneous bits of paper in, only fabricated of fine leather with a hand-stitched handle affixed to the flap. Originally intended to hold, well, documents, they work well with tablets, laptops, and books, though not cameras or headphones. They're also the fussiest of styles because, before you can reach inside, you have to wrestle with locks or straps to get them open.

My two favorite document cases are both dark brown and, from a distance, might be mistaken for one another. The first is an English classic stitched by Ray Clark. One glimpse into the mahogany depths of its dark Havana bridle leather converted me away from the flashier London tan which is arguably more iconic for such cases. There are two compartments and a pair of matched brass locks secure the flap. Then there's the New England-made Lotuff document case whose tumbled cowhide looks like chocolate left to melt in the sun. This one also has two compartments, but adds a rear stash pocket and some internal organization. Instead of a lock, it closes with a pair of straps. In theory, you could slip a newspaper or even an umbrella under these straps, assuming you know what those are.

Parenthetically, let's insert a sub-category here and call it the *attaché case,* by which I mean the style of hard-sided briefcases ubiquitous in offices throughout most of the twentieth century. I have only one of these, but it's a fine example: an

English-made case in the aforementioned flashy tan bridle leather with an upper lid that overlaps the lower compartment instead of fitting flush. Two heavy brass spring latches open with a satisfying thunk to reveal an interior lined in racing green skiver with a bellows pocket for a handful of documents, a slender pen loop, and some stash pockets for fake passports, opera tickets, or what have you. This is the sort of briefcase I imagine handcuffed to the wrists of British agents in the 1960s, with a string of gold sovereigns concealed in the lining. Carrying it in public anywhere elicits wonder, fascination, and suspicion in onlookers.

Finally there are *portfolios*, which are basically leather envelopes intended for carry under the arm. While they don't hold as much, portfolios are perfect for carrying a tablet, some pens, a notebook, and a modern French novel in translation. My most useful portfolios are both from Frank Clegg, one in tan harness leather and a much larger one in chestnut with a brass lock.

Now, if you're still with me, perhaps you can appreciate why that innocent question about graduation gifts threw me. There was no means of answering succinctly, no way to avoid revealing too much, drawing back a curtain on what would no doubt seem an unhealthy obsession. How many briefcases does one man need? The answer might appear obvious to you, but I find it an enigma. The irony, of course, is that I would have to reveal this obsession at all, that it would not be painfully obvious to anyone who has seen me. But it isn't obvious, because to most people one bag looks more or less like another, the way your spouse's shoes are only distinguishable by color, or most cars today are easily mistaken for one another. Only one who shares the obsession will recognize the symptoms.

And yet, I would maintain that this is *not* an obsession, unhealthy or otherwise, and that the problem of what to carry and how to carry it is something fundamental to being human. Whenever I encounter people who don't think about this problem, I am amazed. You just throw everything into a nondescript black backpack? You use a tote from the public radio fundraiser? The same foldable bag you take to the food co-op so you don't have to choose plastic and feel judged? Then you, Reader, have missed the oracle's admonition to know thyself. You are sleepwalking through the days of your life, your bag unexamined, its contents un-meditated-upon.

. . .

A common question from the curious: do you pick a briefcase to fit what you carry, or do you carry what fits in the case you've chosen? Strange as it may sound, this inquiry takes us to the heart of the mystery. The obvious answer might seem to be the analytic one: first lay everything on the table, then calculate the total volume and select a briefcase to fit. Common sense. But most of us don't pack this way. Instead, we choose the bag first and take its dimensions as a built-in constraint, the way poets bind themselves to the strictures of the sonnet. What doesn't fit must be left behind, and if there's room remaining once the essentials are packed, it must be filled. The process, whichever way you begin, forces upon you a series of questions: Do I need to take a laptop *and* a tablet? Will I really find time to read the crime novel *and* the biography? Will I get hungry or not? If I only take the pen with the black ink, will I end up needing to use the red instead? Which devices will need charging and which won't? Whether these are practical questions or existential is not easy to tell.

Definitely frivolous, you might think, the way most of us regard fashion as frivolous. Having a brown briefcase and a black one—and a tan one, too?—is surely just as superficial as having three shades of shoe depending on your outfit, not to mention the belts to match. Yet there are some theologians who argue that dressing in your Sunday best is not frivolous at all, but a way of anticipating the glory of resurrection. Adorning the physical person, making the most of what we are, becomes an iconography of the body to come, a means of dressing yourself up for the eschatological feast. I wonder whether something similar lies behind this preoccupation with the one and the many, with the tools and the bag that contains them.

One way to read the Genesis creation narrative is to see it as a series of forms spoken into existence which are subsequently filled by the divine word. God makes the sky, then fills it with birds. He makes the sea, then stocks it with fish. He makes the land, then packs in the animals, human beings chief among them. In the mind of God, of course, there can be no sequence or discovery, no hesitation over what comes first, the container or what goes inside. He does not make the sky and then wonder what to put in it, or make the fish only to puzzle over how vast an ocean might hold them. He knows all at once how it all goes together, and always has. The dilemma of which comes first, the container or what fills it, is a wholly human one, a problem to haunt the creature alone.

And it does haunt me. The poet Mark Jarman once wrote that every metaphor strives to "make the final unity," to assert the essential wholeness of all things, yet in a broken world every assertion of like-ness inevitably breaks down. No metaphor is ever perfect and, we might add, no briefcase ever holds the right amount. The constant testing and shifting, culling and acquiring, trying different bags or putting different things in them—all of it, like the making of metaphors, is a doomed endeavor that in its very failure suggests a unity just out of grasp.

Whether it is good or not to carry a briefcase, or to overthink the carrying of one, I can't really say. I do it regardless, and so the question is how to think about doing it. I find in the process a reflection of the fundamental paradox of making, the zigzag dance of the forms and what fills them. It is a flawed reflection by necessity, as every inquiry in a mirror dimly must be, but still. Let's suppose that just as one man's frivolity can anticipate glory to come, another broods over the voids of creation, chasing over and over the swirling vortex of divine breath.

MENTORING
Sharing the Road

She had been in my fall first-year seminar class, but, honestly, she had not really stood out. Smart, quiet, attentive, she had blended in with all the other students who seemed exactly like her from my vantage point as the professor. Even when she joined my voluntary small group Bible study in the spring, I still did not really notice her. However, one day during my personal prayer time, God highlighted Emily[1] to me in a striking way: "Tell her I see her desire for greater intimacy with Me and that this longing is the work of the Holy Spirit in her heart. I will teach her to rest in My presence to fulfill her desire."

Such a specific message for a student I barely knew! After our next small group meeting, I pulled Emily aside and shared with her the Lord's words. She responded with absolute shock, admitting that she *had* been yearning to grow closer to God for a long time, but a few weeks earlier had given up on the idea because it just didn't seem possible. God's words encouraged Emily to reignite that longing for closeness with Him and to pursue it intentionally.

But Emily still had a problem: she wasn't sure exactly *how* to "rest" in God's presence or *how* to draw closer to Him. Could I help her, she wondered aloud to me. Although Emily may not have known it at the time, she was asking me to mentor her.

Mentoring has gone by many names throughout the centuries such as *discipleship, apprenticeship,* and *tutoring.* But regardless of what it is called, the practice can be defined as a one-on-one relationship with another individual in which you intentionally invest in them in personalized ways that lead to a mutually-defined goal. For example, professional mentoring helps people develop vocationally, physical mentoring may assist someone in meeting their health goals, and parenting or marriage mentoring supports those who are embarking upon these new life stages. A spiritual mentor, specifically, guides and supports a mentee who wishes to grow in her relationship with God.

When I was in middle school, an established mentoring program in my church paired me with an older woman who taught me that I matter to God because I mattered greatly to her. In college, I studied the Bible with the mother of a close friend of mine who helped me take ownership of my spiritual life and strengthen my practice of the spiritual disciplines. During my late twenties, a believer who lived three thousand miles away guided me through a major shift in my spiritual journey via lengthy email exchanges. All of these relationships were mentorships, and each one changed my life in ways I can never forget or repay.

Spiritual mentoring is a powerful growth tool for many reasons, one of which is the space it creates for someone further along the desired path to guide, support, and encourage the one who wishes to learn. A second advantage of mentoring is that the one-on-one environment enables the mentor to focus on the mentee as a unique individual, thus personalizing the learning experience for maximum effectiveness. And mentoring is just plain fun! Sharing life with another believer as you grow in friendship with each other and in relationship with the Lord is one of life's greatest treasures.

Mentoring brings glory to God specifically by the type of relationship it fosters—one that is both intimate and supportive. The closeness of the mentoring relationship reflects God's desire for intimacy with each one of us. Since the dawn of creation, God has pursued every human with passion and purpose, wanting nothing more than to know us and be known by us. Similarly, God cares for us "as a mother comforts her child" (Isa. 66:13 NIV), and thus the direction, encouragement, and nurture that is part of mentoring displays God's unfailing, custom-made support for each of His children.

A mentoring relationship is an effective tool for growing spiritually and for glorifying God, but all mentorships do not need to look the same to accomplish those purposes. Each unique mentorship should reflect the priorities and personalities of the believers involved, and while there is no right or wrong way to mentor, there are helpful practices that can enhance and enliven this special friendship between followers of Jesus.

First, one should choose a mentor or mentee wisely. One of my first mentees at the university at which I teach pursued a mentoring relationship with me so eagerly that I privately referred to him as my "spiritual stalker." Carlos was in two of my classes in the same semester and appeared at my office door practically every time I opened it. Armed with questions about deepening his relationship with God, Carlos wanted to hear everything I was willing to share about my own spiritual life, and we soon developed a mentorship that continued beyond his time at school.

Mentorships have to start somewhere, and often the starting point is the person who desires to be mentored. But what do you look for in a mentor? Certainly, you should choose someone you admire, someone whose spirituality you respect and would like to emulate in specific ways. Feeling comfortable sharing and spending time with the person also helps. Another consideration is the person's experience and maturity in the areas of your spiritual goals. Do you want to grow in intimacy with God? Do you hope to learn to study the Bible more deeply? Are you seeking a mentor who can guide you on the path of pursuing overseas mission work? Then choose accordingly. As Carlos's desire for understanding vocational ministry grew, for example, he added a mentor to his life who had expertise in that area since I did not. Most importantly, ask the Holy Spirit to lead your mentor choice. Sometimes, God brings together rather unlikely people to form transformative mentoring relationships.

Often, those seeking to mentor others are the ones who initiate the mentoring relationship when they see a need in an individual or when the Holy Spirit highlights someone. Begin moving toward mentorship by asking the believer to meet for coffee, inviting them to your next social event, or texting them that you are praying for them. Notice their response—if they pursue a deeper connection with you, continue growing the relationship and see what develops. If you already know the individual well, the direct approach of suggesting mentoring might work. Either way, if you sense a nudge from the Lord to offer mentoring to someone, resist the fear that you are not equipped for the task and take a step of faith. Every believer has something to share with another.

Second, make sharing life a part of your mentorship. None of my friends or family would ever accuse me of being an exemplary cook, so when I felt led by the Lord to offer a weekly cooked meal to a new Christian friend who had just broken her arm, I seriously doubted the wisdom of the idea. Also, I hate cooking. But Nicole gratefully accepted my offer, and our relationship grew over the months. This friendship, originally unrelated to spirituality, eventually morphed into a short season of spiritual mentorship as Nicole asked me to help her develop some new practices in her prayer life. Without the friendship created through the simple act of sharing food, our time of mentorship might never have happened.

Mentoring is sometimes viewed solely as doing spiritual activities together such as Bible study or service, but a necessary part of a healthy mentorship is sharing life. Mentorship works best when times of "official" mentoring merge with times of real life as believers share both the good and bad of being human. Sometimes sharing life is easy because the connections are natural, like having kids in the same school or belonging to the same church. But even very different folks can enjoy mentoring. Though we have few common life connections, the college students I mentor usually enjoy when we meet for meals, share checkup texts to see how the other is doing, or recommend music or podcasts we think the other would enjoy. Intentionally making "non-spiritual" connections fleshes out the relationship and enriches the times you do spend together focusing on more explicitly spiritual encounters.

Having intentional times to meet for spiritual purposes, however, is the heart of any mentorship, so deciding when your "official" meetings will happen, how they will look, the purpose of your mentorship, and the goals you hope to each meet will make the experience more enjoyable and effective. When your mentorship contains both casual life connections and focused times of spiritual sharing, the happy result is that both believers grow in Christ and become closer through the interactions.

Third, let Jesus take the wheel. Although Danita patiently explained to me why she believed my spiritual gifts were a perfect match for the volunteer ministry position that had opened up at our church, it took many months before I could see myself in the ways Danita did and get up the courage to join the ministry. But Danita didn't worry. She knew Jesus was working in my life and would lead me even when I was resisting her mentoring. And she was right!

Jesus is the head of His church, having given Himself fully for His bride "to make her holy, cleansing her by the washing with water through the word, and to present her to himself as a radiant church, without stain or wrinkle or any other blemish, but holy and blameless" (Eph. 5:26–27 NIV). In our mentoring, then, we can relax and trust our Savior's work in our mentee's life. We don't need to worry or stress, and we can resist unhelpful actions such as pressuring our mentee to comply with our advice, losing patience when they struggle, or missing key opportunities to encourage them. Each mentee's relationship with God is their own, so they are the final authority in all spiritual matters—the practices they adopt, the view of God they hold, the doctrines they believe, and everything in between. We can invest ourselves in the life of our mentee with confidence and joy, knowing our Savior will do His perfect work in their life.

Mentoring is an enjoyable and effective way to bring glory to God as we support and bless each other in Christ. The impact of such relationships can be profound and long-lasting, and every Christian has something to offer. Mentoring is a transformative way to fulfill the command in 1 Thessalonians 5:10–11: "[Jesus] died for us so that, whether we are awake or asleep, we may live together with him. Therefore encourage one another and build each other up" (NIV).

1 All names have been changed.

SMALL TALK

Bread Prices and Domestic Discomforts

One of our overlooked blessings, and increasingly under-realized privileges, is small talk. In an age where many human statements are condensed to a character count, where "conversation" adopts (and adapts to) the functional platforms of texting and social media, the benefits of talking about the insignificant and the trivial can quickly become a lost or despised art. In this essay I want to speak in praise of small talk as a good preoccupation, delivering (I hope) its valedictory speech rather than its eulogy, sending it out into this world rather than marking its translation to the next.

A HOME WITHOUT A HALLWAY

My wife and I, along with our baby daughter, once lived in a tiny apartment in Arequipa, Perú. The compact accommodation had much to commend it, but one of its major drawbacks was that our front door led immediately into our intimate living space. Ours was a home without a hallway. Visitors were immediately ushered into our life with no architectural introduction: shoes and shopping bags, strollers and backpacks proliferated in our tiny quarters, and a small army of ants quickly learned that the space under our front door was an off-ramp to a food debris drive-through. Our longing was not for a palatial entranceway, replete with a sweeping staircase, but just a tiny chamber or space where we and our guests could pause before being in the middle of things.

Small talk is much maligned in many quarters as the most unpleasant of pleasantries, a superficial and formal throwback to a synthetic neighborliness which consumed time but didn't deepen relationships. No doubt some of this is true, but human encounters without small talk give us interaction without introduction, information without intimacy, exchange without proper engagement. In short, they build us a home without a hallway.

Small talk is the space where we linger with one another, where we cautiously remove the outside coats which protect us from the elements, where we hang up our hats and begin to absorb some of the warmth that the house of deep conversation provides. Small talk allows us to transition from the exterior spaces of formal connection to the interior spaces of true contact and mutual esteem. Occasionally small talk allows us to see that this particular encounter won't be a home where we find a seat by the hearth, or that because of different perspectives the doors to the rest of the rooms in the house will be locked without a key.

THE MINISTRY OF MINUTIAE

For more than twenty years I have served as a local church pastor and, as a result, small talk has become one of my main weekly activities. From the outside in pastoral work might appear to be bound up with the important and profound, with the critical counselling needs of a congregation, with the impartation of biblical wisdom to all of life. Some of this is occasionally true, but the more regular work of ministry is small talk: learning the names of adult children and adored pets, hearing about

Stefano della Bella, *Standing sailor in center talking to a seated Levantine man to left, seen in profile, other sailors with a boat to left in the background*, etching

how a recent gardening project has soared or plummeted, chatting about the weather and the whatever, learning the incidental details, the minor passions and major pursuits. Many people do not commonly or consciously think Big Thoughts or want to discuss Big Philosophy or their Big Problems with a pastor who cannot traffic in the trivial and the mundane.

Much as architecture silently expresses the spirit of each age, so small talk gives voice to how individuals think and act and feel. A man's opinion on a recent spate of bad weather days might carry indicators of his optimism or pessimism; a woman's reflections on relating to an employee might open up the wiring which powers a whole network of ideas and assumptions about human relationships; an individual talking at length about their recent vacation will lay bare all sorts of realities about how they view home and holiday, here and there, what they miss when away, what they long to find abroad. The seemingly delicate and fruitless stem of small talk leads the careful listener to the deep roots of another person's life, and opens a way for interaction to develop into conversation, conversation into communion.

In his pastoral reflections from a lifetime of ministry Eugene Peterson insisted that pastors must privilege small talk in their engagement with other Christians,

> If we avoid small talk, we abandon the very field in which we have been assigned to work. Most of people's lives is not spent in crisis, not lived at the cutting edge of crucial issues. Most of us, most of the time, are engaged in simple, routine tasks, and small talk is the natural language. If pastors belittle it, we belittle what most people are doing most of the time, and the gospel is misrepresented.[1]

Old Testament scholar Bruce Waltke contends that part of the ministry of biblical prophets was to pay attention to 'the Importance of trivialities'[2], and this is borne out by the fact that many of their denunciations of the corruption at work in their community centred around knowing the plight of the disenfranchised and voiceless, the widows and orphans. The fact that Old Testament prophets could pronounce on the kinds of scales and measures used in the marketplace, and the crushing economic inequity of their political system, shows that they in no way set aside the small talk of bread prices and domestic discomforts. Only seemingly minor conversations could unearth such major controversies.

A CHILD'S PURSE, FULL OF USELESS THINGS

Aside from the *function* of small talk, granting it a place dignifies the everyday where our lives are lived, privileging the routine and ordinary items that carry the residue and resonances of our most deeply felt realities. Neighbor love prizes the trinkets and downgrade treasures of one another's mundane existence, finding that love lives in the spaces where others might believe that few good returns can be secured. Irish poet Michael Hartnett reflects on this in his evocative piece "Death of an Irishwoman":

> She was a summer dance at the crossroads.
> She was a cardgame where a nose was broken.
> She was a song that nobody sings.
> She was a house ransacked by soldiers.
> She was a language seldom spoken.
> She was a child's purse, full of useless things.[3]

Small talk allows room for the petty passions which reflect the character God has given to each one of us, and marks up the bric-a-brac of the human heart as valuable to Him, and redeemable by Him. We listen to one another in the wealth of words, seemingly about nothing, finding access through them to the *everything* of who we are and what we are becoming in Christ.

One of the charms of Modernist literature is its insistence on recording the ephemeral speech of our insignificant lives. In *Ulysses* James Joyce gives us Dublin on June 16, 1904, in all of its everyday reality, not gilded with Celtic Twilight like the early poetry of W.B. Yeats, but replete with memorized shopping lists, advertizing slogans, and casual conversation in a funeral cortege or a public house. True, the plays of Samuel Beckett appear to back such small talk into the corner of absurdity and inanity, but his record of such speech shows its ubiquity and capacity nevertheless.

A Christian view of the small talk marked by Modernism translates it into a register of permanence and expectation. The new heavens and the new earth will contain speech, but not all of it oratory and exalted prose; it will bring the delight of conversation but not all of it deep. The new cosmos will include the translated and transformed blessing of casual chat, informal conversation, the everyday material more richly embroidered then by the redemptive grace of God. Such small matters will still matter, though robbed of the self obsession and avoidance that can be the parasite of general conversation.

Small talk is a good preoccupation packed with enormous potential. We reject and avoid it at our peril, we engage in it to our great profit, accessing the very self and soul of friends and strangers through one another's "useless things." Small talk is a hallway to the heart, delivering us from mere functionality in our dealings with one another, and providing a way to listen carefully and keenly to the hearts of those whom we encounter.

1 Eugene Peterson, *The Contemplative Pastor: Returning to the Art of Spiritual Direction* (Grand Rapids, MI: Wm. B. Eerdmans, 1993), loc. 1027–1030, Kindle.

2 Bruce K. Waltke and Charles Yu, *An Old Testament Theology: An Exegetical, Canonical, and Thematic Approach* (Grand Rapids, MI: Zondervan, 2007), p. 812, Kindle.

3 Michael Harnett, "Death of an Irishwoman," in *The Penguin Book of Contemporary Irish Poetry*, ed. by Peter Fallon and Derek Mahon (New York: Penguin, 1991), p. 216.

HOMEMAKING
Houses of Cedar and the Home of God

The making of a space into a home—whether a three-room walk-up apartment or a three-story row home—is the work that has kept my hands busy and my imagination active for many, many years. Even when I was a teenager, creating cute, cozy spaces motivated me; I loved decorating my dollhouse with new chairs or dishes, and I would rearrange my bedroom every few months, hoping to find the right direction of warm lamplight falling onto my bed. Wandering through the home furnishing section of the local department store Strawbridge & Clothier as a teenager eventually evolved into taking a spin or two around Ikea's multiple rooms with my husband and daughters while we looked for bedspreads, throw pillows, and other house accessories. Each space I have found myself living in I have sought to make into a place that was not just for sleeping and eating, but for fostering life and love and good memories.

I am not alone in wishing and working for a "home, sweet, home" dream come true. Through the past few decades, decorators such as Martha Stewart and Joanna Gaines have been popular guides for choosing wall colors and tableware; magazines like *House Beautiful* and *Architectural Digest* publish swoon-worthy goals, and reality television shows such as *Fixer to Fabulous* model for us how to accomplish home renovations. Proponents of minimalism or English Country Shabby have Instagram and Tumblr accounts to inspire us. And Barnes & Noble stocks many colorful home and decorating books on their shelves.[1]

Looking at how people live around the world, we see that topography, climate, and resources, as well as cultural traditions, influence how living spaces have been created. Homes in Korea look different than homes in Kansas. The hope for a "home, sweet, home" echoes throughout the world.

The drive for a place and a home, no matter how large or small, is intrinsic to being human. We are wired to make a place where we can protect and care for our people and ourselves. And because we are made in the image of a place-making God, we can cultivate homes that make life and flourishing possible. We can create spaces of beauty and goodness for others to live with.

Yet, because humanity is sinful and broken, we can also make places that are characterized by power, or are places for accumulating more possessions and showcasing wealth. Places where people live have also been places of trauma and abuse.

How do we, people following Jesus and seeking to be formed by Scripture, think about and pursue building our homes and keeping our houses? Can Scripture influence not just how we live together but also how we create our places so they reflect the ways of God and not just the self-centered ways of the world?

God hasn't told us—as people living in the modern age—how to order or arrange our furniture, meal schedules, cleaning practices, or decorations. As Paul writes in the letter to the Ephesians, God has told us how to live together in unity as His people. But since God works in the physical-ness of our lives, then maybe how we think about our homes, how we live in them, and how we arrange them, can mirror who we are as His people. We get these clues from Scripture. As Eugene Peterson said, "The Bible, all of it, is livable; it is the text for living our lives. It reveals a God-created, God-ordered, God-blessed world in which we find ourselves at home and whole."[2]

Encouraged by Eugene Peterson's words about Scripture —"Christians don't simply learn or study or use Scripture; we assimilate it, take it into our lives in such a way that it gets metabolized into acts of love"[3]—I sought to have my vision for homemaking and house-building be formed by Scripture. Several passages in particular animated my imagination.

> But I, through the abundance of your steadfast love,
> will enter your house. (Psalm 5:7)

I'm drawn to the beauty of Psalm 5:7. The words *abundance, steadfast love,* and *enter your house* are rich with promises of God's love and desire for us to be with Him. Entering God's house is about coming to His tabernacle (and then later His temple). God is rich with unfailing kindness and mercy; that He welcomes me to His place and presence is beyond imagining but eternally true because of Jesus' life, death, and resurrection. I love dreaming about what it would be like to quietly come into the tabernacle, knowing that I have been invited by God to enter. His house is offered to me and to others as a place of life and refuge. This welcome of God enlarges my heart to do the same for others.

> By wisdom a house is built,
> and by understanding it is established;
> By knowledge the rooms are filled
> with all precious and pleasant riches. (Proverbs 24:3–4)

This verse teaches me that it matters who I am in my heart and in my mind as I seek to build my house—it matters if I am growing in wisdom and understanding. And how do I know what wisdom is? How do I know what understanding looks like? I keep my eyes on Jesus and on God's word. And fixing my eyes on these things teaches me to practice using my words well, as well as my time and my hands. I pay attention to what I'm striving after and how that influences my emotions, and I think about how I create space for others; I want people to feel welcomed and seen. Am I decorating to show off to others or to offer beauty? As I take care of my home, whether through everyday chores or upkeep, or through adding loveliness to our walls, I try to submit my ways to God's ways.

The next part of the verse—"by knowledge the rooms are filled with precious and pleasant riches"—reminds me how God gave knowledge and wisdom to all the Israelites involved with building the tabernacle and also how the tabernacle was decorated with gold furniture and embroidered linen curtains. These words encourage me to try to cultivate in my home the goodness of human relationships, but also the goodness of lovely things and furnishings. I'm reminded that these things in my home are not treasures to hoard on earth but ways to create spaces of peace and beauty, like those seen in the tabernacle.

Ned Bustard, *Art Maker*, linocut

My husband and I have been collecting original artwork since the early years of our marriage; we desire excellent work created by Christians, as well as work that highlights Scripture. By doing this, we have affirmed the importance of artists, craftsmanship, and storytelling. The artwork hanging on our walls are some of the precious riches we need to remind us that we are God's people.

Exodus 25:8–9 says, "They are to make a sanctuary for me so that I may dwell among them. You must make it according to all that I show you—the pattern of the tabernacle as well as the pattern of all its furnishings" (CSB). Exodus 25–30 is full of specific instructions of the size and the materials used to make the tabernacle. These instructions include all the precious metals and jewels, the good wood, and the lovely materials for curtains that were to be found as part of God's dwelling place. God gave these specific instructions to the Israelites and even gave the Holy Spirit to certain men to be the artists. God gave these plans to the Israelites through Moses, and they were to follow His words. And God's glory would come down to dwell with them. The Hebrews would see what it meant to be set apart as His people.

Reading this section of Exodus leads us to Exodus 36–40, where we can imagine the actual making of the tabernacle, its furnishings, and the priests' clothing. For God's house to be built correctly and for worship to be established according to God's instructions, the builders had to submit to God's ways and words. They walked in wisdom as they built God's house and filled it with precious and pleasant riches. In this, they are our teachers.

Ned Bustard, *Abigail*, linocut

The wisest of women builds her house, but folly with her own hands tears it down. (Proverbs 14:1)

And we who establish our own houses can follow in the footsteps of those who obeyed God's words and directions while building the tabernacle. I'm intrigued by how Proverbs 14:1 correlates with Jesus' words in Matthew 7:24–27. Jesus used the images of building one's house on rock or sand as a way to help His listeners understand the consequences of listening to or not listening to the word of Christ. If one listened and followed His words, it would be like building a house on a rock which would keep the house from being destroyed. A foolish person was one who did not follow Jesus' words, and his outcome would be destruction (Matt. 7:24–27).

The words of Scripture—the words of Christ—form us from the inside out. We hear these words and we want them to form our hearts, our minds, and our motives. And then this formation comes out in our action and our words. But sometimes we just hear the words, and they don't form how we live day to day. And we become the woman who tears down her home because our words and actions don't bring life to those we are living with or caring for.

Our houses are the physical place where we live. They include the rooms where we sit together and talk and laugh and cry, where we share food and drink, and where we sleep and dream. In our homes, we pray and we celebrate. We find out what our callings and creative abilities are. Here as we practice our creativity and interests, we start to learn what it means to follow the cultural mandate found in Genesis 1. But also, in our houses we care for others who come through our doors. Following in God's ways, we make room for people who need enfolding—church members, neighbors, hurting friends, and newcomers to our communities. In our homes we obey God's commands to love God and to love our neighbor.

The word "house" means a place to live in, but it also refers to the generations of a family—the people who come before us and after us. God not only built His house, the tabernacle and then the temple, but He built a house for Himself, made up of His people. Ephesians 2: 19–22 reminds us,

> So then you are no longer foreigners and strangers, but fellow citizens with the saints, and members of God's household, built on the foundation of the apostles and prophets, with Christ Jesus Himself as the cornerstone. The whole building, being put together by Him, grows into a holy sanctuary in the Lord. You also are being built together for God's dwelling in the Spirit" (HCSB).

We are called, as part of God's household, to pray and work towards establishing our house—the people who come after us—to know and serve God, who invites us all into the abundance of His house. Although we do know that the final fruit of our work is in God's hands and purposes, we still seek to walk in God's wisdom as we love and care for our people. God has given us places and people to enfold and care for. And in our homes, while we try to build our house, we are following Jesus' directive to go and make disciples.

From God's first words in Genesis, as He spoke the world into form and planted a lush home in which He could dwell with His creation, to His specific instructions for how He wanted the Hebrews to build the tabernacle so His glory could dwell them, to Jesus coming to Earth to live with His people and thus beginning the building of a new house of worshippers, we finally will arrive to God's New Creation, where we will dwell together with God in Zion for eternity. As Jesus promised, "In my Father's house are many rooms. If it were not so would I have told you that I going there to prepare a place for you? And if I go and prepare a place for you, I will come back and welcome you into my presence, so that you also may be where I am" (John 14:2–4 BSB).

May we be encouraged in our homemaking and house-building as we fix our eyes on the words of God, the ways of Jesus, the work of the Spirit, and the hope of the Home we have in Eternity.

BENEDICTION

"We are filled with the good things
of your house . . ." (Psalm 65:4)

Morning sunshine filling the kitchen windows,
and a yellow knitted throw on my lap,

books lining our shelves,
and laughter around the table,

words in my head that I scribble on lined paper,
songs we sing together Sunday mornings,
water on a baby's head . . .

and every week,
Bread and Wine placed in my hand:
"the Body and Blood, given for you—
take and eat."

1 My two favorite books: *Home: A Short History of an Idea* by Witold Rybcznski, helped me understand the evolution of the home from the Middle Ages to the Modern age. *The Not So Big House: A Blueprint for the Way We Really Live,* by Sarah Susanka, challenged the McMansion way of living and encouraged "rightsizing" the American home with quality materials and personalized details.

2 Eugene Peterson, *Eat This Book: A Conversation in the Art of Spiritual Reading* (Grand Rapids, MI: Wm. B. Eerdmans, 2006), p. 18.

3 Ibid.

PRESENCE

The Gaze of Beauty

When we consider anything, let alone anyone, being "present," we usually imagine its physical properties and location in the world. The chair is present in the room. All students are "present and accounted for" at the beginning of the school day. We "present" ourselves at the doctor's office for our appointment. One way of considering what it means for an object to be present is that that it is "with" us. The food is with us on the kitchen table. I have my wallet with me on the way out the door. When the judge entered the courtroom and was, thereby, present, the people rose to their feet. The food, the wallet, and the judge are with us. Are present to us.

In the context of the biblical narrative, when we consider what it means for God to be with us, something deeper and more mysterious begins to gradually, slowly emerge. For indeed, over the arc of the entire narrative what becomes increasingly real is His presence. The Scriptures are replete with instances indicating that God is with us, either directly through the words God speaks to His listeners, or by the words the writer uses to tell us that this is so. "Have I not commanded you? Be strong and courageous. Do not be frightened, and do not be dismayed, for the Lord your God is with you wherever you go" (Josh. 1:9). "Fear not, for I am with you; be not dismayed, for I am your God; I will strengthen you, I will help you, I will uphold you with my righteous right hand" (Isa. 41:10). "And behold, I am with you always, to the end of the age" (Matt. 28:20).

All of these passages are continuations of what we read on the first page of the Bible. They are more explicit and contextually particular versions of how, in the beginning, "the Spirit of God was hovering over the face of the waters" (Gen. 1:2). God's Spirit was present to—was *with*—the waters of chaos and darkness. In this way, God was not present in the way the chair is present in the room or the wallet in my pocket. He is not simply an inert object who happens to occupy space in the universe. No, rather, His presence, by its very nature, is one that is continually in the business of working to bring order and purpose to chaos. His is a presence of intention. An intention to create beauty and goodness that emerge in response to His very being in that space and calling them forth. In this way, His very presence *is* His activity.

Antonio Tempesta, *The Creation of the World (Orbis fabrica)*, etching

In Genesis 1, God is present to all that is before him; but He is not simply one more object that happens to be there, along with the waters of darkness and chaos. Rather, His presence is one that hovers. He does not intrude. He does not barge in. Nor is He aloof, or unmindful of that with which He is present. He is not afraid of the objects over which He is hovering. Unlike the gods of other neighboring ancient Near Eastern religious cults, the Hebrews' God did not see the chaos as His enemy whom He must battle to subdue, enslave, or destroy, any more than He sees our own traumas as enemies to be subjugated. Instead, He created. He brought order and purpose to what theretofore had been unwieldy, unyielding, and lifeless. His word—an extension of His presence—brought the light into darkness, and the darkness yielded. His presence brought the land up out of the chaotic waters in order to provide the setting for life in all of its potentiality to be given a chance to live. He gave names to all to which He was bringing order, names that in their very essence were the expressions of their purposes. Moreover, they were names that forever attached those objects (Day and Night; Heaven and Earth and Seas, *adam*) to the One who had named them, reminding them, and us, of his presence being forever *with* them. In this way, God reminds what he has created that he is still present with us, even when he has turned his attention more directly to another part of his world in which he is creating beauty and goodness out of chaos. Furthermore, by giving each of those things their names, he also reminds them that his presence *is* his activity. The question, of course, is to what degree we humans are paying attention to this reality.

Additionally, however, in their inimitable style, the Bible's authors weave together multiple layers of story lines to communicate what is going on here. God did not merely bring order and purpose to one dimension of the world and then mindlessly move on to the next and to the next—without pausing to reflect on his work. And upon each reflection, God further names the ordered, purposed object "good" by seeing that it was so. At first glance (no pun intended), we might imagine this "looking" as only a one-dimensional activity. "And God saw that it was good." God, having made something that was good, stands back, takes a long, lingering look, and makes the observation that whatever He has ordered and purposed is good, be that the land, the vegetation, or the animals. He names it good because He sees that it is objectively so. This is not untrue.

But that's not all. The Hebrew word for what we translate in English to be "good" can also easily be translated as "beautiful."[1] What God is making is not only good but beautiful. And it doesn't stop there. Consider: God is not only calling something beautiful that He sees to be so, true as that is. The writer is also drawing our attention to the notion that the beauty that God sees emerges *as a function of God looking at it.* Beauty appears as a direct result of being seen by God. His gaze—His presence—draws beauty forth, for His nature can do nothing less.

Something else we see on the first page of the Bible is that to be human is to be uniquely made in God's image. And on that very same page, one of the first things we see that God is, is an artist.[2] It is as if we have opened the book to find someone working in his studio. And if we have been made to live bearing God's image, one way we are to do that is by, following God's lead, creating beauty by looking for it in places of chaos. And it is, like God, our very presence that is the vehicle that draws forth from the darkness and chaos the beauty—glory—that will not come into being unless we are looking for it. Glory that is to be found by the act of our seeing it where no one else does. As in our stories and those of the people around us.

My work as a psychiatrist involves looking for beauty in the very places we would least expect to find it, those locales that represent the detritus of my patients' traumatic memories, which are held in what they sense, image, feel, and think, in their very bodies. My purpose is to be present to and with every single part of the person with whom I am working, in order to be hospitable to those parts of them that they may hate but do not even know that they carry because they have been buried so long in the recesses of their memory. Buried so deeply because they are too painful to bring to consciousness on their own. It is in the presence of someone else who not merely tolerates but actively beckons and welcomes those bruised and broken elements of our stories into the room, in order for them to be seen, soothed, safe, and secure, that each of us steps into the glory of God that He longs to share with us. Glory that is so weighty that we must practice bearing it in order for us to be ready for the heaven that is coming in which it will be the only clothing we wear. Clothing that is nothing short of God's infinite delight in our joy at His joy in being with us. Glory as that of the Father poured out upon the Son on Good Friday—because He trusted that Easter was coming.

We are largely unaware that the presence of each of us holds the potential, by the gaze of lovingkindness that we can offer to others, to draw beauty forth into the world out of the most mundane moments. Moments in which we can be looking for others who are looking for someone to find the beauty that is waiting to emerge from within them—but simply has yet to be seen by the person whose artistic work it is to call it forth. It can happen anywhere. The grocery store checkout line. The passenger sitting next to you on the plane. Your child. Your spouse, who believes he or she has yet to be seen by you—who may not even know it yet themselves.

But we can only do this—live into the healing power of our presence, through which we bear the image of the One whose presence is first calling forth beauty from parts of our own lives that we hate so much—if we have someone by whom we ourselves are routinely being seen for the beauty that we are becoming. We cannot give what we do not have.

Today, know that your presence is the very face and voice and body of Jesus, and that the glory of God, found in the beauty of those whom you will encounter, is waiting just around the corner for your artistry to call it forth. And what a glorious work of art it will be.

1 Ned Bustard, "God is Good Like No Other," *It Was Good: Making Art to the Glory of God*, ed. Ned Bustard (Baltimore: Square Halo, 2006), pp. 18–20.

2 Dorothy L. Sayers wrote, "The characteristic common to God and man is apparently . . . the desire and ability to make things" (*The Mind of the Maker* [New York: Harper-Collins, 1979], p. 22).

AFTERWORD

About Square Halo Books's Books

On the back page of most every title released by Square Halo Books you will find suggestions for other books we think you might like. As this book honors the amazing work of God over the last twenty-five years, during which He made it possible for us to release over forty books with little to no resources at all, it seems fitting to tell you about all of our titles rather than only highlighting a few.

1997

To start at the beginning of our catalog's history we need to go to the end. The first book from Square Halo Books was *The End: A Reader's Guide to Revelation*. It was built on the understanding that scripture interprets scripture, and contained a glossary defining the meaning of the images in Revelation (gleaned from other parts of the Bible) so that readers could study the book on their own. It sold surprisingly well for a no-name author and a publishing company with no money and no experience. We learned many lessons when we published that book, like "Consigning books with bookstores that go belly-up leads to not getting paid for your books," and "You should print a barcode on the back of a book if you want distributors to carry your it." Little things like that.

1998

The End was followed up with *Digging Deep*, a small workbook Alan designed to help families study the Bible in context so as to get the most out of it. Square Halo probably should have died a quiet death right there, but passion, love, and the desire for the glory of God generated a little miracle.

2000

When I asked the Bauers to publish a book for me on Art and Faith, they dug into their 401(k) and approved the project. Their belief in me resulted in the book *It Was Good: Making Art to the Glory of God.*[1] *It Was Good* was released with a fun release party in New York City, and International Arts Movement (IAM) even built an entire conference around the book. The book sold out in a few years and was replaced with a full-color expanded second edition in 2006.

It was around this time that my dad started warehousing our books and shipping them out for us. He took care of this for us for many years to follow. These days our books are warehoused and distributed by Baker & Taylor.

2002

Due to the fact that there was very little in print in the Art and Faith discussion, it seemed like a good idea to continue to serve the church by trying to fill that need. So *Objects of Grace: Conversations on Creativity and Faith*[2] was created. *Image* journal said of the book: "Here is a dynamic young art critic talking to a group of exceptionally talented visual artists about both contemporary art and Christian faith without a shred of self-consciousness or defensiveness . . . To crown this achievement, the book is itself a work of art, lovingly and vividly designed. If church historians and cultural commentators want to find the cutting edge in American religion today, they should look no further than *Objects of Grace.*"

2003

Image journal was a kindred spirit with Square Halo when it came to creating high caliber materials on Art and Faith, so it isn't surprising that Square Halo released a collection of essays by the founder and editor of *Image* journal (and a contributor to *It Was Good*), Gregory Wolfe called *Intruding Upon the Timeless: Meditations on Art, Faith, and Mystery.* In 2017, we released a revised second edition.

Krystyna Sanderson, another contributor to *It Was Good,* had the distinct honor of being the only photographer allowed to photograph the relief work carried on at St. Paul's Chapel in the wake of the attack on the World Trade Center. Her photographs were going to be hidden away, but instead Leslie and I sat on my living floor with the Bauers and gathered the best of over two thousand photos and paired them with fragments of prayers and Scripture to produce *Light at Ground Zero: St. Paul's Chapel After 9/11.*[3] *Light at Ground Zero* was officially launched at 2003 General Convention of the Episcopal Church in Minneapolis.

2004

Square Halo Books was originally founded to be a theological press, and in 2004 we released the next strictly theological project—Alan's second book, *The Beginning: A Second Look at the First Sin,* a book that affirmed that Adam and Eve were unfallen right up to when they ate the fruit. Art was part of our books from the beginning so it isn't shocking that in conjunction with *The Beginning: A Second Look at the First Sin,* a portfolio of linocuts was pulled by six different artists.[4]

An important detail to know about both the Bauers and the Bustards is that we have a great love for theological conferences. Therefore, with the release of *The Beginning*, it seemed like the right time for Square Halo to host a conference. In 2004 *The New Humanity: A Biblical View of the Fall and Cultural Renewal* was held. The conference featured Carl Trueman as our keynote, an exhibit of "The Beginning" linocut portfolio with the Lime Street Gallery (later known as White Stone Gallery), and a late night concert was presented by Matthew Monticchio and friends. The conference was a load of fun so it was followed up the next year with *The New Humanity: Christian Mysteries for Everyday Saints*. The 2005 conference featured Charlie Peacock and his wife Andi Ashworth as our keynotes speakers. Events like these were a lot of work, and with a disappointing number of actual attendees, it would be many years before Square Halo would host another conference.

2005

Years before Square Halo began, I had become a member of Christians in the Visual Arts (CIVA). As a result, *It Was Good, Objects of Grace, Intruding Upon the Timeless*, and *Light at Ground Zero* all featured CIVA members. Therefore, when it was time for CIVA to celebrate their twenty-firth anniversary, they partnered with Square Halo. This partnership culminated in the release of two deluxe, full-color, hardcover coffee table books: *Faith + Vision: Twenty-Five Years of Christians in the Visual Arts* and *The Art of Sandra Bowden*. Bowden's book was the first in a series of Square Halo books to highlight the work of an individual Christian artist. It would be followed by *The Art of Guy Chase* (2011), *The Art of Edward Knippers: Prints and Drawings* (2018), and *The Art of Bruce Herman: An Unguarded Gaze* (2023).

2006/2009

The next two books from Square Halo could be described as amplified exhibition catalogs. Along with the second edition of *It Was Good*, we released a small book in 2006 called *Mary McCleary: After Paradise*, and in 2009 we released a conversation of sorts between Georges Rouault and Makoto Fujimura titled *Rouault-Fujimura: Soliloquies*.

2011

After publishing *The Art of Guy Chase*, Square Halo and CIVA again partnered to release another large, full-color coffee table book, this time about the artist Sadao Watanabe—*Beauty Given by Grace: The Biblical Prints of Sadao Watanabe*. This book brought to light the extraordinary visual legacy of this remarkable twentieth-century Japanese artist on the eve of the centenary of his birth. Lavishly illustrated, the book featured full page reproductions along with the passages from the Bible which inspired their creation.

2013

Inspired by the many stories of how *It Was Good* had blessed and encouraged so many people, we decided to release a sequel titled *It Was Good: Making Music to the Glory of God.*[5] Jeremy Begbie described it as "Lively, engaging and eminently readable," asserting that it showed that "it is still possible to write about music in a way that enriches our experience of it." The book had two release party concerts—one in Pennsylvania at the The Trust Performing Arts Center and one in Nashville at Belmont. The third book in the series was released in 2018. Of that book Charlie Peacock said, "Like its companion predecessors, *It Was Good: Performing Arts to the Glory of God*[6] is both practical and theological." We also released *C.S. Lewis and the Arts: Creativity in the Shadowlands.*[7] Upon reading this book, Louis Markos, author of *Restoring Beauty: The Good, the True, and the Beautiful in the Writings of C.S. Lewis* remarked, "We need more books like this."

2015

We next published two books which, on paper, sound completely niche (and perhaps they are), but both have found a large number of enthusiastic readers. *Bigger on the Inside: Christianity and Doctor Who*[8] proposed that *Doctor Who* is a rich trove of sci-fi parables that can even illuminate the mysteries of faith. *Revealed: A Storybook Bible for Grown-Ups* offered the reader gripping artwork—from medieval woodcuts to contemporary linocuts—depicting well-known passages along with those shocking stories that are often hidden from view. Both the good and the bad were on display here because to reveal the true scope of redemption, the mystery, sex, and violence found in God's great story must not be glossed over.

2016

Square Halo's next three projects were rather academic books. *Deeper Magic: The Theology Behind the Writings of C.S. Lewis* explored the foundation of Lewis' thought—the theological underpinnings that gave his prose so much power. *Teaching Beauty: A Vision for Music & Art in Christian Education*[9] sought to build a vision for the fine arts, asserting that art and music should be a crucial part of any education. And in *Serious Dreams: Bold Ideas for the Rest of Your Life*[10] a radical idea was defended: that commencement addresses could actually be helpful to young adults in living out their calling in God's story.

2017

This year Square Halo released books to help promote two friends. *Good Posture: Engaging Current Culture with Ancient Faith* was both a vision for civility, hospitality, humanity, and creativity in public discourse and a record of the work of The Row House, an organization founded by Tom Becker. *A Book for Hearts & Minds: What You Should Read and Why*[11] was a festschrift in honor of Byron and Beth Borger. Over the years the Borgers (caretakers of Hearts & Minds Bookstore) have worked tirelessly to create a space for serious, reflective readers. Part of their work has been to serve as unceasing promoters of a certain boutique book company who had no money for marketing. Square Halo wanted to thank the Borgers in a small way for helping our books find readers, so on the thirty-fifth anniversary of the founding of Hearts & Minds, we dropped a box of these books on their counter and sat down with a box of desserts to celebrate.

2018

In addition to *The Art of Edward Knippers: Prints and Drawings* and *It Was Good: Performing Arts to the Glory of God,* in 2018 we published *Godly Character(s): Insights for Spiritual Passion from the Lives of 8 Women in the Bible.* This book looked at eight people who knew and loved their Lord and reflected on how they allowed themselves to be shaped by God over and above their culture and their circumstances.

2019

Godly Character(s) was followed up with a book about church planting called *Don't Plant—Be Planted: Contrarian Observations About Starting a Church.* This book was important to us because I met the Bauers through a church plant and Leslie and I had helped plant the church where we currently are members. In it an experienced church planter gave sound, hard advice about the joys, sorrows, victories, and defeats that come with the arduous task of extending the Kingdom of God.

2020

We followed the snarkily titled *Don't Plant* with a devotional book for people who hate devotional books titled *Nailed It: 365 Readings for Angry or Worn Out People.* Karen Swallow Prior praised this book, saying, ". . . if you, like me, long for a devotional that is sharpening, witty, and downright real, well then, you simply must read this book."

2021

Nailed It was actually a revised and expanded second edition of a book originally published by Kalos Press. We followed that with another revised and expanded second edition of a book first published by Kalos—Margie Haack's gripping (and hilarious) memoir, *The Exact Place: A Search for Father* as well as *This Place: A Few Notes from Home.*[12] But these both came out after *No Place: A Desert Pilgrimage,* an entirely new work by Haack. In 2021 we also released *Naming the Animals: An Invitation to Creativity* (the perfect "prequel" for our *It Was Good* books), which encourages the reader to see creativity as an essential part of God's design for partnership with humanity.

For most of Square Halo's history of publishing "extraordinary books for ordinary saints," releasing one book every year or so seemed like an amazing accomplishment. Therefore, to release the four books described above seemed to be a mammoth accomplishment. But, miraculously that year included four more books. *A Compass for Deep Heaven: Navigating the C.S. Lewis Ransom Trilogy*[13] gave readers background information, historical context, and the literary insight needed to navigate the cosmos of Lewis's science fiction. In *Speaking Code: Unraveling Past Bonds to Redeem Broken Conversations* biblical counselor Diana Di Pasquale asked and answered the question, "Why are our conversations soul crushing rather than soul satisfying?" and gave ther reader a workbook with the tools to begin working through the ideas presented in the book on their own. *J.R.R. Tolkien and the Arts: A Theology of Subcreation*[14] reflected on the implications of Tolkien's ideas, writings, and visual art on artmaking. Finally, poet Malcolm Guite explored how the creative work of poets and other artists can rekindle our imagination for Christ in *Lifting the Veil: Imagination and the Kingdom of God.*

2022

In 2022 it had been long enough for any bad memories from the first two conferences to have faded, so Leslie wanted Square Halo to give it another try. In conjunction with the release of *J.R.R. Tolkien and the Arts* an event was planned called *The 2022 Square Halo Conference: The Inklings—Creativity Collaboration, and Community.* There were lectures, live theater, a pop-up printmaking studio, and more. Our keynote was Donald T. Williams, author of *Deeper Magic*, and the event was topped off with a concert by Andrew Peterson. The event went so well that a follow-up was immediately planned for the following year, *The 2023 Square Halo Conference: Ordinary Saints—Creativity Collaboration, and Community.*

Right on the heels of the conference *Wild Things and Castles in the Sky: A Guide to Choosing the Best Books for Children*[15] was released. This book was modeled after *A Book for Hearts & Minds* and was Leslie's brain child, and she edited it with our dear daughter Carey and our friend Théa Rosenburg. In the summer a festschrift was released called *The City for God: Essays Honoring the Work of Timothy Keller.*[16] This was followed in the fall by *33: Reflections on the Gospel of John; Advent is the Story: Seeing the Nativity throughout Scripture,* and *How to See: Reading God's Word with New Eyes.* This last book was by Alan Bauer and serves as a rather poetic release on the eve of the anniversary of Square Halo Books, bringing the company back to publishing a book by its first author, and one that specifically presents "contextually sensitive biblical studies, and practical instruction consistent with the Doctrines of the Reformation" in hopes of being "useful for encouraging and equipping the saints."

As I think back over our history (and I didn't even mention all the small miracles, book release parties, generous supporters, fabulous conferences, and laughter-filled "planning meetings" in fine restaurants we have enjoyed over the years), I stand amazed by what God has done through this little publishing company that should have never been able to publish a single book.

1 Contributors to the second edition of *It Was Good* include: Sandra Bowden, Karen Mulder, Ned Bustard, Adrienne Chaplin, Roger Feldman, Edward Knippers, James Romaine, Tim Keller, Mary McCleary, Gaylen Stewart, Steve Scott, Dale Savidge, Kimberly Garza, Krystyna Sanderson, William Edgar, Charlie Peacock, Gregory Wolfe, David Giardiniere, Suzannah Bauer, and Makoto Fujimura, Theodore Prescott.

2 Contributors to *Objects of Grace* include: Sandra Bowden, Dan Callis, Mary McCleary, John Silvis, Edward Knippers, Erica Downer, Albert Pedulla, Tim Rollins and K.O.S., Joel Sheesley and Makoto Fujimura

3 Photographs from the book have since been exhibited at Barrington Center for the Arts, Gordon College, The Church of St. Mary the Virgin (New York), and The General Theological Seminary. Photographs from the book were also published in articles in *Episcopal Life* and *The Episcopal New Yorker*, posted on the *National Geographic* website, and even used in the lectures at Harvard Medical School. The 700 Club called it "a moving rendition of the heroism and love that emerged from the explosion of 9/11."

4 The artists are: Chara Bauer, Ned Bustard, Tanja Butler, Matthew Clark, Tyrus Clutter, Edward Knippers.

5 Contributors to *It Was Good: Music* include: Ned Bustard, Brian Moss, David Fuentes, Sandra McCracken, Bethany Brooks, Charlie Peacock, Jan and Mark Foreman, Katy Bowser, Tom Jennings, Brad O'Donnell, Vito Aiuto, Michael Roe, Greg Wilbur, Steve Guthrie, Mark Chambers, Michelle Stearns, Diana Bauer, Doug Plank, Ruth Naomi Floyd, William Edgar, John Patitucci, Hiram Ring, Shai Linne, Gregg Strawbridge, Paul Buckley, Keith Getty, Julius Fischer, Joy Ike, Kirstin Vander Giessen-Reitsma, Drew Holcomb, and Stephen J. Nichols

6 Contributors to *It Was Good: Performing Arts* include: Ned Bustard, Charlie Jones, Robert Bigley, Denis Haack, Chris Cragin-Day, Aaron Craig, Chuck Simmons, Jenifer Ringer Fayette, Martin Landry, Elizabeth Richard, Sean Gaffney, Marlaina Seay, Brian S. Chan, Brian Godawa, Camille Hallstrom, Skip SoRelle, Anthony Guyer, Gaye Jeffers, Abigail Killeen, Elizabeth Dishman, Candace Vance, and Alissa Wilkinson

7 The contributors to *C.S. Lewis and the Arts* include: David C. Downing, Bruce Herman, Scott B. Key, Don W. King, Rod Miller (Editor), Jerry Root, David Rozema, Peter J. Schakel, Charlie W. Starr, Will Vaus, and Theodore Prescott (Foreword).

8 The contributors to *Bigger on the Inside* include: Gregory Thornbury, Carter Stepper, Christian Leithart, Sean Gaffney, Joshua Lickter, Tyler Howat, Christopher Hansen, Ned Bustard, David Talks, Rebekah Hendrian, Sarah Etter, J. Mark Bertrand, Melody Green, and Leah Rabe.

9 The contributors to *Teaching Beauty* include: G. Tyler Fischer, Ken Myers, Gene Edward Veith, John Mason Hodges, Theodore Prescott, Gregory Wilbur, Ned Bustard, Karen L. Mulder, Stephen Richard Turley, David Erb, and Matthew L. Clark.

10 The contributors to *Serious Dreams* include: Claudia Beversluis, Byron Borger, Steven Garber, Richard J. Mouw, John M. Perkins, Amy L. Sherman, Nicholas Wolterstorff, and Erica Young Reitz.

11 The contributors to *A Book for Hearts & Minds* include: Ned Bustard, Calvin Seerveld, Andi Ashworth, Byron Borger, Gregory Wolfe, G. Tyler Fischer, David P. Gushee, Matthew Dickerson, Denis Haack, Daniel Spanjer, Mike Schutt, Karen Swallow Prior, N.T. Wright, Aaron Belz, Eric Bryan, Michael Kucks, Bradshaw Frey, Tom Becker, and Steve Garber.

12 *This Place* was first released as *God in the Sink*. This second edition contains eight new chapters and a new foreword.

13 The contributors to *A Compass for Deep Heaven* include: S. L. Jensen, Julianne Johnson, Jacob E. Meyer, Rachel M. Roller, J. D. Wunderly, Maya Maley, Nolan Andrew, Daniel Z. Hsieh, Daniel Z. Hsieh, Daniel J. Friend, and Evangeline M. Prior.
14 The contributors to *J.R.R. Tolkien and the Arts* include: Ned Bustard, Matthew Clark, Matthew Dickerson, Billie Jarvis-Freeman, John Hendrix, Bryan Mead, Christine Perrin, Bethany Ross, Charlie Starr, Jennifer Trafton, Devin Brown, and Melody Green.
15 The contributors to *Wild Things* include: Luci Shaw, Carey Bustard, Leslie Bustard, Théa Rosenburg, Lynette Stone, Matthew Dickerson, Andi Ashworth, Rebecca Becker, Kimberly Gillespie, Elizabeth Harwell, K.C. Ireton, Carolyn Leiloglou, Joy Strawbridge, Carolyn Clare Givens, Laura Peterson, Christian Leithart, Sarah Etter, Amy Knorr, Katy Bowser Hutson, Missy Andrews, Ashley Artavia Novalis, Pahtyana Moore, Mitali Perkins, Margie Haack, Cindy Ward Rollins, Eréndira Ramírez-Ortega, Quantrilla Ard, Dorene Williamson, Tina Cho, Dorina Lazo Gilmore-Young, Annie Nardone, Matthew Clark, Corey Latta, Elisa Chodan, Shanika Churchville, Anne Kennedy, Junius Johnson, Araceli Cruz, Gypsy Martin, Cindy Ward Rollins, and Amy Baik Lee.
16 The contributors to *The City for God* include: Katherine L. Alsdorf, A.D. Bauer, J. Mark Bertrand, David Bisgrove, Mike Bontrager, Ned Bustard, Jenny C. Chang, Judy Cha, William Edgar, Denis Haack, Bill Kurtz, Sean Lucas, Annie Nardone, John Patitucci, Charlie Peacock, CJ Quartlbaum, Scott Sauls, Daniel Spanjer, and Chris Whitford.

Square Halo Books has been a labor of love for so many people over the years. Following are those who donated of their time and love to this particular project.

A.D. BAUER is the first author to be published by Square Halo. His books include *The End: A Reader's Guide to Revelation, The Beginning: A Second Look at the First Sin,* and *How to See: Reading God's Word With New Eyes.*

TOM BECKER is the founder of The Row House—a forum for engaging current culture with ancient Faith. His first book for Square Halo was *Good Posture: Engaging Current Culture with Ancient Faith*

TRIP BEANS is the Reformed University Fellowship (RUF) campus minister at University Of Maryland, Baltimore County (UMBC). He is a peculiar combination of way-past-his-prime athlete and comic nerd.

J. MARK BERTRAND is a novelist, pastor, and a founding member of the steering committee of the Society of Bible Craftsmanship. He is the author of *Rethinking Worldview: Learning to Think, Live, and Speak in This World.* In addition to writing several mystery novels, he has also contributed essays to Square Halo's *Bigger on the Inside* and *The City for God.*

BYRON BORGER is an avid reader and owns (with his wife, Beth) an eclectic independent bookstore called Hearts & Minds in central Pennsylvania. He speaks often, edited a book for Square Halo called *Serious Dreams: Big Ideas for the Rest of Your Life,* and has written for several journals. You can find his book reviews at heartsandmindsbooks.com.

NED BUSTARD is a graphic designer, children's book illustrator, curator, and creative director for both World's End Images and Square Halo Books. His first book for Square Halo was *It Was Good: Making Art to the Glory of God.*

LESLIE ANNE BUSTARD has been with Square Halo since the beginning, but her first book for Square Halo was last year's *Wild Things and Castles in the Sky.* You can find much of her writing at PoeticUnderpinnings.com.

CAREY BUSTARD was homeschooled classically, graduated from The King's College (NYC), and currently teaches at The Geneva School of Manhattan. She avoided reading any Square Halo titles until last year, but now has written for two.

SANDRA BOWDEN is a painter and printmaker whose work is in many collections including the Vatican Museum of Contemporary Religious Art and the Haifa Museum. Sandra was president of CIVA (Christians in the Visual Arts) from 1993–2007 and co-edited *Faith & Art: Twenty-Five Years of Christians in Visual Arts.* She was featured in Square Halo's *The Art of Sandra Bowden* and *Objects of Grace.*

BRIAN S. CHAN is a professor, pastor, fine artist, and an award-winning martial artist in kung fu (working as a fight choreographer, stuntperson, and trainer for other actors). He is the author of *The Purple Curtain: Living Out Beauty in Faith & Culture from a Biblical Perspective,* the novel *Not Easily Broken,* and he was a contributor to Square Halo's *It Was Good: Performing Arts to the Glory of God.*

SHANIKA CHURCHVILLE has a BA in English from Swarthmore College and an MSEd in Instructional Leadership from Neumann University. She currently teaches writing and coordinates writing services at Lancaster Bible College. Her first writing for Square Halo was in *Wild Things and Castles in the Sky.*

MATTHEW CLARK lives in central Florida where he teaches both art and science at The Geneva School. His MFA is in printmaking and he has been making illustrations for Square Halo books for a very long time. He contributed to Square Halo's *Teaching Beauty* but not to *Wild Things and Castles in the Sky* (that is the *other* Matthew Clark). He has the great joy of having had several of the authors in this book as students and friends.

SHANNON COELHO hails from the wildly beautiful Yukon Territory, but now calls Austin, Texas home. She works part-time writing grants for non-profits and shares her poems and stories in her newsletter, *Foreign and Domestic,* tinyletter.com/ShannonCoelho.

DIANA Di PASQUALE is president of Square Halo Books and runs Third Way Counseling. She contributed to *It Was Good: Music* but her first full book for Square Halo was *Speaking CODE.*

ANDREW FIELD is a pastor at Redeemer Presbyterian Church West Side in New York City. He has also pastored churches in Northern California and Virginia. He enjoys exploring cities with his wife and visiting his grandchildren.

MALCOLM GUITE is a poet and priest, and Life Fellow of Girton College, Cambridge. His books include *Sounding the Seasons, The Singing Bowl, Parable and Paradox, Mariner: A Voyage with Samuel Taylor Coleridge,* and Square Halo's *Lifting The Veil.*

MARGIE HAACK lives with her husband Denis on a small urban lot where she tries to attract bumble bees and hummingbirds with marginal success. Margie's writing includes the *Place* trilogy published by Square Halo Books. You can find her blogging occasionally at Critique-Letters.com.

BRUCE HERMAN is a painter and a teacher whose work can be found in public and private art collections including the Vatican Museums, Cincinnati Museum of Fine Arts, and the Hammer Museum, as well as in various publications including *The Art of Bruce Herman: An Unguarded Gaze.*

SARAH ETTER-HINOJOSA is the youngest person ever to write for Square Halo, contributing to *Bigger on the Inside: Christianity and Doctor Who* while still a teenager. Recently married, she is currently studying International Studies/Spanish.

LIBBY JOHN is a multidisciplinary artist in the fields of music, writing, and dance. She teaches modern dance and choreographs for her dance company, Vivid Artistry Dance Co., and hosts the *Art & Faith Conversations* podcast.

JUNIUS JOHNSON is a scholar, teacher, writer, and french horn player. He is the author of four books, including *The Father of Lights: A Theology of Beauty*. His first contribution to a Square Halo title was in *Wild Things and Castles in the Sky.*

HEIDI JOHNSTON is the author of *Choosing Love in a Broken World* and is also a regular contributor at the Rabbit Room, where she got to know the folks at Square Halo. She lives in Northern Ireland with her husband Glenn and their two daughters, Ellie and Lara.

JESSE JOYNER is a juggler-scholar who is trying to make it through life without ever having a real job. He is one of the few people in the world who have completed a marathon while juggling. He also earned his PhD in Educational Studies from Trinity Evangelical Divinity School. Learn more about Jesse at JesseJoyner.com.

ANNE KENNEDY has an MDiv and is the author of *Nailed It: 365 Readings for Angry or Worn-Out People*, from Square Halo Books. She blogs about current events and theological trends at *Preventing Grace* on *Patheos.com.*

GLENN McCARTY is an author of books for young people and families, including the Tumbleweed Thompson and Dead-Eye Dan series. He lives with his family in Western New York, where he teaches middle school English. He contributes to Story Warren, and is privileged to be contributing to Square Halo for the first time!

TAMARA HILL MURPHY is a spiritual director and author of *The Spacious Path: Practicing the Restful Way of Jesus in a Fragmented World* (Herald Press). You can find her online at TamaraHillMurphy.com and on Instagram @tamarahillmurphy.

SALVATORE MUSUMECI is a socio-cultural historian with an interest in the material and visual cultures of Europe between 1300 and 1600. When not trying to figure out the subtle nuances of Italian history and alimentary habits, he is usually trying to keep up with his son, and not being an embarrassment to his wife.

CHRISTIE PURIFOY is a writer and gardener who loves to grow flowers and community. She is the author of several books, including a book of essays and photographs called *Garden Maker: Growing a Life of Beauty and Wonder With Flowers.* She is blessed to call Pennsylvania home and Square Halo a neighbor.

GEOFFREY REITER is Associate Professor and Coordinator of Literature at Lancaster Bible College and an associate editor at the website Christ and Pop Culture. His scholarship focuses on the intersection of philosophy and genre fiction.

THÉA ROSENBURG is a regular contributor to Story Warren and a co-editor of *Wild Things and Castles in the Sky.* Of late she has been editing all of Square Halo's titles and she reviews children's books for her blog, *LittleBookBigStory.com.*

ANDREW ROYCROFT is a pastor and poet from Northern Ireland who also serves as a visiting lecturer in Biblical Theology at the Irish Baptist College. His first book for Square Halo was *33: Reflections on the Gospel of Saint John.*

KRYSTYNA SANDERSON is a psychoanalyst in private practice in New York and an instructor at the Psychoanalytic Training Institute. Krystyna's connection with the Square Halo started over twenty years ago with *It Was Good: Making Art to the Glory of God,* followed by *Light at Ground Zero: St. Paul's Chapel After 9/11.*

STEVE SCOTT is a British mixed-media artist, writer, lecturer, and performer. He is also the director of the organization CANA (the Christian Artists Networking Association). You can find an essay by (with accompanying art by Gaylen Stewart) in *It Was Good: Making Art to the Glory of God.*

CALVIN SEERVELD is senior member in philosophical aesthetics, emeritus, at the Institute for Christians Studies in Toronto. He is known for *Rainbows for the Fallen World, Aesthetic Life and Artistic Task* as well as for his original translation and oratorio arrangement of The Song of Songs. Learn more about his writings at Seerveld.com/tuppence.html

LUCI SHAW is a poet, an editor, a retreat leader, a lecturer, and the author of forty books, including *Angels Everywhere, The O in Hope,* and *Reversing Entropy.* And last year she wrote the foreword to *Wild Things and Castles in the Sky.*

BRAD SMITH is a Halftime fellow and exploring a career transition from kingdom life in a mid size commercial construction company for thirty-eight years to encouraging and mentoring believers in the workforce.

LISA SMITH is an English professor at Pepperdine University in Malibu, California. Her first book for Square Halo was *Godly Character(s): Insights for Spiritual Passion from the Lives of 8 Women in the Bible,* and her second will be *Hammer & Fire: Lessons on Spiritual Passion from the Writings and Life of George Whitefield.*

SHAWN SMUCKER is the award-winning author of five novels including *The Weight of Memory* and *The Day the Angels Fell.* He produces a podcast with his wife Maile called *The Stories Between Us,* where they host conversations about creativity, writing, and family life.

JOY STRAWBRIDGE grew up in Lancaster, PA, where she regularly stayed out too late at the Bustard house, talking life and literature with Leslie and galavanting with Carey (which they continue to enjoy to this day). Her work as a teacher and nanny inspired her essay in *Wild Things and Castles in the Sky.*

PHAEDRA JEAN TAYLOR was raised on the rocky shores of Scotland, but today she is a watercolor and encaustic artist in Austin, Texas. You can find information about her art and the creative liturgical resources she and her husband make for families and church communities at PhaedraTaylor.com.

CURT THOMPSON is a psychiatrist working with patients at the intersection of neuroscience and Christian spiritual formation. He is married to Phyllis and has two adult children. He is the author of *The Soul of Desire, The Soul of Shame, Anatomy of the Soul,* and the soon to be released *The Deepest Place: Suffering and the Formation of Hope.*

ELISSA YUKIKO WEICHBRODT is an Associate Professor of Art and Art History at Covenant College in Lookout Mountain, GA. The first Square Halo book she read was *It Was Good* and it changed her life. She now teaches and writes about the ways that art and visual culture can help us love our neighbors better, including in her first book *Redeeming Vision: A Christian Guide to Looking at and Learning from Art.*

DONALD T. WILLIAMS is Professor Emeritus of Toccoa Falls College and the author of Square Halo's *Deeper Magic: The Theology behind the Writings of C. S. Lewis.* For more on the theology of God's glory, see chapter five of his book *Ninety-Five Theses for a New Reformation: A Road Map for Post-Evangelical Christianity.*

In Christian art,
the square halo
identified a living person
presumed to be a saint.
Square Halo Books
is devoted to
publishing works
that present
contextually sensitive
biblical studies,
and practical
instruction consistent
with the Doctrines
of the Reformation.
The goal of
Square Halo Books
is to provide materials
useful for encouraging
and equipping
the saints.